KINtop Studies in Early Cinema – volume 3
series editors: Frank Kessler, Martin Loiperdinger

Screen Culture and the Social Question 1880–1914

GW00580114

KINtop. Studies in Early Cinema

KINtop Studies in Early Cinema expands the efforts to promote historical research and theoretical reflection on the emergence of moving pictures undertaken by the internationally acclaimed *KINtop* yearbook (published in German from 1992–2006). It brings a new collection of anthologies and monographs in English by internationally renowned authors as well as young scholars. The scope of the series ranges from studies on the formative years of the emerging medium of animated photographs to research on the institution-alisation of cinema in the years up to the First World War. Books in this series will also explore the many facets of 19th and early 20th century visual culture as well as initiatives to preserve and present this cinematographic heritage. Early cinema has become one of the most dynamic fields of scholarly research in cinema studies worldwide, and this series aims to provide an international platform for new insights and fresh discoveries in this thriving area.

Series editors: Frank Kessler and Martin Loiperdinger

Screen Culture and the Social Question 1880–1914

Edited by
Ludwig Vogl-Bienek and Richard Crangle

British Library Cataloguing in Publication Data

Screen Culture and the Social Question 1880–1914

Series: KINtop Studies in Early Cinema – volume 3

A catalogue entry for this book is available from the British Library

ISBN: 9780 86196 709 4 (Paperback)

Published by
John Libbey Publishing Ltd, 3 Leicester Road, New Barnet, Herts EN5 5EW, United Kingdom
e-mail: john.libbey@orange.fr; web site: www.johnlibbey.com
Direct orders (UK and Europe): direct.orders@marston.co.uk

Distributed in N. America by **Indiana University Press**, 601 North Morton St,
Bloomington, IN 47404, USA. www.iupress.indiana.edu

Printed and bound in China by 1010 Printing International Ltd.

Contents

Richard Crangle and Ludwig Vogl-Bienek

Introduction

The cover illustration for this volume of the *KINtop Studies in Early Cinema* series, taken from a lantern slide of 1890, is a challenging image. The situation it depicts – children in poverty, selling newspapers to raise a meagre income – is an uncomfortable one for most viewers, but equally, the gaze of the boys themselves towards the camera is direct and confrontational. It would be easy to read intentions into that gaze on behalf of these unidentified and long-dead individuals, but any attempts to do so are unavoidably coloured by our need to use them as easy symbols of a narrative we have imposed on their situation, and that realisation is uncomfortable as well. The few certain things it means are that these people existed, they had a position in a social and commercial structure, and they had an individuality that cannot be defined purely in terms of that position or the label applied to them by the producer of the slide.[1]

However, there is another aspect to our choice of image, which works as a metaphor both for our impression of the boys and for our approaches to the medium in which they were originally shown. In simple terms, the picture does not fit the frame: the cover design of *KINtop Studies in Early Cinema* employs a fixed border, based on the common rectangular aspect ratio of film, so when a lantern slide is reproduced in this way we lose part of the image. In our historical approaches to visual media, seen through 120-odd years of film, television and computer screens, we are not used to circular or square projected images as they appeared on screen for much of their history. In the case of the newsboys, we potentially lose telling details like their (lack of) footwear; but in the wider sense, we lose this image's shape and composition, its impact of presenting the boys against a background of posters for popular recreations, not to mention its relation to the other images which preceded and followed it in a projection sequence, its accompanying published commentary, and its relation to the audiences to which it was shown. Several of these would be equally true of an early cinematograph film, of course – both media were fundamentally based on live performance, not just showing of pre-prepared

---

Facing page:
"The Newsboys", slide 6 of STREET LIFE, OR PEOPLE WE MEET (Riley Brothers, 50 slides, c.1887).

materials – but the point is that to approach this material we need to have an idea of the whole picture, and need to see and think a little differently.

Public performances using the magic or optical lantern became a prominent part of the social fabric of the late 19th century in most western cultures. Yet today the impact of this contribution is little-known, and discussion of it limited. Relatively few specialists are researching in this field and know how to find slides and historical evidence in uncatalogued archives or private collections. It is not even clear what terminology we should use for consistent description of the medium. To take three examples: there were contemporary debates about "magic" versus "optical" lanterns (the latter being seen as more serious and educational); there is current controversy in some circles as to the term "pre-cinema" in describing optically based media which to greater or lesser extents contributed to the motion picture industries; and outside a very limited circle of knowledgeable amateurs there is now little or no currency of the technical terms needed to describe with precision the media and their effects.

Two particular terms are, however, quite useful, and on the whole we will use them in the following ways. The historic term "art of projection" (French "l'art de projection", German "Projektionskunst") is quite felicitous, echoing both the tradition of creative fine art to which much lantern material aspired, and the more prosaic sense of a technical craft in which lantern practitioners would become skilled. It covers all aspects of the design of materials for projection, the techniques by which they were projected, creative operation of apparatus as part of a term of performers (lecturers, reciters, singers or musicians), and interaction with a live audience, to name only some features of a complex performance medium. Above all the term "art of projection" signifies a creative potential.

Equally evocative is the term "screen culture", which picks up an approach most influentially made in Charles Musser's essay "Toward a History of Screen Practice".[2] If we can side-step the technological distinctions between (for example) lantern and cinematograph exhibition practice, and look instead at a set of continuities of practice in spectators viewing images on screen, we come closer to a practical understanding of the art of projection in its contemporary contexts. The screen, in the sense of the physical location of the image in relation to its audience, is the common factor in a whole range of communi-cation media practices of the late 19th and early 20th centuries – not necessarily always the centre of the process (music or vocal performance may have taken more of the audience's attention), but always essential.

Between them these two concepts unite the two essential features of lantern and cinematograph media: an image thrown through the air by light, and a surface on which it lands and becomes visible and readable. Successful use of the art of projection requires both aspects, as do all communicative and performative media, and this is reflected in their human dimensions: one or more creators of stories, lectures and/or images, and one or more performers, communicate something to one or more audience members. The overall conception of screen culture gives us a useful framework against which we can begin to place individual examples of topics addressed, techniques used, and impressions taken away.

One of the major public controversies of the late 19th and early 20th centuries in the industrialised world was known by various names, one of the most common of which was the "Social Question". It comprises complex socio-political questions based on a major contradiction, between liberal claims of civil rights and individual freedom on one hand, and prevalent destitution, pauperism and effective lack of rights on the other. Other severe concerns ranged from worries about epidemics spreading out from the slums, to fears that the existing social order could be swept away by uprisings or revolution. The Social Question was oriented towards interventions to change the living conditions of the poor, but also encompassed the debate about their reason and effectiveness. It was raised in many forms and contexts, from political debate and legislation, through campaigning journalism, to popular fiction and poetry. Given the widespread use of projection for public entertainment, it comes as no surprise that the art of projection was used on a large scale to spread concerns and promote solutions to the Social Question. It could even be used for practices of social intervention, by instructing the poor and preparing beneficial and affordable entertainment.

Deployment of screen culture for Social Question discussion took many forms, but, along with travelogue presentations and representations of Christian religious material (both areas which overlap with the Social Question) it represents one of the primary uses of the screen at this period. Among the common slide subjects in the catalogues of contemporary produc-ers are factual lectures using photographic slides to illustrate the conditions of the poor (sometimes with a genuine concern, sometimes with a condescending tone which treats poverty as quaint or entertaining); fictional slide sequences accompanying stories or recitations, often with a propaganda message against abuse of alcohol as a self-destructive feature of poverty; and promotion of organisations offering responses to poverty, particularly some of the organised churches, other religious groups and temperance movements. The overall effect of all these addresses to the Social Question was to promote it as a matter for public concern: more or less by definition, presenting a question to an audience is an invitation to all members of the group, collectively and severally, to take a position on the issue presented. By turning the issue into performance it was constituted as a public problem. There were other methods of doing this (melodramatic stage plays, or the many lecturers or reciters who presented social topics without using images), but the art of projection occupied its own place in this context, using spectacular presentation to impress serious points on its audiences.

In this volume sixteen international scholars address the issues of screen culture and the Social Question from the different perspectives of their individual research, with their essays gathered in three groups uniting related themes and strands of research. Drawing on a rich variety of primary sources they investigate the impact of the lantern and cinematograph in public lectures, entertainments, church services and electoral campaigns. They place the use of the optical lantern in the context of the multitude of visual media in the decades before and after 1900. In every case the relevance of projected presentation becomes obvious: it makes an essential difference for historical research if similar images are printed in books or papers for individual reception, if they are constantly available in exhibitions for examination by small groups or individuals, or if they are projected in deliberately arranged sequences for performances received within public gatherings.

The different approaches of the articles demonstrate altogether the relevance of screen culture in the area where social history and media history overlap. But the media history relevance of the Social Question to the establishment of screen media has hardly so far been examined. Nor have these media been critically investigated as social history sources. All the authors experienced the obstacles of an under-researched field of history, of which the lack of accessible and catalogued archives is one of the most severe.

The articles in the first part of the book reflect the role of screen culture in the public sphere and differentiate varied uses of the optical lantern and early cinema in the contexts of the controversial discourse of the Social Question and for political persuasion. They examine how social reformers like Jacob Riis, as well as charitable organisations, raised public awareness of living conditions of the poor and destitute. They discuss use of visually shocking lectures and adaptations of sentimental stories, like those of Victorian celebrity George R. Sims, to argue for social reform and encourage the audience to help themselves and others. Several examples describe the public interest in the Social Question as a market for the semi-industrial production of photographic lantern slides and early films.

The authors of the second part investigate the use of lantern shows, photography and early films for social prevention by charity and welfare organisations. Case studies demonstrate uses of projection as an agent of social prevention in the context of health and lifestyle. Activities of social intervention like the ongoing temperance campaigns regarded the optical lantern and the art of projection as an ideal medium to combine beneficial entertainment with instruction on desirable social behaviour. Presentations of visual media also turned out to be very helpful to familiarise new activists with living conditions in slums and tenements and to instruct vividly on the work of social institutions. In contrast, increasingly critical standpoints of social reformers against the cinema (at least the commercial cinema) in the 1910s are also reflected.

Finally, approaches to the "hidden history" of screen culture are outlined in the third part of the book, as a basis for proposal of an internationally agreed research agenda, including an introduction to the Lucerna Magic Lantern Web Resource. The lack of access to primary sources, especially lantern slides, is perceived widely as one of the main obstacles to research into screen culture. Several of the articles in this volume underline that the use of lantern slides is known from written evidence but it was impossible to find the slides themselves. It is quite possible that they still exist, since they were originally produced in large quantities, but without a more systematic approach to identifying which resources exist, and where and how they might be accessible, they might as well be lost.

As well as the influence of projected media on the Social Question, the history of the cultural establishment of the screen and its influence on social history needs international research to be better coordinated. More empirical data is necessary to answer economical, political, technical, and design questions and to enable audience research. Comparative analysis of historical screen practice (lantern and early cinema) within the wider context of social and cultural history requires micro-analytical approaches based on an internationally agreed research agenda, a major requirement of which is better identification and accessibility of the considerable historical resources that we do have available.

This volume, then, offers a fundamental step towards substantial research on screen culture in context of media and social history. The articles it contains are based on papers presented at the conference *Screen Culture and the Social Question: Poverty on Screen 1880-1914*, held at the German Historical Institute London (GHIL) in December 2011.[3] This conference was initiated by the Screen1900 research group at the University of Trier.[4]

Complementary to the papers presented, international experts Ian Christie (London, Birkbeck College), Scott Curtis (Northwestern University), Andreas Gestrich (GHIL) and Clemens Zimmerman (Universität Saarbrücken) drew together the individual approaches in summarising comments and conducted the discussion to open questions for future research. Many participants contributed observations based on their own research experience in the history of screen practice and stressed the needs for methodological agreements and an international research agenda. The main areas for future investigation identified as part of such an agenda included (in no particular order):

- material evidence (especially slides and supporting texts);
- technical and creative elements of the art of projection;
- intermedial comparison of the presentation of visual media;
- comparative research on international screen practice;
- investigation of the continuity of non-filmic screen practice with the optical lantern in the 20th century;
- analysis of the interconnections between art, philanthropy, and business;
- examination of the use of lantern shows for social and political persuasion and as practice in social work and pedagogy for instructing the "uneducated" and children;
- questioning the legitimacy of visual representations of the poor, specifically

photographs, created by middle-class producers for middle-class audiences; and

- repetition of motifs as representational strategies in narratives on poverty.

This makes no claim to be anything other than a partly subjective proposition from one series of viewpoints in one particular context. Another conference would have possibly created a different set of priorities. But we have to start somewhere, and the broad principles behind this ambitious outline would, we suggest, help any understanding of screen culture to move forward, with the potential to enrich any number of other areas of study in future.

The editors are particularly grateful to Professor Andreas Gestrich, Director of the GHIL, and his marvellous team who made this conference a fruitful and pleasant time for all participants. The conference, along with the publication of this volume, was made possible by the generous support of the Deutsche Forschungsgemeinschaft (DFG, German Research Foundation) and the GHIL.

Notes

1. The slide image itself is more complicated than meets the eye: it is taken from a set of 50 slides entitled *Street Life: or People we Meet*, produced by the British company Riley Brothers. Known references to the set clearly date it to 1887 or 1888, and in the catalogue listings its image title is "The Newsboy", with an accompanying reading text that refers only to "him". Yet in this image there are two boys, and the posters in the background carry dates from mid-1890. So this slide must be a later replacement for the original image, for some reason which is lost to us (at least) until the earlier version of the image comes to light.

2. Charles Musser, *The Emergence of Cinema: the American Screen to 1907* (Berkeley and New York: University of California Press, 1990), 16–54.

3. Screen Culture and the Social Question: Poverty on Screen 1880–1914. Conference of the German Historical Institute London in cooperation with Screen1900 Project, University of Trier, held at the GHIL, 1–3 December 2011. Conveners: Andreas Gestrich (GHIL) and Ludwig Vogl-Bienek (University of Trier). See Lydia Jakobs, "Screen Culture and the Social Question: Poverty on Screen 1880–1914", Conference Report, in *German Historical Institute London Bulletin*, 34:1 (2012): 191–196.

4. Screen1900 is a research focus in media studies at the University of Trier. Since 2002, several research projects have investigated the history of the screen, the optical or magic lantern and the art of projection in social and cultural contexts. See www.screen1900.uni-trier.de (accessed July 2013).

PART I:

Screen Culture and the Public Sphere – Raising Awareness of the Living Conditions of the Poor

Martin Loiperdinger

The Social Impact of Screen Culture
1880–1914

In 1889, the Liberal Club of Fulham (London) organised a lantern show for 1,450 destitute children. The weekly newspaper *The Graphic* published a picture of this performance in a wood engraving showing a large, packed auditorium decorated with paper lanterns and garlands. The view is toward the stage, whose back wall is covered by a lighted circle almost four metres in diameter in which a larger-than-life-size, bearded man in a nightcap lies in bed while two rodents make for his open mouth. The projection illuminant shines brilliantly in the lantern's housing. A projectionist operates the apparatus, and a second man acting as lecturer points to the image on the screen to underline to the audience his interpretation of what is occurring. A girl sitting on the shoulders of an adult is pointing at the image, as are several people in the first row, expressing the excitement with which they are following what happens on the screen.

The audience is viewing the well-known and popular lantern slide the MAN SWALLOWING RATS. A small painted glass slide rests in the projector, creating the pictorial information for the large projected image. The operator synchronises two mechanisms in the slide to produce movement on the screen. The image tells a story: the sleeping man opens and closes his mouth as both rodents approach in an arc and disappear into his open jaws. Without even noticing, he devours them! Presumably appropriate noises of snoring and smacking lips complete the entertaining performance.

The watching children were moved because presumably they had already experienced more or less frightful encounters with rats in their housing environments (and those who had not were probably afraid of such encounters). Rats were a plague in the slums of London: they outnumbered the human inhabitants of the densely packed tenements. Imagining someone swallowing

Facing page:
Upper: Magic Lantern Entertainment given to 1,450 poor and destitute children by the members of the Fulham Liberal Club and Institute, engraving from *The Graphic* (23 February 1889): 189.
Lower: MAN SWALLOWING RATS, lantern slide with combined rack work and lever mechanism, Carpenter & Westley, England, *c.*1880.

live rats was likely to make the children's skin crawl. Seeing someone unknowingly swallowing rats while sleeping adds a comic effect to the jitters, which might relieve the children's tension as they waver between shuddering and laughter. The fact that evidently contemporary audiences experienced the MAN SWALLOWING RATS with comic relief in the face of the harsh conditions in their own daily lives might explain the tremendous success of this particular "moving image", standard fare in many lantern shows at that time. The performances of this rackwork slide over decades offer an instructive example of the social impact produced by showmen and lecturers who projected pictures and by their audiences who watched them.

Victorian Lantern Shows – the Screen and Social Problems

In the engraving, the girl and the people in the first row pointing to the screen draw the attention of the readers of the *Graphic* to a leading cultural location for experiencing images: by 1889 the screen had become firmly established in Victorian society as a major place of communication through images. Projection technology was the basis of a pronounced media culture, with technical standards, established projectors and illuminants, a differentiated offering of images on slides, reliable channels of distribution and frequent performances. The performance at the Fulham Liberal Club was part of a cultural practice widespread at the time, not only in Great Britain. The term for such slide shows is the Art of Projection, *L'Art de la projection*, *L'arte della proiezione*, *Projektionskunst* etc. As early as the 1870s, apparatus manufacturers, image producers and operators formed a business network of their own, as can be seen in the issues of professional journals bearing the internationally current name of the projection apparatus in their titles: *The Magic Lantern* (London, from 1874), *Laterna magica* (Düsseldorf, from 1875) or *Lanterne magique* (Paris, from as early as 1833).

The manufacturers of devices and images were mainly small or mid-size private businesses situated in the photographic industry, for example Bamforth in northern England. The image selection was spread over various genres: producers' catalogues list geographic and travel images; scientific images; highlights from history; religious themes; current events; dissolving views; and "life model" slides, picture sequences consisting of up to 50 slides using amateur actors photographed against painted backgrounds to illustrate poems, ballads, fairy tales or literary narratives. A spoken text taken from a "reading" normally accompanied the slide set for the performance.[1] Many life model sets told stories of the poor and thus turned social problems directly into performance.[2]

In Britain, the customers for lantern equipment and slides were not only travelling showpeople earning their living by performing lantern shows. As early as 1850, the lantern had become "not only an amusing and rational recreation, but a powerful aid in the work of education".[3] In the 1880s, religious charity and welfare organisations concerned with the effects of social problems relating to industrialisation bought a large portion of the technical equipment and slides offered by specialised enterprises of Britain's photographic industry. Besides the Salvation Army, which was based on Methodist traditions, there were several large welfare and charity organisations in Anglican church circles engaged in poor relief, youth work and the temperance movement: The Church Army (CA), founded in 1882, introduced bands and lantern slides into Anglican services to return poorer groups to the fold of the Church.[4] In 1892 the CA established a Lantern Department, producing around a thousand slides per week, and lent out around 1.5 million slides for projection per year.[5] Starting the same year the CA began using horse-drawn mission vans in rural areas, moving from village to village to proclaim the Gospel with the aid of lantern shows, and by 1898 a fleet of 65 vans was in service.[6] The United Kingdom Band of Hope Union, devoted to complete abstinence from alcohol, organised three million youths in 22,000 local groups and regional associations. The Sunday School Union, in close cooperation with Bands of Hope, reached almost six million school pupils in their Sunday schools in Britain even after the introduction of religious instruction in schools. Bands of Hope and the Sunday School Union favoured using lantern slides to make their performances attractive for their target audiences.

These organisers paid close attention to the "appropriate" mixture of instruction and entertainment. For people for whom electric lighting was unknown, large, brightly shining images from slides were in themselves an attraction. However, the aesthetic qualities of the images alone were not sufficient for successful mission work. Their performance was therefore staged primarily within a social framework using celebrations or entertainments. If there was no occasion such as Harvest Festival, a procession or a parade available, the organiser had to provide a fitting framework, through religious rituals such as prayer service, sermon, hymn singing, or performance in extravagant costumes, humorous commentary or accompanying music. For an audience of poorer people, the serving of food and drink was especially attractive. At the conclusion of their lantern shows, organisations such as the Co-operative Movement customarily distributed samples of food they or the co-operative had produced themselves. Companies from the food industry did the same in their own travelling lantern shows to introduce housewives to their novel, time-saving products such as instant soup.[7] Similarly, the socialist newspaper *The Clarion* organised "Cinderella Clubs" providing free meals for poor children, entertaining them with music, dancing and the magic lantern. The children were given a bun and an orange upon leaving – and a sample copy of *The Clarion* for their parents.[8]

"Illustrated lectures" offered by charities, educational associations and the labour movement contained the projection of slides and an oral commentary in the hall. Projecting technically reproduced material was not sufficient in itself: personal communication was decisive for emotionally experiencing the images, normally via a lecturer explaining or commenting on the projected views.[9] The large charity organisations had professional lecturers with their own repertories to perform their "illustrated lectures". For example, Luther Hinton, a Sunday School Union lecturer, performed his commentary on the set MARTIN LUTHER, HIS LIFE AND TIMES at least 64 times. Performance reports state that, with his entertaining lecture style, he knew how to secure the attention of the audience.[10] If possible, the audience was encouraged to join in: in 1890, for instance, a lantern show by the Co-operative Movement in Greenwich illustrated a popular song, *The Death of Cock Robin*. The children sang along at the top of their voices, so that the singer spontaneously arranged a singing contest between the boys and the girls. Additional slides showed volcanoes and a mine, with the MAN SWALLOWING RATS as a comic filler. There followed a piano and a violin solo; chromatropes with their kaleidoscopically moving play of colours; repeated singing and, the grand finale, distribution of oranges and sweets.[11]

Besides these welfare organisations and political associations, there were entrepreneurs who tried to earn money with lantern work. Only a few prominent figures are known, like T.C. Hepworth, Charles Goodwin Norton or James Williamson in Britain,[12] Carl Skladanowsky & Sons in Berlin[13] or Paul Hoffmann in Vienna.[14] In addition to the few fixed-site commercial venues offering lantern lectures such as the Royal Polytechnic Institution in London or later the Urania in Berlin, Vienna and other cities, most lantern shows, commercial as well as persuasive, were performed by individual travelling town hall showpeople. As already mentioned, charity and welfare organisations in Britain engaged professional lecturers who earned their livings with lantern shows. Experts in lantern performance were also busy in the educational sector, for instance, Jens Lützen, who is said to have performed around 2,500 illustrated lectures from 1890 to 1908 on behalf of the Berlin-based *Gesellschaft zur Verbreitung von Volksbildung* (Society for the Promotion of Public Education).[15]

In Britain, the demand for slides for lectures by non-commercial religious, educational and political organisations constituted a relevant, if not predominant, sector of the market. It is still unknown to what extent lantern shows were arranged for commercial or for persuasive purposes (or for both). Only a few examples exist of enquiries into the local history of lantern shows: for example, Damer Waddington's history of projection entertainment in Jersey from 1814 to the First World War[16] and two samples of lantern shows mentioned in local newspapers over a few months, in Hastings, England, in 1881 and in Middletown, Connecticut, USA, in 1895.[17] To announce shows in Hastings and surrounding locations, the local press used terms like "lantern lecture", "lantern entertainment", "slide presentation", "religious show" and "dissolving view entertainment". Until more exhaustive micro-studies are conducted on the media history of lantern shows on the local level, not much more can be said than, all in all, there were a great number of lantern lectures and entertainments (whatever lecture and entertainment might have meant in the local context and time).

The Commercial Impact of the Cinématographe Lumière

The years before the turn of the 20th century saw the introduction of a new screen technology which was most successful in the entertainment business and, after more or less a decade, was regarded itself as a social problem: a serious danger that threatened young viewers, at least.

In the spring of 1896, cinematograph shows were announced with much ballyhoo and performed with great success as the "wonder of the century". The novelty was limited to the "special effect" of continuous movement. This illusion was produced by the new mechanical device which allowed intermittent projection of sixteen, twenty or more photographic images per second from a celluloid strip called film – including extremely short interruptions of the beam of light every time the film was moved to display the next still photograph. Authors of early film projection handbooks described the film strip as "a multiple lantern slide",[18] and the projector as "a lantern equipped with a mechanical slide changer".[19] Continuity characterised the relationship between lantern and cinematograph not only from the technical point of view, as Deac Rossell has argued:

> The magic lantern was not so much a "precursor" of the cinema as it was the environment into which the cinema was born, the *milieu* which nursed it through its extended period of invention to about 1903, the institution which provided its early business practices, and the medium with which the cinema coexisted for about two decades.[20]

In 1896, when film exhibition switched from Edison's Kinetoscope peepshows to projection, screen practice was already well established in the public sphere. Slide projections were performed in various entertaining and educational contexts and attracted targeted audiences. The field was well prepared for the Cinématographe Lumière and its tremendous success, in both social impact and economic profit.

The Cinématographe, which gave its name to the cinema, was a practical, comparatively light and simply operated all-purpose device to record, project and copy film. It was originally intended as an *appareil de salon* for private screenings of "living photographs" in the homes of amateur photographers. The targeted customers were well-situated people who could afford the pretty sum of 4,000 francs. In 1895, Louis Lumière filmed diverse subjects from family life to introduce the new apparatus to the targeted group of luxury consumers. The resounding success of the first projections in Paris occasioned a thorough alteration in the business model: the intended sale of machines to amateurs was shelved to obtain extra profit from the exclusive showing of their own films. Instead of, for a considerable sum, turning over the apparatus plus unexposed film to a limited number of amateur photographers, the company now charged admission to a potentially unlimited audience to view "living photographs" filmed and projected by the patent-protected Cinématographe.

The reorientation in the business model proved a success. The Cologne chocolate manufacturer Ludwig Stollwerck, who bought the German licence for Cinématographe film showings in March 1896, wrote to a business colleague in New York in April that year:

> Just imagine, in Paris M. Lumière has hired a billiard hall below the Grand Café where you have to go down a rather steep and unpleasant stairs. [...] He charges one franc admission; there are 180 seats and maybe 30 to 40 standing room places. The hall is full almost all day long. In the beginning, he took in 600 francs per day, then the take went up to 800 and 1,000 francs, and when I was in Paris three weeks ago he took in 2,500 to 3,000 francs a day. Now with the good weather and increased tourist traffic, the daily receipts amount to even 4,000 francs. Three weeks ago, he had altogether 12 apparatuses set up, taking in all told 12,000 francs a day on average. You can see what tremendous popularity he has achieved with the audience.[21]

Stollwerck calculated the economic power of the projections: a 20-minute screening of eight to ten 35mm films, each 40 to 50 seconds of projection, could reach more than 200 viewers assembled in front of the screen. A Cinématographe machine performed up to 20 showings a day. Entrance to the show cost 1 franc at first; later the fee was reduced to 50 centimes. Stollwerck's company attracted around 1,000 viewers per apparatus daily with the Lumière machines used in Germany: over the course of 1896 sometimes up to ten Cinématographe machines yielded an income of around 700,000 marks from considerably more than 1,400,000 viewers (price reductions not calculated).[22] All in all, the Societé Lumière earned a net profit of around four million francs from the sale of licences and its own Cinématographe showings in numerous countries.[23]

The projection technique offered ways to present pictures with enormous potential for increasing the number of shows and thus multiplying audiences. In 1896, these effects were well-known from lantern shows. The Société Lumière exploited the well-established practice of screening pictures for its own purposes: simply straightforward business. The protagonist of projection was now no longer a large charity organisation but an internationally active public company for photographic supplies. The business purpose of the Lumière company was to make profit to satisfy its shareholders. On the other hand, audiences paying to watch Cinématographe showings were likely to have experienced the apparatus as a lantern that worked very well, thanks to its sophisticated mechanism, to project living instead of still photographs. Audiences in 1896 were accustomed to sitting down before a screen in the certain expectation that images made from light would appear on the white cloth. The continuity of screen practice cannot be underestimated in explaining the tremendous success which the worldwide showings of the Cinématographe Lumière achieved in 1896.[24]

Screen Business and Moral Questions

Educational or persuasive lantern lectures and commercial shows apparently had to face little intervention by the censor. This applied initially to cinematograph shows as well. It is true that they were submitted to monitoring by the authorities, but, with a few exceptions such as L'AFFAIRE DREYFUS (1899), Georges Méliès' series of one-minute re-enactments of the notorious French court-martial, there were no public debates about film censorship or bans. During the first decade after the success of the Cinématographe Lumière, short film programmes of vaudeville theatres and travelling cinemas evidently aroused only occasional offence with the authorities.

The situation quickly changed with the first founding boom of fixed-site cinemas, which occurred in many countries around 1906. Vigorous economic competition among local nickelodeons or *Ladenkinos* (store-front theatres) favoured sensational fiction films about sex and crime, as well as sensational posters to attract viewers from the street. The risqué subjects of many film dramas could be recognised by any passers-by – thus also by school teachers, judges, clergy etc. While lantern lectures were respected as contributions to the public discourse on the Social Question, the entertaining business of cinema-tograph shows was more and more regarded as part of the social problem itself. Emerging cinema reform committees blamed local cinema owners, mobilised against the "scourge of cinema" and demanded rigorous measures against "trash and filth". They published articles and pamphlets with theories on influence and emulation, maintaining that violence and eroticism on screen would "incite" young people to criminal or morally reprehensible acts. Depic-tions of sex and crime became subject to severe criticism, with the aim of banning all scenes of death, murder, adultery and pre-marital sex. Cinema reform movements influenced public discourse most strongly in the USA and Germany.[25] Rigorous censorship was introduced in both countries around 1910, and as a result numerous film dramas were rendered incomprehensible by removal of key scenes. The film industry saw its economic interests under attack, while audiences felt cheated of promised sensations. From that point on, permanent negotiation and battling began for the integrity of film as intended by the producers in accordance with public demand. The film business relied on the return flow of invested capital with surplus, a matter of life and death for any profit-oriented enterprise.

Screen Culture – Options to Make Use of the Screen

Against claims made by some film historians, the cinematograph did not replace the lantern – on the contrary, lantern lectures expanded after the advent of the cinematograph in the late 1890s and remained stable into the 1910s. This conclusion can be drawn from many contemporary observations. Referring to France in 1905, Laurent Mannoni describes "la manie des projections fixes" in 2,772 secular education associations, in schools, the Catholic Church and particularly in the French army.[26]

Film historian Charles Musser began the first volume of his history of American film and cinema with a reference to *Ars magna lucis et umbrae* by the polymath Athanasius Kircher, whose work appeared in 1646.[27] Except for a few short remarks, Musser unfortunately did not trace the development of the art

Showman from Wales, with tri-unial magic lantern, cinematograph and Edison Phonograph, hand coloured photographic lantern slide, *c.*1900.

of projection in the USA beyond 1897, when film became established. But in the following two decades the similarities between lantern and cinematograph shows came to the fore, at least in contemporary screen practice and reception. Travelling lantern showpeople and travelling cinemas used the *dispositif* of the screen which had been established during the late 19th century as a ubiquitous focal point of public discourse. Urban audiences – and, from time to time, those in rural areas – were accustomed to gathering before a white cloth in the expectation of enjoying large images projected from a lantern. To project slides, the lantern was equipped with a slide carrier or changer; to project films, the lantern was equipped with a mechanical device for intermittent projection of at least sixteen frames a second from a celluloid strip. Many companies offered a projector designed to project slides as well as film strips. Most cinematograph shows included projections of slides, at least for announcing intervals, "take off your hats" reminders and promoting local enterprises. In the first decade after the advent of the Cinématographe Lumière in Britain, many lecturers and showmen combined lantern and cinematograph.

Many Passion Play shows (not just the Oberammergau *Passion Play*) combined lantern and cinematograph projections, for example SOLDIERS OF THE CROSS, a two-hour illustrated lecture by the Salvation Army performed with orchestral or choral music, and consisting of 200 colour images projected from slides and fifteen films running 90 seconds each to tell stories of Jesus Christ and the early Christian martyrs. It was conceived by Commander Herbert Henry Booth, son of the Salvation Army founder William Booth, and produced at the Army's Australasian headquarters in Melbourne. The show was performed in different versions, first in Australia and New Zealand from September 1900 to February 1902, and then in South Africa, Europe, the USA, Canada and again in Australia until 1920. In the course of time, the short films were replaced by extra slides.[28]

Up to this very day, purpose-built venues such as the Urania theatres in Germany and Austria continue to offer illustrated lectures with either slides or films. In the Weimar Republic after the First World War, not only long feature films but also illustrated slide lectures incited public controversies, as a recently published lecture by Armin T. Wegner shows. Wegner was a German medical officer in the Ottoman Empire and photographed the genocide committed during the expulsion of the Armenians into the Mesopotamian desert. His lecture in Berlin's Urania theatre on 19 March 1919 caused tumult in the audience.[29] The lantern maintained its hold in the public sphere, at least as a supplement to the predominantly commercial entertainment of the cinema.

So from the 1900s, the lantern and cinematograph screen culture offered various options for different purposes: religious welfare organisations enhanced their sermons with impressive slide projections; temperance activists performed life model slide stories against the demon drink; food companies and Co-operative movements projected images to promote their products; travelling showpeople entertained audiences to earn their living; film operators employed by emerging cinema chains entertained audiences to satisfy those companies' shareholders; surgeons screened films, and art historians projected slides, to teach medical and fine arts students respectively; political parties, the churches, public health campaigns, navy leagues and colonial associations, as well as trade unions, used enlarged images projected from slides and films to make their persuasive efforts more effective for large audiences. Performers chose to use either slides or films, or both, for an illustrated lecture or an entertaining show depending on access and suitability for their purposes. In teaching, slides were preferred over films, as time for comments was limited by running times of films while slides allowed a free hand in timing the lesson.

So it was only after the First World War that screen practice in many countries showed a trend toward separation in the use of slides and films. The education sector preferred slides to films, whereas in the entertainment business of commercial cinemas the use of slides became more or less limited to announcements and local adverts. But film programmes never entirely excluded illustrated slide lectures from the public sphere.

Notes

1. See Richard Crangle and Ann Hecht, "Life Model Slides", in David Robinson, Stephen Herbert and Richard Crangle (eds), *Encyclopaedia of the Magic Lantern* (London: Magic Lantern Society, 2001), 172; and also Ludwig Vogl-Bienek's article in this volume.

2. See Ludwig Vogl-Bienek, "Turning the Social Problem into Performance: Slumming and Screen Culture in Victorian Lantern Shows", in Marta Braun et al. (eds), *Beyond the Screen: Institutions, Networks and Publics of Early Cinema* (New Barnet, Herts: John Libbey, 2012), 315–324.

3. Carpenter and Westley's *Companion* (1850), quoted in Mervyn Heard, *Phantasmagoria: the Secret Life of the Magic Lantern* (Hastings: The Projection Box, 2006), 213.

4. See Stephen Bottomore, "Projecting for the Lord – the work of Wilson Carlile", *Film History* 14:2

(2002): 195–209; Frank Gray, "Mission on Screen: the Church Army and its Multi-Media Activities", in Braun et al., *Beyond the Screen*, 27–34.

5.   Ludwig Vogl-Bienek, "Projektionskunst und soziale Frage. Der Einsatz visueller Medien in der Armenfürsorge um 1900", in Jörg Requate (ed), *Das 19. Jahrhundert als Mediengesellschaft: Les medias au XIXe siècle*, Ateliers des Deutschen Historischen Instituts Paris, vol. 4 (Munich: Oldenbourg, 2009), 162–177, here 168.

6.   Torsten Gärtner, "The Church on Wheels. Travelling Magic Lantern Mission in late Victorian England", in Martin Loiperdinger (ed.), *Travelling Cinema in Europe: Sources and Perspectives*. KINtop Schriften 10 (Frankfurt and Basel: Stroemfeld, 2008), 129–141.

7.   Best known is the Swiss company Maggi, cf. Yvonne Zimmermann, "Maggis Wandervortragspraxis mit Lichtbildern. Ein Schulmädchenreport aus der Schweiz von 1910", *KINtop* 14/15 (2006), 53–65.

8.   See www.wcml.org.uk/contents/creativity-and-culture/leisure/clarion-movement/pages-from-the-clarion-scout/ (accessed 27 March 2013).

9.   See Joe Kember, *Marketing Modernity: Victorian Popular Shows and Early Cinema*. (Exeter: University of Exeter Press, 2009), 44–68.

10.   See Torsten Gärtner, "*The Sunday School Chronicle* – eine Quelle zur Nutzung der Laterna magica in englischen Sonntagsschulen", *KINtop* 14/15 (2006), 25–35.

11.   See Karen Eifler, "Between attraction and instruction: Lantern shows in British poor relief", *Early Popular Visual Culture* 8:4 (2010): 363–384.

12.   Stephen Herbert, "Charles Goodwin Norton", and Martin Sopocy, "James Williamson", both in Stephen Herbert and Luke McKernan (eds), *Who's Who of Victorian Cinema: A Worldwide Survey* (London: British Film Institute, 1996); also Stephen Herbert, "Hepworth, Thomas Craddock" in Robinson et al., *Encyclopaedia of the Magic Lantern*, 135.

13.   Hauke Lange-Fuchs, "Die Reisen des Projektionskunst-Unternehmens Skladanowsky", *KINtop* 11 (2002), 123–143, and Janelle Blankenship, "'Leuchte der Kultur' – Imperialism, Imaginary Travel and the Skladanowsky Welt-Theater", *KINtop* 14/15 (2006), 37–51.

14.   See Detlev Hoffmann and Almut Junker (eds), *Laterna magica: Lichtbilder aus Menschenwelt und Götterwelt* (Berlin: Frölich und Kaufmann, 1982).

15.   Jens Ruchatz, *Licht und Wahrheit: Eine Mediumgeschichte der fotografischen Projektion* (Munich: Wilhelm Fink, 2003), 257.

16.   Damer Waddington: *Panoramas, Magic Lantern, Cinemas: a Century of "Light" Entertainment in Jersey 1814–1914* (Jersey: Tocan Books, 2003).

17.   Stephen Herbert, "A Slice of Lantern Life: Lantern Presentations in and around Hastings in Early 1881", and Terry and Debbie Borton, "How Many American Lantern Shows in a Year?", both in Richard Crangle, Mervyn Heard and Ine van Dooren (eds), *Realms of Light: Uses and Perceptions of the Magic Lantern from the 17th to the 21st Century* (London: Magic Lantern Society, 2005), 185–192 and 105–115 respectively.

18.   Henry V. Hopwood, *Living Pictures: Their History, Photo-Production and Practical Working* (London: The Optician and Photographic Trades Review, 1899), 188, quoted in Deac Rossell, "Double Think: The Cinema and Magic Lantern Culture" in John Fullerton (ed.), *Celebrating 1895: the Centenary of Cinema* (London: John Libbey, 1998), 30.

19.   C. Francis Jenkins, *Animated Pictures* (Washington, D.C.: published by the Author, 1898), 100, quoted in Rossell, "Double Think", 35.

20.   Rossell, "Double Think", 30.

21.   Ludwig Stollwerck to John Volkmann, New York (16 April 1896), quoted in Martin Loiperdinger, *Film & Schokolade: Stollwercks Geschäfte mit lebenden Bildern*. KINtop Schriften 4 (Frankfurt and Basel: Stroemfeld, 1999), 122–123.

22.   Ibid., 187–191.

23.   Ibid., 192.

24.   See the numerous entries of Cinématographe Lumière premieres in Deac Rossell: "'The New Thing with the Long Name and the Old Thing with the Name that Isn't Much Shorter …': A Chronology of Cinema 1889–1896", *Film History* 7:2 (1995).

25. See Lee Grieveson, *Policing Cinema: Movies and Censorship in Early Twentieth-Century America* (Berkeley, Los Angeles and London: University of California Press, 2004), and Sabine Haake, *The Cinema's Third Machine: Writing on Film in Germany, 1907–1933*. (Lincoln and London: University of Nebraska Press, 2003), 27–60.

26. Laurent Mannoni, "Plaque de verre ou celluloid? Lanterne magique et cinéma: la guerre d'Indépendance", *1895*, no. 7 (1989), 3–6.

27. Charles Musser, *The Emergence of Cinema: the American Screen to 1907*. History of the American Cinema, vol. 1 (Berkeley, Los Angeles, London: University of California Press, 1990), 17–24.

28. See www.nfsa.gov.au/collection/documents-artefacts/soldiers-cross/ (accessed 28 March 2013).

29. Armin T. Wegner, Andreas Meier (ed.), *Die Austreibung des armenischen Volkes in die Wüste: Ein Lichtbildervortrag*, (Göttingen: Wallstein, 2011).

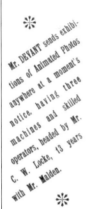

Stephen Bottomore

The Lantern and Cinematograph for Political Persuasion before WWI: Towards an Introduction and Typology

I t is apparent from examining a variety of sources that the projected image was often used for political persuasion, propaganda and campaigning from the late 19th century to the Great War. However, not much has been published on this theme by film and lantern historians, and almost nothing has appeared in terms of an overview. Given the large size of the field, this article will inevitably be something of a "lightning tour", but it is worth offering this rapid and sketchy excursion for three reasons: firstly to try to suggest some differences between the "social question" (the main theme of this collection) and what I will call the "political question" with reference to the screen; secondly to attempt to delineate some sub-categories of political uses of the screen; and thirdly to try to stimulate more research into screen propaganda, especially in this early film era.

Before going any further, and in case lantern-oriented scholars should be surprised at the omissions, let me mention two aspects of the political screen which I will *not* be covering. I will not be dealing with the magic lantern as depicted in drawings or caricatures for purposes of political satire (even though this was perhaps the first conjunction of politics with the lantern).[1] And I will not be dealing with uses of the lantern to display the results of elections, for although that was probably the first *practical* employment of screen media for political purposes, it did not constitute political persuasion or campaigning as such – it was essentially a form of news.[2] For the same reason I will not include film newsreels about politics and the like, because these are not in principle propaganda but are meant to take a non-partisan view.

Having fenced out these two areas that I will not cover, I will explain how I have divided up the remainder of the territory of political uses of the screen.

Facing page:
In Britain, the Primrose League attracted a large membership for the Tory cause by featuring famous performers such as magician David Devant and his new "animated photographs". Advertisement from *Primrose League Gazette*, 1 December 1896.

Firstly, some attempt at definition. The term "politics" was originally defined as the art or science of civil government, but in more recent times the meaning has been broadened to cover almost any relationship of power and authority between people and organisations.[3] This range of meaning, both narrow and broad, is convenient for my purposes because I plan first to deal with political uses in a more general sense, then move into more specific uses, and end on the most *strictly* political application of all (according to that original definition), by which I mean screen campaigns to win governmental elections.

Varieties of political persuasion on screen

I have consulted a large number of sources (books, journals, etc.) about lantern and early film history from a variety of countries, and I find that political uses of the screen, if such are mentioned, tend to fall into a limited number of types or categories. I suggest that uses of the screen for political persuasion in the pre-WWI era may be divided into five categories, several of which can be refined in further sub-categories, and I intend to deal with them under these headings and in this order:

1. Social issue campaigns and narratives.

2. Anti-establishment and liberation campaigns.

3. Pro-establishment censorship and regulation.

4. Pro-establishment campaigns.

5. Electoral campaigns.

1. Social issue campaigns and narratives

I start with the use of screen media to depict social deprivation and other such issues. This is probably the most questionable of my five categories, because it is not clear whether many of these types of screen production were really political at all. Such lantern slide sets and films were mainly made about, or to publicise, issues of social deprivation such as poverty, child labour, slums, etc. Usually they were made commercially, sometimes they were sponsored. In this category I would include, firstly, life-model slides based on texts by authors such as George R. Sims and produced by makers such as James Bamforth or York & Son; secondly, the social-documentation slides of Jacob Riis, Lewis Hine and the like; and thirdly, "social films" as Kevin Brownlow calls them, made by various companies especially in America, up to the 1910s.[4]

I question whether many of these were truly political because, although they depicted poverty and injustice, they rarely addressed the causes of such deprivation. Colin Gordon has argued that life-model slides presented poverty as an issue to evoke sympathy, and not a *problem* requiring political or legislative intervention; indeed poor people in these slides were sometimes presented as merely picturesque or "interesting", or even somehow ennobled through suffering.[5] Similarly, although Jacob Riis showed images of dire poverty in New York, he apparently believed that the solution to these problems was

Lantern slide showing social concern: Slide 5 of TED'S TATTERED JACKET (G.M. Mason, 14 slides, 1900s). While perhaps not directly political, this type of story addressed social issues facing its audiences: here the hero loses a job because his jacket is too shabby; the family's poverty is only relieved when the father gives up alcohol.

reform or charity, not fundamental change and redistribution of wealth or power.

I have not been able to establish what percentage such slide sets represented of all lantern sets, but "social films", my third sub-category, apparently made up around 8% of films released in the early 20th century.[6] Although some of these have been portrayed as radical, and many of them depict working class settings – for example LILY OF THE TENEMENTS (Griffith, 1911) – on the whole they use these settings merely as suitable locations for melodramatic stories, with an implication that a personal intervention rather than a political one can best solve characters' problems.[7] On rare occasions these commercially-made "social films" do venture something more critical, especially when they contrast poor with wealthy people, in such films as THE KLEPTOMANIAC (Porter, 1904) or A CORNER IN WHEAT (Griffith, 1909). But in these cases the implication is usually that particular wealthy individuals are at fault rather than government or the system. So to sum up: these "social" issue slide and film productions only rarely and marginally campaign or argue for political change.

2. Anti-establishment and liberation campaigns

We now move into more truly *political* territory, also moving from productions which were usually made for *commercial* exhibition, to those which were more often made as *sponsored* slide and film productions, though this is not a hard-and-fast rule.

In this category of political screen campaigns I include three subcategories: labour, women's suffrage and national liberation.[8] One might call all of these broadly "left wing" campaigns, although people involved in the latter two – suffrage and nationalist campaigns – might not necessarily have categorised themselves as leftish. Nevertheless, their aims were certainly to broaden political rights in opposition to the existing state of affairs, so their agendas were in that sense anti-conservative.

In the first subcategory I place those few lanternists who presented a radical agenda for social change, and perhaps the best example is the campaigner from the *Clarion* newspaper, William Palmer (1860-1941), alias "Whiffly Puncto".[9] In the mid-1890s Palmer travelled through Britain giving shows in which he projected slides of both luxurious and poverty-stricken communities, alternating the two extremes to create a visual dialectic to counter gross inequality and the status quo; his shows were accompanied by sarcastic commentary and music.

A broadly socialist agenda may also be found in a number of film initiatives before the Great War. From around 1903, the Co-operative organisation in Britain made and exhibited films to promote their ideas of mutual aid, and to condemn low wages.[10] A decade later there were various attempts to establish union-run cinemas in industrial areas of Britain.[11] In France the "Cinema du Peuple" project exhibited socialist films, including their own productions about working people, and even produced a film about the Paris Commune.[12] Meanwhile in the USA between 1911 and 1914 at least three left-wing films were made by "worker filmmakers", as Steven Ross calls them.[13] In other countries there were a handful of ventures such as the "Red Cinema" in Amsterdam.[14] Altogether this sounds quite an extensive list of early radical screen initiatives, but, with the possible exception of the Co-operative movement's work in Britain, these were piecemeal and transitory efforts.

The female suffrage campaigns of the years before the Great War also spawned a considerable number of films. Most of these were commercially-made dramas, especially satires of the movement; however, a few actual campaigning films were made, notably in the United States, sponsored by suffrage organisations and sometimes featuring the movement's leaders.[15] In Britain it seems that the suffragettes had another approach: being skilful in publicity, they

Advertisement for a socialist lantern show presented by "Whiffly Puncto" and featuring the celebrated campaigner, Robert Blatchford. *The Clarion* 19 December 1896.

organised events that they believed would be filmed by newsreel companies, thereby creating a regular presence for themselves on screens.[16]

In my third subcategory, "national liberation", I place the various instances of screen propaganda to campaign for nationalist or anti-colonialist aims. An early example came when campaigners for Irish rights and home rule showed lantern slides at the House of Commons in 1890 to attack English imperialism in

Ireland and draw Parliament's attention to their concerns.[17] I suspect that there were instances of lantern shows or campaigns in or about other countries under foreign domination during the late 19th century (only further research will tell). Early films were also used to convey some of the various nationalist messages of the time onto screens. For instance, D.G. Phalke's mythological films made in India from 1913 offered a symbolic argument for independence from Britain.[18] Meanwhile, some early film showmen in colonised countries managed to generate their own nationalist messages by choosing suitable pre-existing films sometimes with an anti-authoritarian theme; they might then localise the message by subtle use of commentary during the screening. Some instances of this are emerging through research on cinema in the colonised Philippines and Korea, and in partitioned Poland.[19]

3. Pro-establishment censorship and regulation

It is often forgotten when discussing political cinema that what is withheld from the screen is as important as what is shown. While I have not found instances of lantern slides or lantern shows being censored or banned for political reasons, this certainly happened with films – mainly applied by, or on behalf of, the establishment to silence their opponents.[20] Perhaps the first film to be barred in this way was Georges Méliès' 1899 depiction of the controversial Dreyfus affair, L'AFFAIRE DREYFUS.[21] In the silent era, in countries including Germany and Czarist Russia and in certain colonised states, films were banned (and film shows closed down) which promoted left-wing or subversive opinions.

Particularly likely to be banned were any films that depicted sympathetically or seemed to encourage strikes or industrial action by workers, or that challenged the authority or dignity of elites. Thus in Berlin in 1911 a film that included scenes of a workers' strike (and sabotage) was completely banned, and was only allowed to be screened when the offending shots had been deleted. German censorship was markedly strict on these kinds of issue: later that year a trade writer noted that "no film which in any way suggests a rising of the down-trodden is permitted".[22]

Censors were equally concerned about references to the other end of the social spectrum, and in countries such as Russia, Germany and Japan any on-screen criticism of their rulers or high authorities was banned. In Japan it was forbidden "under severe penalties" for a film to ridicule any person holding Government office. The Japanese Emperor was, of course, never to be criticised, so an early Pathé film depicting the French Revolution and fall of King Louis XVI was prohibited in case comparisons were drawn between the possible fates of the French and Japanese rulers.[23] Even in supposedly tolerant Britain, after film censorship was introduced in the early 1910s, the censors would eliminate scenes "tending to disparage public characters and institutions" (these included monarchs, government ministers and judges).[24]

There were also attempts to encourage self-censorship; this happened in the USA for example, with exhibitors being advised not to show controversial or socially critical films which might conjure up in their spectators' minds "unhappy thoughts".[25]

4. Pro-establishment campaigns

I have seen little evidence that broadly "right-wing" films or lantern slides were curbed through censorship, even though such productions were far more numerous and widely shown than the left-wing variety. I divide such conservative productions into three types: colonial, militarist and miscellaneous.

The topic of colonial screen propaganda is very extensive. I have discussed this theme in separate papers where I proposed further subdivisions, the main distinctions being whether the slide set or film in question was primarily designed to be shown in the colonised or in the colonising country, and whether it was produced commercially or was sponsored.[26] To mention briefly some examples of the various permutations: in Europe, lantern sets giving a rosy view of the colonies were widely shown to the public from the late 19th century; while early in the 20th century businessmen viewed films sponsored by colonial administrations or companies which promoted investment in various parts of Africa. Meanwhile in the French colonies of North Africa and Indochina local people were shown films specifically selected to demonstrate the military and economic power of their colonial masters; and commercially-made fiction films shown in such countries often reinforced a message of colonial supremacy. Whatever the venue, the audience or genre, the message of colonial slides and films was much the same: that it was right and proper for one nation or people to control the affairs of another.

My second, sometimes related, category is early screen militarism, a theme which, like colonialism, was expressed in multiple forms and genres, and produced in various countries by various makers. Several lantern and early film showmen inclined to the nationalist point of view, and needed little prompting to bend their lantern or cinematograph projector to the chauvinist task. In addition, there were a number of organisations, including the naval leagues, most notably the German one, which sponsored screen presentations for large audiences from the late 1890s, to demonstrate both the power of the nation's forces and the need to develop them further.[27] During wartime, such militarist screen displays increased enormously in number and belligerent tone: as examples one need only mention the many films and slides screened about the Spanish-American and Anglo-Boer wars, usually in support of the dominant side.

My third subcategory, "miscellaneous", comprises screen productions sponsored by other broadly right-wing organisations. One might include certain industrial and business-booming films, for example; and slides or films for various patriotic leagues and institutions, which supported a broadly reactionary agenda of tradition, patriotism, armed force and empire. Organisations such

Many cameras (including film cameras) covered President McKinley's Inauguration on 4 March 1901, but US Presidents in this era rarely used film for actual campaigning.

as Britain's Empire League helped to mount spectacular imperial events, pageants and coronations (several occurred in Britain in 1911) which were effectively "designed to be filmed", and acted as soft propaganda for the monarchy and empire. In some cases these leagues and institutions worked so clearly for right-wing *party* political ends that I subsume their screen activity into my fifth category.

5. Electoral campaigns

For historians of propaganda this may be the most intriguing category, because electoral campaigning is the most blatant form of political persuasion, indeed the most literally "political" of my categories according to the original definition of that word.

I have found scant information about the use of magic lantern slides for electoral campaigning, apart from in Britain which I will come to in a moment, though there are several examples of the use of early *film* in this role, in various countries. The cinema trade press carried brief reports of film used in electoral campaigns, including instances in Australia in 1909, Venezuela 1911, France 1913, and Sweden in 1914.[28] However these are cursory references, and I suspect that they describe not *sustained* screen campaigns, but one-off experiments. Almost equally meagre, surprisingly, are the data for the United States up to the early film era.

One might expect that both the lantern and film in its early years would have been widely used in American political campaigning, but other than Charles Musser's recent article on the subject I have not so far seen much evidence for this, though it might be buried in newspapers of the time.[29] I did find a few

Header for an article about electoral campaigning in Britain on the Tariff Reform issue, using a horse-drawn van fitted with a magic lantern and rear-projection screen. *Focus,* 17 February 1904.

instances of the lantern used in regional political campaigns in New York in the mid-1890s, but thereafter it seems that remarkably little screen campaigning was done nationwide in the period up to the First World War, by candidates for Presidential office at least.

For instance, although William McKinley for his 1896 and 1900 campaigns established a press office and had a photographer trailing him, he apparently made little effort to employ screen media. He was filmed by Biograph in his home town, and these scenes were shown in various theatres and other venues, but strictly speaking that does not constitute a screen *campaign*.[30] Theodore Roosevelt has sometimes been called the "first media President" because he was so often filmed.[31] But these shots were taken by newsreel companies, and Roosevelt himself had no particular interest in film as a medium for campaigning or anything else, according to one of his biographers.[32] In the 1908 election William Jennings Bryan did have a film of himself made (and possibly in his 1900 campaign too), but a single film surely does not make a campaign. Incidentally, his rival Taft, who was reluctant to use any publicity methods, won the 1908 election. Perhaps the first presidential candidate to take film seriously as a campaigning instrument was Woodrow Wilson in the 1912 and 1916 campaigns,[33] though the details of this are still obscure – as with so much else in the history of early screen campaign politics.

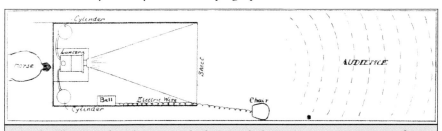

Another illustration from the same article, depicting the lantern/van arrangement as seen from above. The bell is to signal slide changes to the lantern operator inside the van.

So to Britain, where I suggest that screen projection was taken rather more seriously as a means for campaigning than it was in other countries. There were some piecemeal steps in this direction from the late 19th century by various parties and groups. In the London County Council election of 1894 to 1895 both major parties used lantern projection to demonstrate to the electorate the alleged improvements – or lack of them – that had been made to the Capital. On a national scale, from the 1890s the Liberals used lantern projection to promote their free trade policy, with Winston Churchill being a particularly keen advocate of this tool of visual propaganda.[34] All these, however, were somewhat limited and short-lived uses of screen media, as was true with the above-mentioned examples from other countries. By contrast, I suggest that deployment of screen and other visual media for national campaigning and electoral persuasion by the British Conservative Party was in a different league. What makes the pioneering effort of the Conservatives different, I suggest, is that it was on a large-scale, was sustained over many years, and involved the lantern, early film and other media. I will briefly outline some of the pertinent points.

The Conservative screen propaganda effort began around the 1880s when lantern slides promoting the Party's policies were shown throughout the country at gatherings of the Primrose League.[35] The League had a huge membership, and promoted Tory policies on issues such as "Tariff Reform" (protection of imperial trade), control of immigration and opposition to wealth taxes. The Conservative screen propaganda effort then moved outward to the general public, and the Party increasingly used visual media in electoral contests from the mid-1890s, especially in London. This type of campaigning grew in scale, and in 1907 an entire fleet of specially-equipped vans toured Britain, showing slides and films to promote the policy of Tariff Reform. Thousands of public meetings were addressed up and down the country, and – according to reports in the Conservative Party archives – literally millions of spectators in Britain saw this projected propaganda.[36] A similar campaign was mounted in 1910, with numerous projectors being set up nationwide, showing films to counter Lloyd George's wealth-taxing budget. Incidentally, in this same year the Party produced other forms of campaign publicity materials in abundance: over a million posters, 2.8 million postcards, and 46 million leaflets. The Conservative Party had reached a high degree of organisational sophistication by this stage, and the screen was just one means among several to reach out to the electorate.[37]

I would suggest that this screen propaganda effort by the Conservatives was comparable in scale to the Soviet agit-train programme of the 1920s (though that is probably not a comparison the Conservatives themselves would appreciate). In short, this was the first major, long-term political campaign using screen media, a campaign which had developed over some 30 years from the 1880s to the eve of the Great War, and then was resumed in the 1920s.[38] Much more could be said about this pioneering screen media campaign by Britain's Conservatives, but that will have to await further investigation.

I have tried here to develop a typology for a subject – the origins of political campaigning on screen – which is not the main subject of this book. However, one can certainly see points of contact in this pre-Great War era between social issues and political issues promoted via screen media, most obviously in the first of my five categories with the "social films" I have described. And there is another parallel worth mentioning, for if the "social question" in the context of screen projection has been somewhat neglected by scholars, even more unjustly neglected has been the "political question". The use of lantern and cinematograph for political persuasion and propaganda is a subject which – to employ that familiar phrase from the academic world – "deserves further research".

Notes

1. Illustrators from the 18th century, in drawing satirical images about politics, sometimes used the magic lantern as a symbol of truth, to contrast with the deceptions of statesmen or monarchs.

2. The use of the magic lantern to show election results possibly took place as early as the 1868 US Presidential election campaign, though the first hard evidence I have seen of such use was during the 1872 election. The employment of lanterns for election results continued into the early cinema era. See Leora Wood Wells, "The Magic Lantern in Politics", *ML Bulletin* (September 1980): 2; and illustration in *Frank Leslie's Illustrated Newspaper* (23 November 1872): 161.

3. This or similar meanings are given in various online dictionaries.

4. See the Introduction to Kevin Brownlow, *Behind the Mask of Innocence* (London: Cape/Knopf, 1990).

5. Colin Gordon, *By Gaslight in Winter: A Victorian Family History Through the Magic Lantern* (London: Elm Tree, 1980), 52, 83–84.

6. Miriam Hansen finds that in a sample of 150 films from the years 1905 to 1916, about a dozen deal with themes such as poverty, slum life and ethnic difference. See Miriam Hansen, *Babel and Babylon: Spectatorship in American Silent Film* (Cambridge, Mass.: Harvard University Press, 1991), 70.

7. Hansen, *Babel and Babylon*.

8. These are virtually the same three movements which George Dangerfield depicts as so crucial in his account of Britain in the pre-WWI era. See George Dangerfield, *The Strange Death of Liberal England, 1910–1914* (New York: Capricorn Books, 1961 [1935]).

9. See *The Clarion* (19 December 1896): 404; and *The Clarion* (27 March 1897): 100. His name is sometimes spelled "Whiffley".

10. See Alan Burton, *The British Consumer Co-operative Movement and Film, 1890s-1960s* (Manchester: Manchester University Press, 2005).

11. See for example "A Working Man's Cinema", *The Bioscope* (6 November 1913): 467.

12. Tangui Perron, "'Le Contrepoison est entre tes Mains, Camarades': C.G.T. et Cinéma au Début du Siècle", *Le Mouvement Social*, no. 172 (July–September 1995): 21–36.

13. Steven Ross, *Working-class Hollywood: Silent Film and the Shaping of Class in America* (Princeton: Princeton University Press, 1998).

14. Bert Hogenkamp, "De roode bioscoop", *Skrien*, no. 136 (Summer 1984): 33–35. The well-known socialist leader, Hendrik De Man, also had early plans to use film for propaganda. See also Daniel Biltereyst, Philippe Meers and Lies Van de Vijver, "Social Class, Experiences of Distinction and Cinema in Postwar Ghent" in Richard Maltby, Daniel Biltereyst and Philippe Meers (eds), *Explorations in New Cinema History: Approaches and Case Studies* (Oxford: Wiley-Blackwell, 2011).

15. Martin Norden, "A Good Travesty upon the Suffragette Movement: Women's Suffrage Films as Genre", *Journal of Popular Film and Television* 13, no. 4 (Winter 1986): 171–177.

16. See Lisa Tickner, *The Spectacle of Women: Imagery of the Suffrage Campaign, 1907–14* (London: Chatto & Windus, 1988).

17. Fintan Cullen, "Marketing National Sentiment: Lantern Slides of Evictions in Late Nineteenth-Century Ireland", *History Workshop Journal*, no. 54 (2002): 162–179; and see *The Times* (21 June 1890): 7. See also Kevin Rockett and Emer Rockett, *Magic Lantern, Panorama and Moving Picture Shows in Ireland, 1786–1909* (Dublin: Four Courts Press, 2011).

18. See Brigitte Schulze, *Humanist and Emotional Beginnings of a Nationalist Indian Cinema in Bombay. With Kracauer in the Footsteps of Phalke* (Berlin: Avinus, 2003).

19. See for example Sheila Skaff, *The Law of the Looking Glass: Cinema in Poland, 1896–1939* (Athens: Ohio University Press, 2008), 48. See also Germain Lacasse, "The Film Lecturer", in André Gaudreault, Nicolas Dulac and Santiago Hidalgo (eds), *A Companion to Early Cinema* (Oxford: Wiley-Blackwell, 2012), 492–493.

20. Robert Goldstein, "Political Censorship of Cinema in Pre-World War I Europe", *Michigan Academician* 21, no. 1 (1989): 45–65; Daniel Czitrom, "The Redemption of Leisure: The National Board of Censorship and the Rise of Motion Pictures in New York City, 1900–1920", *Studies in Visual Communication* 10, no. 4 (Fall 1984): 2–6.

21. See Stephen Bottomore, "'Zischen und Murren'. Die Dreyfus-Affäre und das frühe Kino", *KINtop*, no. 2 (1993): 69–82.

22. Heide Schlüpmann, "Early German cinema – Melodrama: social drama", in Richard Dyer and Ginette Vincendeau (eds), *Popular European Cinema* (London and New York: Routledge, 1992), 218–219. See also *Moving Picture World* (2 December 1911): 720.

23. *The Cinema* (19 February 1914): 23; Donald Richie, *A Hundred Years of Japanese Film* (Tokyo: Kodansha, 2005), 21–22.

24. *The Bioscope* (19 February 1914): 729; *Daily News* (6 November 1912): 5.

25. Quoted in Tom Gunning, "Weaving a Narrative: Style and Economic Background in Griffith's Biograph Films", *Quarterly Review of Film Studies* 6, no. 1 (Winter 1981): 15.

26. Stephen Bottomore, "Early Missionary Filming and the Emergence of the Professional Camera-man", in Marta Braun et al. (eds), *Beyond the Screen: Institutions, Networks and Publics of Early Cinema* (London: John Libbey, 2012); and Stephen Bottomore, "Imperialism and Early Cinema", unpublished paper. See also Wolfgang Fuhrmann, "Locating Early Film Audiences: Voluntary Associations and Colonial Film", *Historical Journal of Film, Radio and Television* 22, no. 3 (August 2002), 291–304.

27. Martin Loiperdinger, "The Beginnings of German Film Propaganda: the Navy League as Traveling Exhibitor, 1901–1907", *Historical Journal of Film, Radio and Television* 22, no. 3 (August 2002): 305–313.

28. See for example "Electioneering by Cinematograph", *The Bioscope* (21 October 1909): 27; and a news item in *Westminster Gazette* (30 March 1914): 10.

29. See Charles Musser, "Cinema, Newspapers and the U.S. Presidential Election of 1896", in A. Quintana and J. Pons (eds), *The Construction of News in Early Cinema* (Girona: Museu del Cinema, 2012), 65–84.

30. Jonathan Auerbach, "McKinley at Home: How Early American Cinema Made News", *American Quarterly* 51, no. 4 (December 1999): 797–832; Margaret Leech, *In the Days of McKinley* (New York: Harper & Row, 1959) covers aspects of film and photography in McKinley's campaigns.

31. Karen C. Lund, "The First Presidential 'Picture Man': Theodore Roosevelt and His Times on Film", *LC Information Bulletin* 58, no. 9 (September 1999): 212–214.

32. Edward Wagenknecht, *The Seven Worlds of Theodore Roosevelt* (New York: Langmans, 1958), 78.

33. See for example an item in *Universal Weekly* (5 October 1912): 3–4.

34. Some Liberal slides are detailed in "The Lantern and the Election", *Review of Reviews* (February 1895): 172–173; and see Frank Trentmann, *Free Trade Nation: Commerce, Consumption, and Civil Society in Modern Britain* (Oxford: Oxford University Press, 2008), 92–93, 122–125.

35. Janet Robb, *The Primrose League, 1883–1906* (New York: Columbia University Press, 1942), 87-93,

182–218; Martin Pugh, *The Making of Modern British Politics, 1867–1945* (Oxford: Blackwell, 2002), 71. They are also available on microfiche (Brighton: Harvester Press Microform Publications, 1982).

36. This information comes from my cursory examination of the files, "Minutes and Reports of the Conservative Party Conferences, 1867–1946" for the period 1907 to 1911. These papers are held in the Conservative Party Archive, Bodleian Library, Oxford. They are also available on microfiche (Brighton : Harvester Press Microform Publications, 1982).

37. Other techniques introduced at Conservative Party headquarters included indexing their opponents' speeches (with a card index) and analysing the voting records of MPs; there was a major effort at further Party reorganisation in these pre-War years.

38. T.J. Hollins, "The Conservative Party and Film Propaganda Between the Wars", *English Historical Review* 96, no. 379 (April 1981): 359–369. See also Alan Burton, "Early political films in Britain" in Vanessa Toulmin and Simon Popple (eds), *Visual Delights 2: Exhibition and Reception* (Eastleigh: John Libbey, 2005), 135–144.

Ludwig Vogl-Bienek

A Lantern Lecture: Slum Life and Living Conditions of the Poor in Fictional and Documentary Lantern Slide Sets

Slide 1. Magic lantern show

The screen culture of the 19th century was based on the "art of projection". This historical term describes the various ways of creating live performances with the magic lantern: carefully arranged image sequences projected on screen, interspersed with colourful visual effects and dissolves from one image to the next. The images and effects were projected by creative lanternists who operated the lantern in a way similar to playing a musical instrument. The series of projections were always accompanied by a lecture, recitation, singing or music. In French and German the equivalent terms were "l'art de projection" and "Projektionskunst". The art of projection firmly established the screen as a cultural locale that integrates virtual realities into public performances. No previous medium had a comparable potential for the visual presentation or re-presentation of distant realities or fictions in public gatherings or meetings. Large-scale projections mediate impressive experiences which can be shared by a great number of people. They easily evoke the impression of being witness to the events, or at least support a belief in a realistic representation. This belief was even stronger when the images were created with the aid of photography.

For historical research on the "rapidly compacting public communication in the course of the 19th Century"[1] examination of the art of projection's function is indispensable. As a medium of communication it takes an important intermediate position in the structuring of the public sphere: it links public gatherings or meetings to a visual mass medium that nevertheless leaves a certain creative leeway within live performances. In the second half of the 19th century the art of projection followed the controversial social discourse of industrialisation often called the Social Question or Social Problem. The utilisation of

Facing page:
[Slide 1] *Upper*: Engraving from *Catalogue and Price List of Stereopticons, Dissolving-View Apparatus, Magic Lanterns, and Artistically-Colored Photographic Views on Glass* (New York: T.H. McAllister, 1891). *Lower*: A lantern lecturer of the Gilchrist Trust, 1890. Engraving from *Illustrated London News* (18 October 1890).

illustrated lectures and melodramatic screen entertainment featuring impoverished protagonists turned the Social Problem into public performance.[2] But several thousand lantern slide sets on social topics have not so far been taken into consideration in historical research on the Social Question; nor have most early moving pictures on the topic. This is typical of tens of thousands of works in the art of projection, which in cultural and social history are known only to a very exclusive circle of specialists, because they have not been made accessible in a media-historical context. The only way to explore them is interdisciplinary, and this cannot be achieved by a few. This obstacle to research can be removed effectively by generating critical digital editions of works in the art of projection which consider its unique nature as a performance medium. This brief "lantern lecture" exemplifies how projection was used in live performances to influence the formation of public opinion concerning the Social Question in the late 19th century.

2. Short report of the Photographic Society of Ireland

In June 1890 a short report of a recent meeting of the Photographic Society of Ireland appeared in the *Optical Magic Lantern Journal and Photographic Enlarger* [*OMLJ*].[3]

PHOTOGRAPHIC SOCIETY OF IRELAND. — On the 22nd May this society concluded the winter session by a public lantern exhibition in the theatre of the Royal College of Science. There was a large attendance. During the evening two hundred and twenty slides were passed through the lanterns by Mr. J. Carson, C.E.; they were described by the secretary, in the absence through illness of Professor J. Alfred Scott. A large number of the slides were made from negatives used in hand cameras, those causing most amusement having reference to street life in Dublin, particularly in some of the slums of the city.

[2] From *OMLJ* (June 1890): 8.

This short notice is worth dwelling on for two reasons: first because at its time it was nothing out of the ordinary, and second because it points to the highly developed technical potential of the optical media with which the social environment could be represented at public gatherings. It is nothing out of the ordinary because it is only one of many similar reports of magic lantern shows. But that is exactly what makes it so remarkable as an example of the widespread screen culture of the 19th century.

[3] Engraving from *Illustrated London News* (18 October 1890): 488.

3. Gilchrist Science Lecture

This illustration from *The Illustrated London News* of 18 October 1890 conveys a vivid impression of a magic lantern lecture: a "Gilchrist Science Lecture to working men" is shown in which the magic lantern was applied for the education of the working classes. The related report says that these events were regularly attended by 700 to 1,200 people.[4] The lecture theatre at the Royal College of Science in Dublin, mentioned in the previous reference, was slightly smaller but still accommodated more than 500 people.[5]

4 (Repeat of 2). Short report of the Photographic Society of Ireland

The Photographic Society of Ireland used the magic lantern to show numerous photographic slides to a large audience. But there is a difference between simply showing images and creating an appealing public event. Obviously, the organisers were experienced in the art of projection: they chose the slides very carefully and asked an eloquent speaker for a lecture that fitted the slides well. They also highlighted the possibilities of mobile photography with so-called hand cameras which were already available in different variations in 1890.

[5] From *OMLJ* (June 1890): viii.

5. Advertisements for hand cameras

In the same issue of the *OMLJ* as the report of the Dublin meeting appeared a number of different advertisements for hand cameras. These enabled photographers to shoot the candid street scenes that caused such great amusement when projected, and made it possible to show the "foreign" world of the slums to the audience. So the second reason for which I consider the event in Dublin remarkable is this: it approaches the social environment by means of the most modern optical media of the time. Often unnoticed everyday scenes become attractions on the screen and the living environment of the excluded becomes a picturesque event at public gatherings.

[6] STREET LIFE: OR PEOPLE WE MEET, no. 15, Riley Brothers, Bradford, *c.* 1887.

6. The Stone-breaker

Striking images of street scenes were also produced by companies of the optical trade as ready-made sets of glass slides. "The Stone-breaker" is an example belonging to the set STREET LIFE: OR PEOPLE WE MEET, produced and distributed by Riley Brothers, a slide making and hiring business in the industrial city of Bradford in northern England. The accompanying published lecture "reading" text comments: "His is not a pleasant life nor a well-paid one". The viewer of the slide learns about the difficulties of the stone-breaker's work, including the assertion that in earlier times it "was performed by the most ignorant and stupid labourers of the district".[6]

[7] STREET LIFE..., no. 1.

7. Introductory slide of STREET LIFE: OR PEOPLE WE MEET

Overall 50 different street scenes are shown in this set, with the intention "to bring you face to face with a number of people – some poor, others by no means wanting in this world's goods – who claim no relationship with each other, but who, collectively, give life and animation and colour to the gloomy streets of our great cities and towns".[7] The accompanying reading texts are informative, entertaining and at some points even humorous, as a few examples will suggest.

[8] STREET LIFE..., no. 16.

8. The Stonemasons

The Stone-breaker is followed in the set by the Stonemasons, who in contrast are young men with qualified work "who earn a good wage".[8] It is said that they like their work and enjoy singing or whistling to the rhythm of their hammer's blows. This is the starting point for a humorous episode relating the story of a puritan priest who, as the stonemasons' employer, demands an appropriate selection of the song that is to be whistled. But when he notices that the slow rhythm of the religious piece of music leads to a significant downshift of the work speed, he asks the stonemason to continue his cheerful song.

[9] Street Life..., no. 17.

9. Tinker at his Stall

Before the next change of slide the continuation of the imagined journey is described:

> Down away towards the East end of the city we might come in contact with some street characters who would decidedly object to be photographed, as they submit to that operation only under compulsion, and at the expense of the State; but the Tinker at his Stall has no such reluctance, and he very willingly, and as we think, with something almost akin to pride, permits us to examine his store. What a heterogeneous collection he has![9]

The Tinker presents a wondrous variety of goods taken from all the things others no longer need, for the most part "household requisites [...] and these are chiefly procured at second or third hand from the drunken and improvident of the neighbourhood".[10] After a comic episode describing a drunken fellow who sells his bed to the Tinker (a story which originated in the humorous collection *Joe Miller's Jests* from the mid-18th century) the journey continues.

[10] STREET LIFE..., no. 18.

10. The Italian and Monkey

We see a little way before us the aesthetic figure of the unmistakable Italian with his faithful little monkey companion. If we were to follow for a short distance, we should see him make his way slowly towards the better-class neighbourhood, where there are likely to be a number of children, whom the monkey's antics and drolleries will draw to the windows.[11]

These sample images illustrate in the designated sequence a liberal but integrative tendency of the whole series. Workers and the labouring poor are shown more or less managing their lives, but succeeding.

[11] STREET LIFE..., no. 31.

11. Disabled Sailors and Piano

Even the needy add a service for the enlivenment of street life with the street piano. Incidentally, the issue of governmental social services or private welfare is left out. Rather it is depicted as a matter of course that the so-called "better classes" accept the offered services and pay adequate wages to the workers.

[12] STREET LIFE..., no. 12.

12. The Shoeblack

The Shoeblack is a symbolic figure whose regular occupation was held as an approved scheme against the destitution of children (for example in the London "shoeblack brigades") by providing respectable labour and income. Here he is presented as a successful businessman. The praise of his profession culminates in a report of how a young fellow joined in a fundraising campaign after the Great Chicago Fire of 1871: he "put up a notice: 'Black your boots for 2d. to-day for Chicago.' and he actually sent over £4 to the fire fund".[12]

The social success of the Shoeblack is expressed by the fact that he himself becomes a benefactor.

[13] STREET LIFE..., no. 50.

13. The Policeman

The presentation of photographic images on the screen for the STREET LIFE production is determined by a liberal view of life in the city. Thus it is hardly surprising that at the end of the day the state appears only in the function of Ferdinand Lassalle's "night watchman state": "the last man we meet is the lonely Policeman, whose night watches are about to commence. We cannot follow him on his monotonous rounds, nor do we wish to do so."[13]

The author's social notions and hope that an enlightened awareness might be able to improve the social conditions are clearly expressed again in this last appeal:

> And so I say if you would seek to gain a knowledge which will enlarge your mind and fit you for the duties of life, you must go into the streets; you must get to know something of the lives of your fellow-men, that you may be able to sympathise with their hardships, to understand their difficulties, to interpret their peculiarities, that by this "... knowledge we may learn ourselves to know / And what to man and what to God we owe".[14]

14 (Repeat of 7). Introductory slide of STREET LIFE: OR PEOPLE WE MEET

The creation of an elaborate media product was linked to the expectation of success in shows and on the market. This expectation was obviously justified by the concept of these magic lantern slides. The *Indispensable Handbook to the Optical Lantern* of 1888 emphasises this series as an outstanding highlight in the choice offered by Riley Brothers:

> These are not made up from life models in the ordinary understanding of that phrase, that is, live people suitably attired photographed in a studio in front of a consistent background. But they are taken directly in the street, and show the natural surroundings. [...] The slides we have seen are extremely good and realistic.[15]

Riley Brothers included this praise as promotional material in their sales catalogue.

The differentiation from images of "life models" taken in studios leads to a clear detachment between fictional and documentary images. The fictional life model slides were often used to tell sentimental stories of the life of the poor. The author of the reading for STREET LIFE clearly distances the actual production from this view: "my lecture is not intended to reveal to you any of the heartrending scenes of poverty and degradation which are only too-commonly met with in street life. These would scarcely come within the scope of my subject."[16] This unsentimental commentary pursues a strategy of social inclusion for the formation of public opinion. This strategy depends on the better classes to comply with their duties of life and on the labouring poor, such as the Stone-breaker, to be content with a humble living.

The often unnoticed character of the elusive everyday life can be met with concentrated attention in its presentation as an illusion on screen: with the latest modern means of contemporary visual media a virtual form of inclusion is medially staged in a public performance. But through this inclusion into the field of attention of well-to-do audiences a borderline of social exclusion is established imperceptibly and without explicit intention. Excluded from visibility for the audience and from the possibility of receiving attention are all those who cannot be integrated in the demonstrated principle of successful self-sufficiency.

15. The Newsboys

Due to its image material the concept of the series has some limitations. This becomes noticeable when the Newsboys' miserable glance falls on the audience. Even the author of the reading cannot avoid addressing the hideous living conditions of these children: upon their success "in bringing a few coppers to the family store depend a frugal supper, and perhaps the escaping of a severe thrashing".[17] The author reveals that the poor children's destiny also touched the hearts of well-meaning people who were close to liberalism:

[15] STREET LIFE..., no. 6.

And yet perhaps, there are no child-toilers who engage our attention so much as those who earn a precarious living by the sale of daily papers; for they are made the subjects – heroes and heroines in a humble way – of the greater part of those stories of child-life of which we never seem to tire.[18]

The hopeful concept of social inclusion by means of self-help and its support by the better classes was effective only to a limited extent, and thwarted by social reality often enough; at least as seen from a conservative charitable as well as from a progressive liberal view. For a considerable number of the other characters on the screen in this set it could be questioned, too, how quickly the border of social exclusion came closer: what happens to the Stone-breaker when he is too old and frail to work? Is the Stonemason's income sufficient for the social coverage of his family in case of serious accidents? Will the Italian still be a welcome foreigner in old age when he is no longer able to show an impressive monkey, but needs help? All the characters we "met" on the street have the potential of being quickly transformed into humble heroes and heroines in heartrending stories of poverty and degradation.

[16] THE NEWSBOY'S DEBT, no. 1, James Bamforth, 1888.

16. THE NEWSBOY'S DEBT (Bamforth)

Such stories were often illustrated by "life model" posed photographic slides and projected on to the screen, as here in THE NEWSBOY'S DEBT, a pathetic poem about a poor boy's honesty. Life model slide sets on sentimental and elevated stories about the destinies of the poor were very popular in the late 19th and early 20th century and made up a great part of the range of various magic lantern slide manufacturers and distributors.

[17] GOLDEN LINKS, no. 21a, James Bamforth, 1895.

17. GOLDEN LINKS: OR, LED BY THE LORD (Bamforth)

Tales of widows, orphans and impoverished old people focussed on the border of social exclusion and the necessity of social help for those who are unable to care for themselves. With educational intentions the social, familial and health-related effects of alcoholism were shown as well as successful ways to flee poverty. These slide series were reproduced photographically and hand tinted when colour was required.

No. 5.—
Mr. Jas.
Bamforth
painting a
background
in 40
minutes.

[18] Photograph from "Bamforth's 'Life Model' Picture Postcards, Bamforth's 'Life Model' Pantomime Songs, Bamforth's New Premises and Studios, 1905–06", offprint from *The Caxton Magazine and British Stationer* (Holmfirth: Bamforth, 1906).

18. James Bamforth painting a background

For the production of life model slides, painting and photography were combined. This image from a printers' trade paper of 1905 shows James Bamforth, one of the most successful manufacturers of life model slides, painting a background himself. These backdrops were used for sets in professional photographic studios similar to the scenery on a theatre stage.

[19] *Caxton Magazine* offprint 1906.

19. How the Life Models are taken

The photographs for life model slides were taken in this kind of studio setting.[19] Painted backdrops and set designs allowed the producers to place the social actors of the stories in any desired environment. The costumed life models could represent anybody from any walk of life. Ordinary people living close to the producers, or sometimes their family members, were commonly chosen as models:

> The models are simply Mr. Bamforth's neighbours, who take a great interest in his work and are generally willing to sit.
>
> Of course, the photographer selects, as far as possible, persons whose faces readily lend themselves to the expression of the emotion or character desired. Thus it has happened that some of his bold, bad villains have been really most respectable and law-abiding townsmen while some of the awful drunkards have been in private life the most sober of men.
>
> At the same time it must be admitted that the taproom of the local public-house has afforded some excellent models.[20]

No. 8.—
Part of the
Store
Room for
back-
grounds.

[20] *Caxton Magazine* offprint 1906.

20. Store room for backgrounds

The universal scope of fictional magic lantern slide sets to address social issues far exceeded the options offered by documentary productions on these subjects, and it can be assumed that they were more popular. This was a good reason for the Riley Brothers business to include life model slides in their slide production. Although they presented their production STREET LIFE: OR PEOPLE WE MEET with a certain distance, this series marks a turning point in the firm's range. Riley Brothers were not only producers of magic lantern slides; their main business was the sale and rental of slides from all major British manufacturers.[21] STREET LIFE was one of the early items in their catalogue and is listed as item number 53. The catalogue was complemented by yearly supplements which were added to the existing range, and reached item number 1,903 in the last supplement for the season 1914/15. We don't know if the numbers of the early items reproduce the original order of addition to stock, but it is significant to see that after STREET LIFE the Riley catalogue began to offer a wide range of life model sets mainly on social topics. The extensive choice of fictional slide sets was still supplemented by occasional single social reports for the screen.

[21] From *OMLJ* (October 1892): iii.

21. Advertisement for SLUM LIFE IN OUR GREAT CITIES by Archer and Sons

A series titled SLUM LIFE IN OUR GREAT CITIES appears as item 597 in the Riley Brothers catalogue. The manufacturers and dealers Archer and Sons, of Liverpool, advertised this set in their monthly advertisement in the *OMLJ* from October 1892 until February 1895.

This series crosses the border of a virtual social inclusion that was constructed in STREET LIFE. It penetrates a living environment that George R. Sims called "a dark continent that is within easy walking distance of the General Post Office".[22] The inhabitants of this dark continent are shown from the distanced point of view of virtual *slumming*. Those who did not want to follow the fashion of confronting themselves with the living conditions of the outcasts *in situ* could follow the exciting slumming experience on screen in a safe environment accompanied by reporters who showed an informed manner.[23] The description of taking pictures with a detective or hand camera has an almost adventurous touch: "it need scarcely be mentioned that this was a work of no small difficulty and at times of danger also, for many of the inhabitants in these districts strongly object to have their portraits taken or to be photographed or noticed in any way".[24]

[22] SLUM LIFE IN OUR GREAT CITIES, no. 1,
Archer & Sons, 1892.

22. Introductory slide to SLUM LIFE IN OUR GREAT CITIES

The reading text accompanying Archer's slide set claims that "the pictures give a true insight to the character and habits of the people who live in these districts, as well as the natural expressions on their faces which can be obtained in no other way".[25]

Right from the beginning of the reading the shocking conditions found in the midst of wealth and prosperity are bemoaned, and the next sentence already makes explicit accusations: "It is generally admitted that drunkenness is the source of the largest proportion of poverty, of vice, of crime, of poorly-clad and ill-fed children ...".[26]

[23] Slum Life ..., no. 7.

23. Slum Life, Slide 7

The remarks in the reading for this set are not nearly as eloquent as those accompanying Riley's Street Life. They follow a simple scheme of outrage about the illustrated conditions, for which drunkenness and depravity are repeatedly made responsible. Above all children are depicted as victims, but on the other hand ...

[24] SLUM LIFE ..., no. 16.

24. SLUM LIFE, Slide 16

... many children are described as stubbornly resistant to all attempts to rescue them. It is claimed that they tend to be in bad company and that they elude control. But abruptly contrary statements are made, too, as in the following scene:

[25] SLUM LIFE ..., no. 41.

25. SLUM LIFE, Slide 41

Again a group of people can be seen posing for the camera. The reading text tells the story of events before and after: the "venerable looking fish woman" we see here "has just been slapping a workingman's wife on the back with the smaller portion of a fish knife" while praising her fish.[27] Immediately after this quiet scene excitement came up again because the knife had disappeared, just like the two boys. The reporter leaves open though, the question of whether the boys were the thieves or not: "There are many noble boys in the slums, and it is satisfactory to know that the majority are honest".[28]

[26] Slum Life ..., no. 38.

26. SLUM LIFE, Slide 38

In this case the reading text claims that the camera operator was faster and was not noticed until after the picture was taken. The shot catches a market-woman who drinks beer during work: "when she saw the camera coming she swallowed the beer very rapidly and retired".[29]

[27] SLUM LIFE..., no. 40.

27. SLUM LIFE, Slide 40

The tone changes again from denunciation to acknowledgement when an interview with "Old Rosy" is rendered, who prefers: "to live in a low neighbourhood and in an uncomfortable house ... because of the sympathy and help of poor neighbours."[30] The observers of life in the slums admit "it was an object lesson of great value to see how many of the respectable poor placed a copper in her hand".[31]

[28] SLUM LIFE..., no. 54.

28. SLUM LIFE, Slide 54

The closing slide of the set shows two ragged boys with the drink shop in the background. The profits of the gin-palaces are contrasted in the reading with the hardship of men and women "who are really not accountable for the money they spend ... . To be drunk with these people means to be happy".[32]

Consequently change in the slums is not represented, in the closing appeal, as the responsibility of its inhabitants: "We felt that such an experience as we had ought to fall to the lot of those who by their wealth and influence could do a great deal to stamp out such unnatural and disgraceful conditions of Slum life in our great cities".[33]

In contrast to the lantern slides by Jacob Riis, presented by Bonnie Yochelson in this volume, the main reason for the production, sale and rental of SLUM LIFE IN OUR GREAT CITIES can be found in its spectacular entertainment value rather than in serious socio-political intentions. Nevertheless its potential influence on the formation of political opinion should not be underestimated. Which living conditions can be defined as poverty and justify support for the concerned? Which of the poor should count as respectable and in need of support, in contrast to those who are held personally responsible for their circumstances and do not deserve help?

Most of the lantern slide sets on social topics that survive today were produced for religious, charitable, philanthropic or progressive liberal events, but could be shown just for entertainment as well. In socio-political contexts they mainly supported tendencies which led to social and welfare state reforms.

29. Advertisement for the Fabian Society

---

*   *   *

SLIDES FOR THE FABIAN SOCIETY. — The Fabian Society, 276, Strand, are desirous of obtaining free lantern slides (in aid of their work), such as sets on Slums and Slum Life, Life and Labour, Municipal Development, etc.

*   *   *

---

[29] From *OMLJ* (September 1896): 139.

Lantern slide sets which were made in the context of working class movements were a lot rarer, and so it has only been possible to reconstruct them in a rudimentary way.[33] Independent production could be obstructed by high costs for organisations that were less well-off, but they could still make use of the scope of the art of projection by employing existing image material and presenting it with their own texts. An 1896 advertisement for the socialist Fabian Society is exemplary for this: the Society is "desirous of obtaining free lantern slides (in aid of their work), such as sets on Slums and Slum Life, Life and Labour, Municipal Development, etc."[35]

In the last decades of the 19th century the art of projection provided the infrastructure to broach social issues based on visual representation in live performances. The examples discussed in this "lantern lecture" convey an impression of how the established screen was employed to gain influence over the formation of public opinion concerning the Social Question.

Notes

1. Jörg Requate, "Öffentlichkeit und Medien als Gegenstände historischer Analyse", *Geschichte und Gesellschaft* 25 (1999), 5.

2. See Ludwig Vogl-Bienek, "Turning the Social Problem into Performance", in Marta Braun et al. (eds), *Beyond the Screen: Institutions, Networks and Publics of Early Cinema* (New Barnet, Herts.: John Libbey, 2012), 315–324.

3.   "The Photographic Society of Ireland", *Optical Magic Lantern Journal and Photographic Enlarger* [OMLJ] No. 13 (June 1890): 8.

4.   "Science for the People. At a Gilchrist Lecture", *Illustrated London News* (18 October 1890), 487–488.

5.   *Twentieth Report of the Science and Art Department of the Committee of Council on Education, with Appendices* (London: Her Majesty's Stationery Office, 1873), 537.

6.   *Street Life or People we meet, a lecture to accompany a series of photographic transparencies for the lantern*, (Bradford: Riley Brothers, n.d. [c.1887?]), 11. The reading is anonymous but may be the work of Willie Riley (1866-1961), a partner in the Riley Brothers business and later a successful popular novelist.

7.   Ibid., 4.

8.   Ibid., 11.

9.   Ibid., 12.

10. Ibid.

11. Ibid.

12. Ibid., 9.

13. Ibid., 30.

14. Ibid., 31. The quotation is from the poem "The Tears of the Muses" (1591) by Edmund Spenser (c. 1552–99).

15. Walter D. Welford and Henry Sturmey (eds), *The "Indispensable Handbook" to the Optical Lantern: a Complete Cyclopaedia on the Subject of Optical Lanterns, Slides, and Accessory Apparatus* (London: Iliffe & Son, 1888), 328.

16. *Street Life or People we meet*, 4.

17. Ibid., 6.

18. Ibid.

19. See Richard Crangle and Ann Hecht, "Life Model slides", in David Robinson, Stephen Herbert and Richard Crangle (eds), *Encyclopaedia of the Magic Lantern* (London: Magic Lantern Society, 2001), 172.

20. Philip Reynolds, "Sentiment to order", *Harmsworth Magazine* 5.28 (October 1900): 340.

21. See Richard Crangle, "Riley Brothers", in Robinson et al., *Encyclopaedia of the Magic Lantern*, 255.

22. George R. Sims, *How the Poor Live* (London: Chatto & Windus, 1883), 5.

23. See Seth Koven, *Slumming: Sexual and Social Politics in Victorian London* (Princeton and Oxford: Princeton University Press, 2006).

24. *Slum Life in our Great Cities* (Liverpool: Archer & Sons, n.d.), 4.

25. Ibid., 4.

26. Ibid., 5.

27. Ibid., 18.

28. Ibid.

29. Ibid., 16.

30. Ibid., 17.

31. Ibid.

32. Ibid., 24.

33. Ibid.

34. For example the lantern shows of the Welsh labour leader Jabez Jones are discussed in Richard Keen, *Coalface* (Cardiff: National Museum of Wales, 1982), 30–33. See also Karen Eifler, "Between Attraction and Instruction: Lantern Shows in British Poor Relief", *Early Popular Visual Culture*, 8 (2010): 363–384.

35. *OMLJ*, no. 88 (September 1896): 139.

Joss Marsh and David Francis

"The Poetry of Poverty": The Magic Lantern and the Ballads of George R. Sims

George R. Sims: journalist and writer; born 1847, died 1922. Knighted by the King of Sweden and Norway in 1905, he "never received a native honour". "Panache" and "an indulgent sense of fun", concludes Philip Waller in the *Dictionary of National Biography*, acidly, "often made him appear trivial". "I have always been very vague", the secretary to the Oxford University Press had written to a contributor to the *Dictionary*'s Supplement, in 1934; "about the importance of G.R.S.".[1]

But Sims was important – not least for his impact on late 19th- and early 20th-century visual story-telling and the representation of urban poverty. Both the importance and the repeated put-downs stemmed from his unparalleled success, his extraordinary versatility, his celebrity, and his astoundingly prolific output: for example in one week of 1921, at age 74, he told an interviewer, he had written "an act of a new play, two songs, [...] a Grand Guignol story", and "10,000 words of newspaper copy".[2]

Sims was an inventive and almost compulsive fiction writer; he was a hit playwright, whose *Lights o' London* (1881) made him indubitably, liberatingly rich; he became, in the 1910s, a master-purveyor of fanciful topical panto-mimes – one of which launched a character called "Cinema Man" into the world of Sleeping Beauty. He was the quintessential multi-media figure of late-Victorian London.

But as those 10,000 words indicate, Sims was first and foremost a journalist and a "Bohemian", who made his first contacts during drinking sprees at the Unity Club. He identified strongly with Henry Mayhew, Thomas Hood (author of the bitter "Song of the Shirt"), and, above all, Charles Dickens – a lineage of imaginative investment in social activism.

Sims's first break as a journalist and writer came in 1872, on the *Weekly Dispatch*. He began writing for *Fun*, a major rival to *Punch*, in 1874, and shot to fame when its editor Henry Sampson launched a new Sunday sports and entertain-

Facing page: George R. Sims: frontispiece to *The Dagonet Ballads* (1879).

ments paper, *The Referee*, in 1877, and took Sims with him to create its "miscellaneous" column. He took the pen-name "Dagonet" – the jester to Sampson's "Pendragon", a figurative name for King Arthur.

Sims's "Mustard and Cress" was a pioneer gossip column, with a Dickensian dislike for "cant". "I like candour", Sims remarked in 1878: "The man who when asked why he had changed his domicile replied, 'To be nearer the pub', ought certainly to go up two [points in public estimation]".[3] The writing is fresh, kindly, cynical, with the occasional sting of wit, and bursts of genuine earnestness (as in an entry, alternately touching and hilarious, on his New Year's resolutions for 1886).[4] The column was "a sort of public diary",[5] an idea Sims liked to tinker with, and hooked two generations of "Refereaders". It acknowledged and created Sims as a personality, even a personality at play, in the new era of personality journalism: "Dagonet" became the late-Victorian epitome of the "familiar stranger" of modern celebrity studies, famous for being the famous George R. Sims.

You might not expect a jester to be a serious urban investigator and a founder of the Welfare State. But Sims lived up to his suffragist mother and Chartist grandfather in series after series of unsparing "crusading" reports in newspapers and journals like *The Pictorial World* and *The Daily News*. Beginning in 1883, with *How the Poor Live*, he brought the dispossessed of the nation and its "Monster City", the "Outcast" and "Horrible" London, into the homes of middle-class readers. In some, Sims took as co-investigator the black-and-white artist and fellow "Bohemian" Frederick Barnard, who had made his name illustrating Chapman and Hall's Household Edition of Dickens in the 1870s: where they penetrated, Sims said, a camera would not have been tolerated.[6] He sometimes went direct from the theatre, in full evening dress, using his celebrity status to get his foot through slum-dwellers' doors. The series were not written for gain: unlike many who professed "sympathy" with the poor, wrote hard-nosed William Archer, even in his plays, Sims never used "the lower orders" as "paying material".[7] And they were taken seriously: in 1884, for example, Sims was called as an expert witness before the Royal Commission on working-class housing.

It was on behalf of children, above all, that Sims campaigned; two series from 1907, *The Cry of the Children* and *The Black Stain*, are entirely devoted to them. His work made these "most helpless subjects of the crown" present to the imagination in all their palpable reality – beaten, neglected, "farmed" out, "in a state of nervous terror", in "surroundings that are unprintable".[8] In one "Black Hole ... of Babydom" in South London, for example, hanging over "a horrible bed, on which three ... vermin-tortured, half-starved children were ... huddled together", Sims sees, and as a result we see, "a framed picture of the Saviour with the little children gathered around Him. Beneath the picture I read these words: 'Feed My Lambs'".[9] The cases tumble out, one after another: a drunken mother gives birth on a bed of dirt; a baby drowns head downwards in a pail; a girl's rags are "fastened on her with French nails and a couple of curtain hooks".[10] Sims's work put dinners on school tables, for the first time; it helped secure the first-ever legislation for the rights of children. There was value in his unlikeliness, as well as his celebrity: if *he* could care, who should not?

The various pieces of Sims's multifarious personality cohere completely in one part of his enormous production, the remarkable series of ballads he wrote, principally for *The Referee*, some for Edmund Yates's raffish journal "for Men and Women" (code for "adult" readers), *The World*.

The "Dagonet Ballads" are hard-hitting, heart-rending, sharply seen, dexterously verbal, and poundingly rhythmical, without losing the cadences of speech: classic pieces of Victorian literature-with-a-purpose, minus the overt moralising, and with a more than usually radical bent. The first *Referee* ballads appeared soon after the launch of the paper, and regularly from 6 January 1878. The first of three collections, *The Dagonet Ballads*, was published on 1 March 1879 – very soon after their newspaper publication. It sold in the tens, perhaps hundreds, of thousands, at a time when the average print run of a three-volume novel was 500 copies. Two further collections followed: *The Ballads of Babylon* in 1880, and *The Lifeboat and Other Poems* in 1883. The three were republished, bound together, as *Ballads and Poems*, in 1883.[11] A fourth volume, *The Land of Gold and Other Poems*, was a slimmer afterthought in 1888.

The ballad form was traditional, medieval, popular, simple and narrative: a

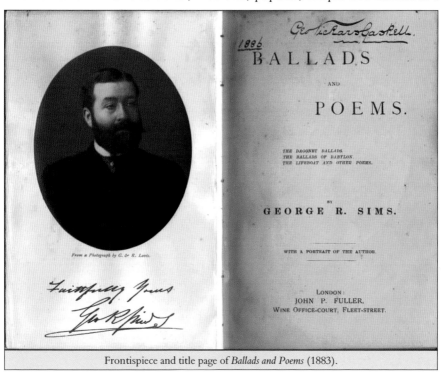

Frontispiece and title page of *Ballads and Poems* (1883).

Postcard illustration of "Billy's Rose" (c.1910).

quatrain stanza, sometimes stretched to six or doubled to eight lines, Sims's preferred length. Revived in the 18th century, it was widely used by popular poets – Kipling, most famously. Sims's fellow *Fun* contributor W.S. Gilbert played "topsy-turvy" variations upon the form in the 1860s. Sims borrowed it most directly, however, from the *Pike County Ballads* of the American Civil War hero and biographer of Lincoln, Colonel John Hay, first published in the *New York Tribune* in 1870 and widely circulated: Sims was a fully cognisant part of the transatlantic entertainment exchange of the 19th century. "Wall, no!" begins "Jim Bludso, of the 'Prairie Belle'", the ballad that first struck him, "I can't tell

Frontispiece and title page of illustrated edition of "In the Harbour".

whar he lives, / Becase he don't live, you see".[12] The essence of the "Dagonet Ballads" is all there: the story-telling situation; the mingling of the vernacular and the grotesque with the heroic and the pathetic; and the silent interlocutor who is not himself one of the down-home "folks", through whom Sims would often manage the intrusiveness of his ballads' social investigation.

More than the *Pike County Ballads*, Sims's "Dagonet Ballads" live up to their broader ballad inheritance of protest and revolutionary feeling, as in Blake's 1794 *Songs of Experience* and Wordsworth and Coleridge's radical 1798 *Lyrical Ballads*. For Sims, the ballad was the ideal form of record for "common alley tragedy".[13] The "Dagonet Ballads" are witnessings of the downtrodden and the fated, last testaments of the desperate and the helpless poor: the slum girl who dies to bring a rose to her fading brother ("Billy's Rose"); the farmer who hurls himself under a train to free his young wife to marry the man she loved, and thought dead, the father of her unborn child ("The Level Crossing"); "Crazy Kate", whose mad heart bursts with joy when her drowned husband seems to wash up on the shore, unchanged after twenty years ("In the Harbour"); the battered wife who rescues her husband from his burning bed, only to have him again abandon her – her face scarred by molten lead – for the floozy who left him to the flames ("Sal Grogan's Face"). For Sims, the "Woman Question" was an urgent part of the "Social Question".

Some of the ballads have happy endings; a few venture out of the city; some feature working-class heroes of the industrial age like railway signalmen; a few feature upper-class (usually tarnished) men and women. All have an

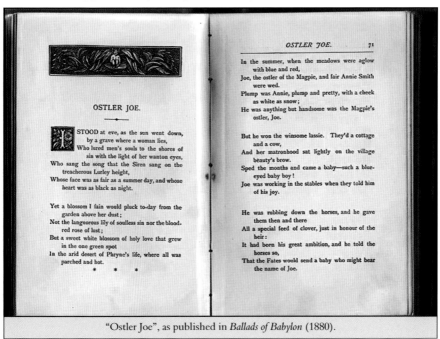

"Ostler Joe", as published in *Ballads of Babylon* (1880).

Split-second action in THE MATRON'S STORY (Bamforth, 1890).

uninhibited, late-night feel. And indeed they were written in the small hours, in the smoke-filled rooms of the club, well lubricated with booze, with self-censorship at a dead-of-night low. It was thus, ironically, as a "seasoned worshipper of the vine-wreathed god" that Sims penned some of the most biting Victorian indictments of parental inebriation.[14] The startlingly unorthodox "Ostler Joe", for example, in which a faithless wife crawls back from a lurid high-life to die in the arms of her husband, who is made *happy* by her return; this poem attracted a press barrage against the "indecent" author (presumed, with some logic, to be Swinburne).

Part of the appeal of Sims's ballads was dramatic, as might be expected of a master-craftsman of the late Victorian stage. Part of their appeal was narrative – the appeal of the ballad form itself, whose ABAB rhyme structure refuses quite to "close" (as theorists of poetry would say), and thus propels us forward into the story. But what is most remarkable about the "Dagonet Ballads" is the moment in Sims's career they came into being – not *after* he launched himself

The slum girl dreams of her pantomime transformation, in A MUSLIN FROCK (Bamforth, 1899).

into investigative journalism, but *before*: the ballads predate the first of his urban series by at least five years. For George R. Sims, poetry was not a by-product or development of that hard-core training in social criticism. Rather, poetry preceded and precipitated his concern with poverty. It was the "Dagonet Ballads" that brought "Dagonet" to all aspects of the "Social Question".

That Question brings us to the brink of another, and very different one: why did visual story-telling – including magic-lantern story-telling, combining the projection of images with vocal narrative and sometimes music – develop to so high a degree in Britain, in the last quarter of the 19th century?

One reason may have been the era's passion for narrative painting: all painting, Victorians believed, "rises in the scale of art in proportion as it is a story".[15] Another may have been the determination of Temperance activists to capitalise on the powerful impact of George Cruikshank's series *The Bottle*, transferred to the lantern screen shortly after its first publication in 1847. Lantern slide propaganda flowered into screen stories that required ever finer and finer

York's THE LIFEBOAT (1886).

psychological choices and visual breakdown of critical action – like the decision to reach for the bowl of cherries on the bar counter in the Reverend James Kirton's BUY YOUR OWN CHERRIES.[16] It used to be believed that "high" literature inspired the development of screen language and screen culture, but that development owes far more to popular and propagandist stories like these: screen culture did not trickle down, but percolated up. The unique influence of Dickens was a direct result of the "popularity" that earned him the sneers of the *cognoscenti*.

Thus we arrive at Sims's place in the history of screen culture, and the bearing of his work on the "Social Question" in relation to that culture.

The catalogues of the major lantern slide makers and distributors in the 1880s and 1890s – James Bamforth, York & Son (the premier producers of Sims slides, with 21 and 14 sets each), Riley Brothers (who distributed 31 Sims sets, 24 of the ballads), J. Lizars, the Church Army and the Band of Hope Union – all contain at least a full page of titles by Sims: THE MATRON'S STORY, NELLIE'S

Bamforth's competing version of THE LIFEBOAT (1899).

PRAYER, THE STREET TUMBLERS, TICKET-O'-LEAVE, TOLD TO THE MISSIONARY, and all the titles mentioned above except SAL GROGAN'S FACE.[17] There were more slide sets for works by Sims than by Tennyson (the Poet Laureate), Longfellow (an international favourite), Thomas Hood, Robert Burns or Walter Scott (the pre-eminent author of the Romantic generation, popular throughout the 19th century). By the mid-1890s all of these were dead, their fame already pronounced by posterity, thus safe bets for slide producers. Sims was virtually the only living writer in Britain whose name sold slides.[18] Only Dickens rivalled him for lantern slide popularity – and emphasis on the "Social Question".

What made Sims's ballads appeal to the reading public – their drama, narrative, relevance, daring, and literary quality – appealed also to slide makers. Nearly every one of the 24 ballads adapted for the lantern featured working-class protagonists. Almost all Sims-based sets were "Life Model" slides, in which real people are posed against sets and painted backdrops (or occasionally exterior locations and actual rooms). A few of Sims's short stories – particularly compressed narratives one might almost call prose ballads – were also adapted for the lantern, including A MUSLIN FROCK, from *The Social Kaleidoscope* (1881), of which a beautiful 24-slide Life Model series was produced by Bamforth. Illuminated by the best photographic artists of the magic lantern world, the Sims lantern slide ballad series are pinnacles of lantern achievement, vivid presentiments of cinematic art.

We have found no evidence that Sims wrote with lantern presentation in mind; the popularity of Life Model slides came after the first vogue for the "Dagonet Ballads", and the first Sims slide sets to be registered for copyright, IN THE SIGNAL BOX and THE LIFEBOAT (both by York & Son) on 15 January 1886, follow the poems they illustrate and interpret by three years.[19] The bulk of the Sims-based slide sets date from the 1890s. There is no lantern-related correspondence in the archive of Sims materials in the Rylands Library, Manchester.

But Sims must in some sense have authorised lantern slide adaptation of his work. Manufacturers and distributors sometimes directed renters and purchasers to his books, sometimes republished the ballads as lantern readings; the notice "copyright" on individual sets was intended to protect their own investments, not Sims. Had he objected to lantern adaptation, given how much of it there was, into the 1920s, some evidence would be likely to survive. Sims was a shrewd businessman, far excelling Dickens as a multi-media manipulator, and much is still extant of his dealings with theatre producers, with some scraps concerning film production, in which he seems personally to have invested. Some of the ballads were filmed, besides many of his plays, and his name features prominently in publicity – for example, in advertisements for the highly effective 1914 British film of his most famous, most angry ballad (CHRISTMAS DAY IN THE WORKHOUSE, G.B. Samuelson Co., dir. George Pearson).[20] Just as he published the ballads at affordable prices, Sims may conceivably have given away the rights to their lantern slide visualisation, wanting their social message to spread through that medium. He understood and valued the visual: both as a playwright and as what he called a "versifier", he wrote with his eyes as well as his ears. His preferred master-metaphors were strikingly visual: the "social kaleidoscope" (1881); the "cinematograph" of urban existence (from the "Prologue" to *Living London*, 1901–03);[21] the cosmopolitan "moving scene" and "life-Picture" (from the 1902 volume *Biographs of Babylon*).[22]

Slide sets were shot, of course, in black and white. But, for those who had money, or for professional lanternists who needed a star attraction, they were available hand-coloured. Sometimes delicate, sometimes exuberant, the coloured sets have a real claim to visual beauty – to making "poetry" out of "poverty". They present the same problem as that posed by D.W. Griffith's brutal and beautiful *Broken Blossoms* (1919); by the Chaplin *oeuvre*; by Steinbeck's 1939 *Grapes of Wrath* and Ford's 1940 film adaptation; by James Agee and Walker Evans's 1941 *Let Us Now Praise Famous Men*, a work that offers the beauty they found in a hard-scrabble Alabama sharecropper family as an antidote to the "obscenity" of the artists' intrusion into their lives.[23] The beauty crystallises in the figure of their daughter: not to fall in love with her, Agee eventually comes to believe, would ultimately have been a greater insult than to feel her attraction. For Sims, equally – and certainly for York and Bamforth, both adapting the ballad "The Magic Wand" – the slum child who waves a pantomime wand over her dying mother, is "a poor little London blossom / The alley had not defiled".[24]

But we are forgetting sounds. No lantern shows were silent – and the ballad form was not only popular, but also (and crucially) *oral*. Ballads were originally composed and recited by traditional bards; the form is explicitly designed for memorisation and performance, in a communal setting. Sims's ballads spoke directly to that oral tradition, in its new Victorian manifestation – recitation. Thus "Ostler Joe" scandalised America in 1886 not when it was read but when it was *recited*.

Catherine Robson has written memorably of the special terror to which generations of children were subjected by the new educational codes of the 1860s and '70s: the recitation on "Examination Day", when the rods and canes of "every teacher of every rank" reminded them of their performance duty before the dreaded school inspectors.[25] But recitation was also a chance to shine for adult readers: Kipling was an immediate favourite of the adventurous; 'Jim's Wife' (Mrs Clement Nugent Jackson), author of the earnest *Gordon League Ballads* (also much adapted for slides) offered extensive advice for reciters, from choice of ballad to tone of voice to suitable costume, in three long Prefaces; late-Victorian publishers put out innumerable collections of recitable pieces. His ballads, wrote Sims in 1917, "were never put forward by me as poetry, but were intended for reciters who wanted something dramatic".[26]

Most likely, it was the measured structure and performative exuberance that made the ballads sure-fire reciters' pieces; they were also mercifully short, in an age when most recitations stretched the capacity and attention spans of both speakers and audiences. And – what may most have made them such catnip to lanternists, profoundly amenable to visual adaptation – they had the pounding narrative drive of the ballad form (to which Sims the journalist-dramatist, trained above all in telling a story, powerfully responded) and an almost physically palpable rhythm, since poetry that is recited is keyed to the sensations of the reciter's body, heart and breathing. These factors enabled visual break-down, generated a parallel "poetic" rhythm on screen, and enhanced the creative interplay, during lantern projection and reading, of word and image.

The ballads specialised, too, in symbolically charged objects that were also part of the stories' naturalistic *mise en scène*. The precious rose Nell dies to bring her brother, for example, in "Billy's Rose":

> Lo that night from out the alley did a child's soul pass away,
> From dirt and sin and misery to where God's children play.

Lo that night a wild, fierce snowstorm burst in fury o'er the land,
And at morn they found Nell frozen, with the red rose in her hand.

Billy's dead, and gone to glory – so is Billy's sister Nell;
Am I bold to say this happened in the land where angels dwell:–
That the children met in heaven, after all their earthly woes,
And that Nelly kissed her brother, and said, "Billy, here's your rose"?[27]

The rose is perhaps the most thumping symbolic *cliché* Sims could produce. But that is part of the point: the rose, like the stock characterisation of the child, gives the ballad a known emotional language. It is a prop used with the same kind of effectiveness as the flower for which the girl's heart, starved of beauty, yearns in Griffith's *Broken Blossoms*. In this final moment of the ballad, the rose *is* Nell.

The ballads of George R. Sims, their adaptation for the lantern screen, and the bearing that both ballads and slide sets have on the "Social Question" are a

"Night after night went Sally, / Half starved, to the splendid scene / Where she waved a wand of magic / As a Liliput fairy queen": THE MAGIC WAND (York, 1889).

The culminating moment of THE MAGIC WAND (York, 1889).

THE MAGIC WAND (Bamforth, 1889).

challenge to history and to interpretation. We conclude with four propositions that they provoke:

– First, that "po'try" and its recitation may have had a very considerable impact on the development of visual story-telling.

– Second, that funny people can have very serious agendas: like Dickens, arguably both the greatest humourist and greatest social critic of his age, and Mayhew, who was not only a pioneer sociologist but also a comic writer, Sims mounts a stiff challenge to our modern habit of compartmentalisation.

– Third, that posterity was misled by Oscar Wilde and the "high Modernists". In being "melodramatic" and "sentimental" the "Dagonet Ballads" challenge us to revise our contempt for Victorian "melodrama" and "sentimentality". Far from being embarrassing modes of excess, "melodrama" and "sentimentality" could be highly effective in raising political awareness of the "Social Question" – opening, not closing, possibilities for greater social understanding. Modern audience experience is relevant here: when we performed THE MAGIC WAND at a children's charity event in 2009, audience members audibly wept. And its power stems from the unlikeliness, and extreme sentimentality, of its central metaphor – the Christmas pantomime fairy's wand, which the slum child who earns a few pennies on stage pathetically believes can save her mother.

– Fourth and finally, that emphasis on the individual, which is the spring of all narrative, and propels the Sims ballads forward, is not politically emasculating but politically effective; the belief that it must always inevitably retard analysis is a self-righteous *canard*, which Sims and a great many other Victorians would have recognised as such. "From Babylon the mighty the monster chorus swells", Sims wrote in the "Overture" to *Ballads of Babylon*, "A cry to one vague heaven from all the million hells".[28] The lines shunt aside the undifferentiated mass, the agglomerate of misery, of "the monster chorus", to enter, individually, in the individual ballads, "all the million hells".

The best test case for this last proposition is the only Sims ballad which has permanently entered the lexicon of British poetry, "In the Workhouse, Christmas Day", the angry and uncompromising testament of an old pauper whose wife died for want of bread last Christmas Day. It is to this poem, for example, that the doctor-hero of Robertson Davies' novel *The Cunning Man* (1994) turns in a desperate attempt to restore the shell-shocked and disabled servicemen committed to his care. When he leads off his first Reading Hour with "Christmas Day in the Workhouse" [*sic*] the men laugh aloud. "Everybody knew some parody of the poem, and there were roars of – *'I wish you a Merry Christmas', said he; / The paupers answered BALLS"*. But "I gave it everything I had", "lay[ing] on the pathos firmly". The men laugh, clap, weep – and begin to recover. "The grim old story had hit the mark".[29]

For this ballad is an argument, on multiple levels, for the importance of the individual. The pauper who faces down the smug charity of a workhouse Christmas Dinner, is a number claiming a name and the right to tragedy. The dreaded Workhouse was the most frequent target of Sims's ballads, as of his journalism. Lest we forget, the New Poor Law of 1834 effectively criminalised poverty, and stored men, women, and children in separate wards – the provision of all provisions that most nakedly turned individuals into statistics and

Postcard illustration of "In the Workhouse, Christmas Day" (*c.*1910).

Malthusian numbers. That provision is the key to the enduring power of this ballad, and its lantern and cinema adaptations (Bamforth, 1890; G.B. Samuelson, 1914): the pauper couple will not accept "relief" that means separation. But, by a final twist of cruelty, the wife dies, alone, as the husband seeks a crust to keep her from that last resort:

> Yes, there, in a land of plenty,
> Lay a loving woman dead,
> Cruelly starved and murdered
> For a loaf of the parish bread.

> At yonder gate, last Christmas,
> I craved for a human life.
> You, who would feast us paupers,
> *What of my murdered wife!*

★ ★ ★

> 'There, get ye gone to your dinners
> Don't mind me in the least;

Think of the happy paupers
Eating your Christmas feast;
And when you recount their blessings
In your smug parochial way,
Say what you did for *me,* too,
Only last Christmas Day.'[30]

Notes

1. Philip Waller, *DNB*, quoting a letter held in the Oxford University Press archives.

2. *The Return of G.R. Sims (A record of Mr. G.R. Sims's experiences in two worlds). By a friend of his, in collaboration with R.H. Saunders* (London: Hutchinson, [1924]), 31.

3. *The Referee*, 27 January 1878.

4. *The Referee*, 3 January 1886: 7.

5. Arthur Calder-Marshall, *Prepare To Shed Them Now: The Ballads of George R. Sims* (London: Hutchinson & Co. Ltd., 1968) 2.

6. "It was ... a Bohemian like myself ... who drew my attention to the babies and little children in the crowded bar in which we frequently found ourselves late at night." George R. Sims, preface to *The Black Stain* (London: Jarrold & Sons, 1907), xiii, xi.

7. William Archer, *English Dramatists of Today* (London: Sampson Low, Marston, Searle & Rivington, 1882), 311.

8. Sims, *The Black Stain*, 4, 14.

9. Sims, *The Black Stain*, 25.

10. Sims, *The Black Stain*, 31-32.

11. George R. Sims, *Ballads and Poems* (London: John P. Fuller, 1883).

12. Colonel John Hay (ed. Henry Morley), *Pike County Ballads and Other Poems* (London: George Routledge & Sons, 1897), 13. Hay's ballads were first published in book form in 1871.

13. George R. Sims, *The Social Kaleidoscope* (London: John P. Fuller, 1881), 104.

14. George R. Sims, *My Life: Sixty Years' Recollections of Bohemian London* (London: Eveleigh Nash, 1917), 61.

15. *The Leader*, 1865, cited in Julia Thomas, *Pictorial Victorians* (Athens, Ohio: Ohio University Press, 2004) 3.

16. At least four slide versions of this Temperance classic are known from the 1870s to the 1920s, one from about 1904, the year it inspired one of R.W. Paul's most dexterous films.

17. Images of slides from most of these sets are in the *Lucerna* web resource (www.slides.uni-trier.de), and original slides are held in many private collections including the Francis Collection.

18. In the absence of data on sales or circulation of slide sets it is impossible to be definite, but the only likely rivals to Sims in terms of slide adaptations would be socially and religiously concerned writers like Hesba Stretton (Sarah Smith, 1832-1911, author of *Jessica's First Prayer* and many other titles), though she did not have the same popular "name recognition" enjoyed by Sims.

19. British copyright registration practice at this time was to deposit a copy of the image (for slides, a paper photographic print) at the Stationer's Hall – sometimes with a selection of images rather than the full set. The records are now held at the National Archives, reference COPY 1, and are available online.

20. This 1914 film, and the earlier slide set IN THE WORKHOUSE (Bamforth, 9 slides, 1890) are included in the DVD-ROM *Lichtspiele und Soziale Frage: Screening the Poor 1888–1914* (Munich: Film & Kunst, 2011).

21. *Living London* I: 3.

22. George R. Sims, *Biographs of Babylon* (London: Chatto & Windus, 1902), viii.

23. James Agee, Prologue to *Let Us Now Praise Famous Men* (Boston: Houghton Mifflin, 1941; reprinted 2001), 6.

24. George R. Sims, *The Lifeboat and other Poems*, 12.

25. F.H. Spencer, *An Inspector's Testament* (London: Unwin, 1938), 73. Cited in Catherine Robson, "Standing on the Burning Deck: Poetry, Performance, History", *PMLA* 120.1 (January 2005): 155.

26. Sims, *My Life*, 182.

27. Sims, *Dagonet Ballads*, 50–51.

28. Sims, "Overture" to *Ballads of Babylon*, 1.

29. Robertson Davies, *The Cunning Man* (Toronto: McClelland & Stewart, 1994), 225–228.

30. Sims, *Dagonet Ballads*, 14–15.

Bonnie Yochelson

The Jacob A. Riis Collection: Photographs for Books and Lantern Lectures

As a New York City police reporter in the 1880s, Jacob Riis earned a reputation for tenacious investigative work and colourful writing, in which he described newsworthy crimes and advocated for improving the inhumane living conditions of New York's poor. In 1887, when he learned about the recent invention of flash photography, he imagined that photographs could amplify his verbal descriptions. He secured the help of two amateur photographers, Richard Hoe Lawrence and Henry G. Piffard, and they arranged for Riis to present his "flashlight" photographs at the Society of Amateur Photographers of New York, where they were members. Riis invited the press, thus transforming the club's monthly lantern slide demonstration into a media event. He expanded the lecture into an article and then a book, *How the Other Half Lives*, which became a bestseller and catapulted Riis to the forefront of the American social reform movement. He subsequently took his own photographs, wrote nine more books and dozens of articles, and continued to lecture nationally with the aid of the lantern until his death in 1914.

Alexander Alland, himself a photographer, discovered Riis' photographs and brought them to public attention with the 1947 exhibition, "Battle with the Slum", at the Museum of the City of New York. He produced 50 dramatic prints from Riis' negatives, which established Riis' identity as a pioneer of "concerned photography" and led to the Museum's acquisition of the collection. An amateur historian, Alland subsequently spent years researching Riis' life and work, and his beautifully produced book, *Jacob A. Riis, Photographer & Citizen*, published by Aperture in 1973 and reprinted in 1993, has inspired generations of admirers. Riis' most famous image is *Bandit's Roost*. The version of the image that is best known appeared on the cover of Alland's book.

Bandit's Roost illustrates the interpretive problems posed by the Jacob A. Riis Collection. There are no vintage prints of *Bandit's Roost*, but there are two negatives – or rather, a stereographic negative that has been divided in two. Unlike Alland's print, the negative is vertical. Alland cropped the image,

Bandit's Roost, halftone reproduction of print by Alexander Alland, in Alexander Alland, *Jacob A. Riis, Photographer & Citizen* (Millerton: Aperture, Inc., 1973), 97.

Jacob Riis, Richard Hoe Lawrence and Henry G. Piffard, *Bandit's Roost,* two halves of stereoscopic negative.

deleting the tunnel-like alley hung with laundry in the background to enlarge and dramatise the foreground figures. Riis used a simple camera that made four-by-five-inch negatives. The 34 stereographic negatives in the collection, which measure eight by five inches, were made by Richard Hoe Lawrence and Henry Granger Piffard at Riis' direction. Some of these negatives remained whole, but most were broken into four-by-five-inch halves for the production of lantern slides. The *right* half of the stereographic negative was used to make the lantern slide of *Bandit's Roost*, and the existence of three slides of this image suggests that Riis used it often in his lectures. One of the three was hand-coloured, which renders the scene less menacing and more picturesque than the black and white versions.

Bandit's Roost appeared in Riis' 1890 book, *How the Other Half Lives,* as a full-page halftone illustration made from the *left* half of the stereographic negative. That Riis used both halves of the negative – the right features a menacing "bandit" at the right edge of the composition and the left features a woman with two small children at the left edge – suggests that Riis did not prefer one to the other.[1] In 1890, halftone technology was in its infancy, and the illustration of *Bandit's Roost,* which is approximately the size of an index card, is crude and fuzzy. Its unimpressive appearance may explain why the photographs in Riis' controversial book were hardly mentioned by reviewers.

Jacob Riis, Richard Hoe Lawrence and Henry G. Piffard, *Bandit's Roost*, hand-coloured lantern slide.

Bandit's Roost, How the Other Half Lives (New York: Scribner's Sons, 1890), 63.

In 1987, I was appointed Curator of Prints and Photographs at the Museum of the City of New York, which owns the Jacob A. Riis Collection of Photographs. The collection was unlike any I had ever seen: it consists of 415 glass negatives, 326 lantern slides, and 191 prints in a variety of formats taken by different photographers. As an art historian and art museum curator, I was accustomed to caring for artists' exhibition prints. By contrast, the Riis Collection was a hodgepodge – a journalist's raw materials that he used to prepare lectures and publications.[2] The curatorial challenge of working with the collection was compounded by the unceasing demand by museums and scholars for Riis exhibition prints and reproductions. It took several years to devise a strategy to meet the demand in a way that did not misrepresent Riis as a 20th-century photojournalist like Dorothea Lange or W. Eugene Smith.

At the heart of my study has been the close inspection of the collection and its uses to untangle these puzzles of authorship and dating. When I first arrived at the Museum, researchers were shown a set of 8 x 10 inch enlargements made in the 1950s from Riis' negatives. These lacklustre prints were sometimes cropped, either to enlarge the figures within the composition or to mask the fact that many of the negatives were copies of prints by other photographers.[3] Scholars who studied *only* these copy prints – neither the original glass negatives nor the lantern slides and vintage prints – were not given the opportunity to understand the nature of Riis' photographic practice. In 1994 I wrote an article called, "What Are the Photographs of Jacob Riis?" which described the interpretative problems posed by the collection.[4] That year, the National Endowment for the Humanities awarded the Museum a grant to produce a new set of contact prints from the negatives on printing-out paper and a set of colour transparencies from the lantern slides. These new "vintage material" prints and transparencies gave the public access to an accurate transcription of the original glass for the first time. Since then, the Museum has used only these materials for exhibition and reproduction purposes.[5]

By 1994, I had left the Museum staff to work as an independent curator for the Museum and other organisations. To work further on Riis, I collaborated with Daniel Czitrom, Professor of American History at Mount Holyoke College, who brought to the study of Riis his understanding of New York City politics, law enforcement, housing reform, and immigration. In our book, *Rediscovering Jacob Riis: Exposure Journalism and Photography in Turn-of-the-Century New York*, Czitrom focused on Riis' journalism, and I analyzed Riis' photographic practice.[6] What follows is a brief summary of my findings.

Jacob August Riis was born in 1849 in the cathedral town of Ribe, Denmark. A rebellious child, he performed poorly in school, apprenticed to a carpenter in Copenhagen, and, at age 20, left Denmark to make his way in America. For five years he struggled as an itinerant worker, taking various jobs but failing to get a foothold in his new country. A newspaper job proved a turning point, and by 1877, he was a police reporter for the *New York Tribune* and had married his childhood sweetheart, whom he brought to New York from Denmark.

In his 1901 autobiography, *The Making of an American*, Riis explained that the police reporter "is the one who gathers and handles all the news that means trouble to some one: the murders, fires, suicides, robberies, and all that sort, before it gets into court".[7] The police reporters' office at 301 Mulberry Street, across the street from police headquarters, was in the heart of Lower Manhattan's immigrant community, and Riis, working at night on crime stories, became intimate with the worst doings of New York's poor. Leaving work between two and four in the morning, he walked through Five Points and Mulberry Bend in the Sixth Ward, past the cheap entertainment halls and lodging houses of the Bowery, through the city's oldest tenements in the Fourth Ward, to the Fulton Street Ferry, where he crossed the East River to his Brooklyn home.

Riis's search for answers to the housing problems of the poor began in earnest in 1884, when the *Tribune* transferred him from night to day work. He explained: "A new life began.... I met men now in whose companionship [my impressions] began to crystallise, to form into definite convictions; men of learning, of sympathy, and of power. My eggs hatched."[8] With an intimate understanding of the challenges facing the newly-arrived immigrant – from his own early years and from his newspaper beat – Riis began to understand the larger social picture: New York was experiencing an unprecedented flood of immigrants, who were living in the world's most crowded, unsanitary, crime-ridden slums. In his earlier reporting, Riis had been criticised for his "altogether editorial and presuming" writing style, but as he focused on the human costs of poor housing, his editorialising only increased. So did his frustration: "I wrote, but it seemed to make no impression".[9]

In October 1887, Riis read a four-line notice in the newspaper about the German invention of a magnesium flash powder, which could provide enough light to capture a photographic image in the dark. This "instantaneous flash-light" suggested a way for Riis to "[put] before the people what [he] saw" on his late night trips. Riis, however, had no intention of operating a camera himself and "began taking pictures by proxy". His friend Dr John T. Nagle, a member of the Society of Amateur Photographers of New York, enlisted two fellow Society members, Dr Henry Granger Piffard and Richard Hoe Lawrence, to follow Riis into the city's "darkest corners". Together with "a policeman or two", the four men set out on several outings; the photographers' interest was "centered in the camera and the flashlight", and Riis was "bent on letting in the light where it was so much needed". Riis called the group a "raiding party", which, armed with magnesium flash powder loaded into cartridges in a revolver, "carried terror wherever it went".[10]

In January 1888, Riis delivered his first lecture, "The Other Half, How It Lives and Dies in New York", at the Society's monthly lantern slide meeting. The lecture showcased the "flashlight" photographs taken by Lawrence and Piffard, but Riis proselytised for two hours, showed 100 slides, and invited his colleagues from the press, who published extensive reports in the local papers. From these articles, many of which included wood engravings based on the photographs, it is possible to outline Riis' talk and identify approximately half of the 100 photographs.

Riis led his audience on a slum tour, from the infamous Gotham Court on Cherry Street, a "model" tenement where it was said a thousand people lived; to Bandit's Roost, a narrow, filthy alley in Mulberry Bend; to Corlears Hook on the East River, where the Short Tail Gang sat under the docks drinking beer. Among the indoor scenes were a "black-and-tan dive" on Wooster Street, where "the white and black races meet in common debauch"; Happy Jack's Palace, a seven-cent lodging house on Pell Street; and an opium den on Pell between Mott Street and Chatham Square. His tour complete, Riis showed slides of charitable organisations, such as the Five Points House of Industry and the Children's Aid Society, as well as scenes from a police station, the city jail known as "The Tombs", and the penitentiary on Blackwell's Island in the East River. He concluded with images of "how the other half dies in New York", presenting Bellevue Hospital, the city morgue, and Potter's Field on Hart's Island.

Even before the lecture took place, Riis' photographic helpers had tired of their nighttime excursions, and Riis hired a professional to take, for example, *Prayer Time in the Nursery – Five Points House of Industry*. That photographer, however, used Riis' negatives without his permission, and Riis hired a lawyer to reclaim them. Without other options, Riis bought a simple four-by-five-inch box

Jacob Riis and unknown photographer, *Prayer Time in the Nursery, Five Points House of Industry*.

Jacob Riis, *The Potter's Field, The Common Trench*.

camera and tripod. *Potter's Field* was Riis' first photograph, and he describes the experience of taking it as a comedy of errors.[11]

Setbacks notwithstanding, Riis began delivering his lecture to church groups throughout the New York area, and in the 1889 Christmas issue of *Scribner's Magazine* – a national magazine for upper-middle-class readers – appeared a condensed version of the lecture with 21 illustrations. The title, "How the Other Half Lives, Studies Among the Tenements", was considerably more genteel and less local than "The Other Half, How It Lives and Dies in New York".

Of its illustrations, ten were new photographs taken by Riis, including *Five Cents a Spot*, which depicts the interior of an illegal flophouse. The following year, Scribner's published the book, *How the Other Half Lives*, which included another batch of new photographs by Riis, such as this image of a sweatshop on Ludlow Street. To take these photographs, Riis continued to function like a "raiding party", entering a crowded, dark space with a sanitary or law enforcement official and photographing by surprise. *A Ludlow Street Sweater's Shop*, for example, depicts the moment Riis entered the room: "The boy and the woman alone look up at our entrance ... . The men do not appear to be aware even of the presence of a stranger." Riis took his photograph before he established rapport with his subjects. Only afterwards did his Yiddish-speaking

Jacob Riis, *Five Cents a Spot.*

guide help him conduct an extensive interview in which the "wife of the boss ... disinclined to talk at first ... [grew] almost talkative".[12] These photographs, in which the intimacy of the setting, the harsh light, and the element of surprise create a sense of shock in the viewer, are the photographs for which Riis is most famous, and in the 1980s, was most severely criticised. The invasive nature of the "raiding party" and Riis' reliance on racial stereotypes to organise his tour of the slums led scholars to question Riis' motives and to characterise him as a bigot and a police agent.[13]

In *How the Other Half Lives*, Riis used every means of entertainment and persuasion he could muster to move his audience to action, and one could argue about the character of his intentions. What is beyond doubt and little known, however, is that after that book, Riis revised his approach completely, abandoning the raiding party and the slum tour.

The Children of the Poor, the sequel to *How the Other Half Lives*, was published in 1892. Focusing on the plight of children, Riis devoted the early chapters to describing the types of children at risk – ragpickers, gang members, sweatshop workers, and truants – and the latter chapters to describing institutional programs to help them – kindergartens, industrial schools, and boys clubs. To capture the interest of his readers, Riis introduced individuals he encountered and illustrated his anecdotes with photographic portraits. When photographing

Jacob Riis, *A Ludlow Street Sweater's Shop*.

Jacob Riis, *"I Scrubs", Little Katie from the West 52nd Street Industrial School.*

Katie at the 52nd Street Industrial School, for example, he found his title for the picture, *I Scrubs,* when he asked her what kind of work she did. She stood for her picture "without a question and without a smile", he noted, but later she invited Riis to her home on West 49th Street, which he found "all clean, if poor".[14] Thus for his second book, Riis reversed his work process: first he made a personal connection with his subject, and then he asked her to pose for a photograph. I would suggest that this change in technique was not due to a change of heart but to a shift in rhetorical strategy and an increased ease with the camera.

Between 1890 and 1892, Riis made more photographs than at any other time. In addition to taking the photographs for *Children of the Poor,* he launched three public health campaigns – against upstate pollution of New York's water supply; illegal ragpicking; and the degrading and dangerous conditions of police station lodging houses, which comprised the city's only refuge for the homeless. For all three initiatives, he made photographs, which were published as wood engravings in newspapers. *Under the Dump at Rivington Street* is one of nine photographs he made of ragpickers living illegally in the city's dumps.

Thereafter, Riis' use of the camera dwindled, and in 1895 and 1896, he hired professionals to take photographs to illustrate specific articles.[15] In 1900, he published *The Ten Years' War,* a book reviewing his years fighting for housing

Jacob Riis, *Under the Dump at Rivington Street.*

IN SLEEPING QUARTERS—RIVINGTON STREET DUMP.

In Sleeping Quarters, Rivington Street Dump, "Extra, Real Wharf Rats", *The Evening Sun*
(18 March 1892).

Lewis Hine, *In the Oyster Camps, Child Labor in Louisiana*.

reform, and in 1902 *The Battle with the Slum*, a lightly revised and heavily illustrated version of the same book.[16] *The Battle with the Slum* inspired Riis to seek out photographs from government agencies like the New York City Board of Education and social service organisations like the Charity Organization Society to illustrate new initiatives to help the poor. In the course of the decade, the improved quality of halftone illustration had created increased demand for such photographs, and a corps of professional photographers had developed to meet it. Approximately half of the photographs in the Riis Collection are photographs like these, most by unidentified professionals and some by well-known photographers like Lewis Hine.[17]

To conclude, here is a brief summary of Riis' photographic practice. In 1888, when he conceived the idea of using flash photography to expose the way the other half lived, Riis was compelled to commission photographs or take them himself. His period of active engagement with the camera occurred between 1887 and 1895 (a handful of photographs can be dated to 1898). By 1900, photographs of settlement houses, schools, and playgrounds were available through the agencies that built or ran them. When in his autobiography Riis remarked, "I am downright sorry to confess here that I am no good at all as a photographer", he meant it.[18] He was a polemicist, not a photographer, and although photographs were integral to his polemic, he did not consider himself a photographer, and he did not value photographs apart from his message.

My conclusions are based primarily on a comparative study of the Riis Collection with published writings. Although his lectures were as important to him as his writings – and earned him as much if not more income – evidence of them is thin. Riis spoke extemporaneously, without a script, and his papers include only some rough lecture notes. There is one published transcript of a lecture that Riis delivered in Washington, D.C. in 1891, which indicates the images he showed and even mentions audience reactions, such as laughter and applause. I have recently contracted with the Museum of the City of New York to prepare a complete catalogue of the Riis Collection, which will be published in 2015. An exhibition to accompany the publication is being planned, and its centerpiece will be the re-creation of a slide lecture based upon the 1891 transcript.

Notes

1. I contend that Riis was not particularly sensitive to composition. Maren Stange, by contrast, assumes that the cropping of *Bandit's Roost* was intentional. See *Symbols of an Ideal Life: Social Documentary Photography in America, 1890-1950* (New York: Cambridge University Press, 1989), 6–12. For another influential interpretation of Riis as a self-aware artist of the camera, see Peter Bacon Hales, *Silver Cities: The Photography of American Urbanization, 1839-1915* (Philadelphia: Temple University Press, 1984), 193.

2. Riis prepared his papers for donation to a public collection, and his family donated them to the Library of Congress, Washington, D.C. By contrast, he did not save his photographs, which were found in the attic of the Riis family home in Queens, New York, only after Alexander Alland urged Riis' son, William Roger Riis, to look there. See Alexander Alland, Sr., *Jacob A. Riis, Photographer and Citizen*, Aperture, Inc. (Millerton, New York: Aperture Inc., 1973), 43–48.

3. In many of the copy negatives, the edges of the prints tacked to a board are visible. In others, negative numbers and/or titles inscribed by commercial studios are visible.

4. Bonnie Yochelson, "What Are the Photographs of Jacob Riis?" *Culturefront*, vol. 3, no. 3 (Fall 1994): 28–38.

5. The reproductions seen here were made from the vintage-material prints that the Museum commissioned in 1994 by Chicago Albumen Works, Housatonic, Massachusetts.

6. Bonnie Yochelson and Daniel Czitrom, *Rediscovering Jacob Riis: Exposure Journalism and Photography in Turn-of-the-Century New York* (New York: The New Press, 2007). From 1997 our work was supported by a National Endowment for the Humanities grant for collaborative research.

7. Jacob A. Riis, *The Making of an American* (New York: MacMillan, 1901), 203.

8. Ibid., 242.

9. Ibid., 267.

10. For his description of taking up photography, see Riis, *Making of an American*, 265–269.

11. Riis, *Making of an American,* 270–271.

12. Jacob A. Riis, *How The Other Half Lives, Studies Among the Tenements of New York* (New York: Charles Scribner's Sons, 1890), 125–126.

13. For example, see Sally Stein, "Making Connections with the Camera: Photography and Social Mobility in the Career of Jacob Riis", *Afterimage* (May 1983): 9–16.

14. Jacob A. Riis, *The Children of the Poor* (New York: Charles Scribner's Sons, 1892), 60–61.

15. For example, "Goodbye to the Bend", *The Evening Sun* (24 May 1895) includes seven photographs by a *Sun* photographer named "Collins". At that time, Riis worked for *The Sun*, and there are nine negatives by Collins in the Riis Collection.

16. Jacob A. Riis, *The Ten Years' War: An Account of the Battle with the Slum in New York* (Boston and New York: Houghton Mifflin & Co., 1900) and Jacob A. Riis, *The Battle with the Slum* (New York: Macmillan, 1902).

17. In preparing "A Modern St. George, The Growth of Organized Charity in the United States", *Scribner's Magazine* (October 1911): 385–402, Riis acquired eight prints by Hine, seven of which appeared in the article.

18. Riis, *Making of an American*, 263.

Caroline Henkes

Early Christmas Films in the Tradition of the Magic Lantern

Christmas is coming. This can be observed in so many signs of everyday life. Businessmen are arranging their shops, nobody wants to fall behind. The same goes for our cinema owners. For them it's a question of existential importance not to fall behind in the season's competition by ensuring that they can offer films which are in keeping with the thinking and endeavours of this special time of the year.[1]

As this quotation from the German trade paper *Der Kinematograph* illustrates, Christmas was already connected to economic factors at the beginning of the 20th century, but, despite all the competition, it was also always accompanied by a specific mood of giving and sharing, which had to be reflected in Christmas films as well. Therefore many films would present heart-warming scenes, where (for example) rich children shared their food and gifts with poor children, or generous rich parents brought gifts to a poor family.

However this article will focus on early Christmas films which, at first glance, lack a happy ending. These films tend to present ambivalent attitudes towards poverty and suggest to the audience approval or condemnation of the protagonists with regard to generally accepted moral standards. The Christmas films discussed thus presumably function as a reinforcer or intensifier of existing societal attitudes. By concentrating on three divergent but exemplary films – THE LITTLE MATCH GIRL (GB 1914), CHRISTMAS DAY IN THE WORKHOUSE (GB 1914)[2] and WEIHNACHTSTRÄNEN (Christmas Tears) (Germany 1910)[3] – this article will show how early Christmas films discussed poverty by using generic representational conventions and strategies of emotional response in the tradition of the magic lantern.

Elementary for this analysis is the fact that the two British films directly refer to well-known magic lantern sets, whereas the third (German) film essentially resorts to commonly used lantern narratives. This initial situation allows a

---

Facing page: CHRISTMAS DAY IN THE WORKHOUSE (GB 1914).
Upper: The protagonist isolated from the other workhouse inhabitants.
Lower: Death as the only resolution for the old man's critique.

direct comparison between these two popular practices of screen performance around 1900 with a focus on the discussion about deserving and undeserving poor as well as on facets of intermediality. The first part of the article therefore focuses on divergent ways of representing poor characters with regard to the content, whereas the second part examines continuities regarding the representation techniques of early cinema and the magic lantern.

Starting with the plot analysis, these three short films feature protagonists who present different points of view towards the role and representation of poor people: a young, innocent child, an old and desolate man, and a desperate, ill-fated mother. The social questions addressed within the plots of the films differ widely: the main theme in THE LITTLE MATCH GIRL is a child neglected by her alcoholic father; CHRISTMAS DAY IN THE WORKHOUSE offers a critical examination of the British workhouse system; and WEIHNACHTSTRÄNEN deals with a mother's grief, self-reproach and solitude on Christmas Eve, because her child died in a car accident. These variations concerning the protagonists and themes allow a detailed discussion of different ways of representing poverty.

All three films present generally acknowledged poor characters and consequentially allow the filmic discussion of the poverty problem, especially with reference to the representation of the poor protagonists. In the late 19th century, paupers were conventionally regarded as "deserving" poor, meaning those who were poor because of external circumstances and not responsible for their own poverty, or "undeserving" poor indicating self-inflicted poverty because of e.g. alcohol abuse or laziness. This question of the deserving or undeserving poor was still widely discussed around the turn of the 20th century and crucial for public opinion with regard to their treatment. In considering the cinematic portrayal of the protagonists, I will analyse why and how these characters are able to evoke compassion amongst the audience, and if this is related to their representation as deserving poor, thus allowing us to draw conclusions about the audience's possible perception of poverty and the films' intended messages.

THE LITTLE MATCH GIRL is an adaptation of Hans Christian Andersen's well known story about a poor neglected girl trying to sell matches in order to survive, who ultimately dies outside in the cold, accompanied by visions which symbolise a functioning family life. The child's position in this film allows no ambiguities: the audience's compassion is clearly evoked by her innocent portrayal. She is pictured as pretty, lonely, hard-working, and fearful, but nevertheless obedient towards her drunkard father. Her death is ultimately a consequence of her father's recklessness and alcohol abuse. This girl is obviously deserving poor, a character deserving the audience's compassion. THE LITTLE MATCH GIRL illustrates the precarious situation an innocent child can fall into due to external circumstances, and condemns the undeserving poor like the child's father, implying that alcohol abuse is the source of all evil. Poverty as suffered by this protagonist emphasises the difference between deserving and undeserving poor and underlines the need for charity. However, the sad fate portrayed in this short film arouses exactly the kind of emotion the audience demanded on screen around Christmas: spectators wanted to see sad fates in order to "virtually help" these characters and feel superior to (for example) the passers-by in THE LITTLE MATCH GIRL. This plot construction also was very popular in magic lantern slide sets where, by arousing feelings of superiority and pity simultaneously, spectators could be subtly manipulated for charity.[4]

CHRISTMAS DAY IN THE WORKHOUSE tells the story of a poor old man whose wife died because of a lack of charity. The protagonist, John, can be described as deserving poor as well: he and his wife had led a strenuous life in Devon where he worked as a trader, before they had to move to the city. Due to unfortunate circumstances they descended into poverty. However, the deserving pauper criticises the Workhouse and the "guardians and their ladies"[5] – and herewith a certain ambiguous moment is established in the storyline. But the reason for his critique is still presented as comprehensible to the audience: on Christmas Day the previous year, his wife died from starvation because the workhouse's benefactors refused to let him take away food for her. The fact that John is deserving poor and lost his wife as a result of adverse circumstances explains his critique, but this is only possible because he is clearly isolated from the other workhouse inhabitants and presented as a single case.[6] However his articulated critique causes an ambiguous moment regarding his societal position (is he still deserving after he criticises the charity organisation?) which – at least in the film version – can only be resolved by John's death. In contrast to the magic lantern version where the original Sims ballad is fully reproduced, and which ends with the articulation of John's critique, the film doesn't have this open ending. Instead the film version of CHRISTMAS DAY IN THE WORK-HOUSE even leaves parts of his critical words out altogether.[7] Another more pragmatic reason for John's death might be that it had to be guaranteed that the story is self-contained. This could only have been achieved through John's death (and thereby his 'eternal union' with his wife). In CHRISTMAS DAY IN THE WORKHOUSE, poverty is depicted as a burden imposed by society's absence of understanding of the urgency of a situation of non-self-induced poverty, which caused the death of John's wife and eventually his own.

The protagonist in WEIHNACHTSTRÄNEN is the most ambiguous figure presented in this article. The film shows a woman who has "fallen" after having lost her child in a car accident. However, she wants to spend Christmas with her dead child, steals a Christmas gift and finally dies on her daughter's grave. At first glance, this woman embodies characteristics clearly attributed to the undeserving poor, especially her abusive alcohol consumption and resulting poverty; a negative impression that is increased by her shabby appearance. The reason for her behaviour, however, lies in the emotional trauma caused by her child's deadly accident, a situation for which she can't really be blamed. Consequentially the film adopts a rather neutral position towards its female protagonist, showing her sad fate and at the end presenting her as a loving mother despaired by her child's death. Here again the film focuses on the individual fate of a poor woman, with her poverty depicted as caused by external circumstances. Ultimately the woman is liberated from her suffering through death on her child's grave, an iconography more usually applied the other way around. This ending shows a close similarity with some lantern slide sets, where a person's death on the grave of a loved one was often the sad climax of a melodramatic story.[8] The mother's death can therefore be interpreted as a release from worldly suffering and hence from her position as undeserving poor.

In addition, through the means of money a social inferiority is emphasised between the three protagonists and their (possible) benefactors: all three characters are dependent on charity in order to survive. The protagonist in THE LITTLE MATCH GIRL dies because nobody stops in the cold and buys matches, the old man is dependent on benefactors because he doesn't have the money to buy food for his wife, and the mother in WEIHNACHTSTRÄNEN experiences charity when, in her submissive position (sitting on the steps in front of a theatre), she evokes pity amongst rich theatregoers. The contemporary audience was familiar with these scenic constructions from magic lantern stories as they illustrate the protagonists' dependence on charity, or in some cases the charitable acts of the passers-by. Representations of acts of charity (or the refusal to act charitably) were deliberately inserted to arouse the audience's sense of justice and to connect charity with ethics. All three films show people

Mother kneeling in front of her daughter's grave, shortly before dying. WEIHNACHTSTRÄNEN (Germany 1910).

who could be helped with a small amount of money; however ignoring their need leads to their tragic endings.

In these Christmas films poverty is shown as a portion of individual tragedies and the reasons for the protagonists' poverty lie in external circumstances. All three protagonists share an isolated position within the films: they are all on their own, family members are either dead or neglect them. This focus on individual cases facilitates the audience's identification with and understanding for the sometimes ambiguous characters. The construction of a scene of injustice within the storyline additionally allows the audience to take the protagonist's side and put oneself in his/her position. The injustices which the three characters have to endure form the main narrative plot lines in each story, and eventually lead to the protagonists' death which underlines the melodramatic nature of the stories. The protagonists are represented as deserving poor, or at least change into deserving (or saved) poor at the end of the story, because only then can compassion be evoked and feel justified amongst the audience.

Child kneeling on her mother's grave. Lantern slide from ORA PRO NOBIS (Bamforth, 1897).

Three-dimensional versus painted scenery.
THE LITTLE MATCH GIRL (GB 1914).

This might have been useful to open up the audience's mind for charity organisations which could have been present at or after the screen performances.

Besides the relationships between their content, the continuities with regard to the representation techniques of two types of popular screen performance around 1900 – the magic lantern and the cinematograph – are worth examining. The chosen films adopt various modes of representation concerning the established visualisation techniques of the magic lantern – and with regard to early cinema this consequently leads to a discussion of the term *intermediality*. In *Film and Attraction*, André Gaudreault characterises early cinema by emphasising the "diversity of cinematographic connections in the intermedial context of the turn of the 20th century". He states that "the so called 'early cinema' is also the result of multiple cultural practices linked to images, whether photographic or not, moving or not – and socially recognised practices at that".[9] A further concern of the present article is the demonstration of some of these intersections of intermediality with the magic lantern, by looking at the narrative style and representational techniques in the selected films.[10] The intermedial approach applied by Gaudreault especially for the very first years of cinema is extended into the period of the ongoing institutionalisation of cinema (from c. 1910 onwards) in order to demonstrate that these three Christmas films produced between 1910 and 1914 still share visual and narrative representation styles with the magic lantern. These Christmas films borrow familiar representational techniques and narrative patterns from lantern performances to illustrate and narrate their stories attractively.

Two of the films – THE LITTLE MATCH GIRL and CHRISTMAS DAY IN THE WORKHOUSE – are based upon well-known narratives: a tale by Hans Christian Andersen (1805–75) and a ballad written by George R. Sims (1847–1922), both also familiar to the audience through lantern slide sets. This made their understanding easier and allowed film producers to focus on attractive illustration, rather than on detailed reproduction of the narrative.

As an illustrative example, I will examine the narrative structure of THE LITTLE MATCH GIRL. The story's content is unchanged with the exception of some small details, such as a change in the day the story takes place, to Christmas Eve instead of New Year's Eve – Christmas obviously provided a more melodramatic context for the story due to the greater importance of Christmas in Britain.

The film maintains the tale's original linear structure and narrative, however a frame narrative where the child's father is shown in a pub, drinking, and the child is fearfully waiting for him in their humble hut, is added. When he finally arrives home and notices that his daughter didn't sell any matches, he kicks her out of the hut and warns her not to come back home without money. These scenes take about one third of the total film length and frame the narrative to accentuate a conflict between father and child. Seven different intertitles provide the audience with missing information about the girl's context and explain the plot ("Father will hit me", "Go away and don't dare to come back without money"), whereas in the second part of the film the same number of intertitles is sufficient to structure a plot which lasts twice as long as the first part. This *bipartite structure* can be explained by the shift from this new frame narrative towards the already known storyline, and thus also towards a narration and visualisation technique in the tradition of the magic lantern.

This is also maintained with regard to the stage setting: the scenes in the hut seem more realistic than the subsequent scenes, and the narrative film style of the first part is substituted in the second part by a tableau-like imagery. When the child is outside in the cold, trying to sell matches and looking for shelter at the corner of two houses, the single frames last longer. The film's iconography is based on this tableau-like representation and narration style which focuses on the attractive visualisation of an already known storyline. In contrast to the first part of the film, where the intertitles tended to explain the action,

Portrayal of movement. THE LITTLE MATCH GIRL (GB 1914) and lantern slide from THE LITTLE MATCH GIRL (Arger & Son, US 1905, design by Joseph Boggs Beale).

the second part rather uses them to differentiate between the separate scenes or visions, but without adding a character's thought or information which couldn't be seen on the screen anyway ("Barefoot", "What she saw in her vision when she lit the second match"). The child's staging, especially when she lights the matches and has her visions about an oven, a richly set table with a turkey moving towards her, a huge Christmas tree and finally her dead mother (in Andersen's original, she sees her grandmother) is similar to the composition of the lantern slide set of this story produced by McAllister in 1905.[11] When the girl has these visions, due to the filmic possibility of capturing movement, she stands up and moves towards her vision, but otherwise the structures of these different scenarios look very much alike. The huge item which she sees is at the centre of the frame, and the girl is a marvelling observer of her own vision. In both film and lantern versions the gleaming or the movement of the object attracts the audience's attention and might therefore be called a *visual attraction*.

So the visual composition of key scenes of the film demonstrates a close connection to the composition practice of magic lantern slides. Because there was no need to explain the story and the child's behaviour to the audience, the challenge was rather to create attractive visual highlights – e.g. the moving turkey or the huge radiating Christmas tree – a device of the cinema of attractions. In his article "Now You See It, Now You Don't", Tom Gunning pointed out the close connection between early cinema and the importance of visual stimuli, in contrast to the increasing concern for narrativisation with the ongoing institutionalisation of cinema.[12] The second part of THE LITTLE MATCH GIRL however clearly focuses on the attractive visualisation by using established representational techniques of the magic lantern.

This also becomes evident from the scenic composition of CHRISTMAS DAY IN THE WORKHOUSE. The whole film stands in the *oral narrative tradition* of the magic lantern because virtually each filmed scene is separated from the next one by long intertitles consisting of the verses of the ballad. The individual scenes' main function is to illustrate and not to narrate the story – similar to the function of lantern slides. The scenes of course include information relevant for the story, whose details are more easily and quickly understood when visualised – e.g. the woman's bad health – but nevertheless the illustrative aspect of the individual scenes is more important than forward movement of the narration. One can hardly imagine that this film was shown without a narrator who read the intertitles aloud to the audience. In *Marketing Modernity* Joe Kember points out the wide variety of performance styles from other entertainment media as a substantial resource for early filmmakers: "For example, the staging, costuming, and gestural language of life model lantern slides could deliver a great deal of information to audiences, and early film-makers familiar with these techniques tended to translate these to moving pictures".[13]

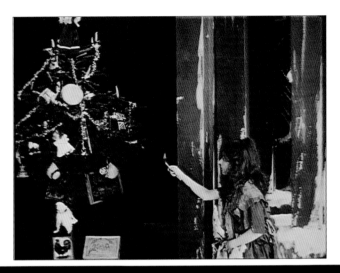

The girl as a marvelling observer of her own vision. THE LITTLE MATCH GIRL (GB 1914) and lantern slide from THE LITTLE MATCH GIRL (Arger & Son, US 1905, design by Joseph Boggs Beale).

Examples of gestural language. WEIHNACHTSTRÄNEN (Germany 1910).

Visions and daydreams play a major role within all three Christmas films.

In WEIHNACHTSTRÄNEN the actress adopts a *gestural language* to show her desperation right from the beginning. This acting style enabled the audience to recognise and immediately identify the protagonist's situation – a method which was also important for the production of life model slides. If we look at the different actors performing in these three films, we can notice standardised interpretations of emotions with overacted gestures of fear, dismay, anger, grief etc. In early film practice this traditional repertoire of a "naive visual expression system" was still widespread, as Jörg Schweinitz demonstrates in his book *Film und Stereotyp*.[14] This specific acting style reveals the proximity between early film, theatre and the magic lantern, where explicit gestures were required to facilitate and guarantee the understanding for the audience. In addition the plot is visually supported by the actors' exaggerated poses.

All three films include visions experienced by their protagonists. At a certain point of the stories, the protagonists *imagine something* – a visualisation of dreams or a vision, an illusion within the filmic illusion itself. The visions in THE LITTLE MATCH GIRL offer the girl a "way out" of the cold, to satisfy her hunger and finally end her poverty through the celebration of faith which is represented by her ascension to heaven. In CHRISTMAS DAY IN THE WORKHOUSE, the film's inner plot consists of a flashback showing the old man's situation at Christmas one year ago; within this he and his dying wife share a vision about their past life in the countryside. In WEIHNACHTSTRÄNEN, the woman's vision right at the beginning resembles a nightmare: she dreams about the accident in which her child died and "sees" Father Christmas who refuses to give her a doll for her dead daughter. These visions and/or dreams illustrate a further important alikeness between Christmas films and lantern slide sets where this kind of visualisation also was highly popular. Furthermore, all three protagonists see or dream of a beloved but already dead family member, their connecting factor to the afterlife. In WEIHNACHTSTRÄNEN the mother's vision about her dead child induces the protagonist's turn towards the afterlife and her final salvation; a salvation also from being "undeserving poor".

These intermedial aspects within early Christmas films show that performance practices of the magic lantern were still applied in films around 1910, especially when cinematic tales were narrated. The oral narrative tradition of these films, their representational and narrative techniques with tableau-like scenes, their gestural acting style and the importance of visions allow the films to focus on more clearly visual storytelling.

Christmas seems to have been a preferred reason for exploring poverty on screen. The Christmas films discussed in this article deal with individuals' tragic fates, their salvation through death as the only possible way out of poverty: if they can't have a nice Christmas, at least they should find salvation and be united with their loved ones. However these protagonists remain social types without specific individual characteristics, and in this way illustrate the societal discussion about "deserving" and "undeserving" poverty. Poverty in Christmas films was presented as caused by external circumstances – or in the Christmas fairy tales with happy endings it was used to illustrate charity. Christmas films didn't intend a critical discussion of poverty as a societal problem but rather tried to arouse compassion or thankfulness respectively amongst the audience and provoke an emotional impact. These films fit well into the apparent charity boom, which according to contemporary newspaper articles seems to have been widespread: they formulate a plea to the audience's sense of responsibility. Christmas films invite the audience's contemplation and might have moved them to generosity.

In addition these films are a perfect example of early cinema's high level of intermediality, the "dependence of cinema on other mediums and cultural spheres",[15] a "process whereby form and content are transferred and migrate among media".[16] Intermediality therefore becomes a key word when describing the complex evolution of visual media culture at the turn of the 20th century, especially with regard to the connections between the magic lantern and cinematograph. Even though by 1910-14, when these Christmas films were produced, the institutionalisation of cinema had begun, the narrative style and the visualisation techniques applied still evoke performance styles of the magic lantern. The magic lantern mode of presentation offered visual and narrative means of design that were suitable and thus intentionally applied in early Christmas films in order to increase the emotional impact on the audience. The development of cinema is therefore closely bound to earlier entertainment and screen performance practices and cannot be viewed in isolation.

Notes

1. *Der Kinematograph*, no. 256 (22 November 1911).

2. A lantern slide set and film of THE LITTLE MATCH GIRL, as well as CHRISTMAS DAY IN THE WORKHOUSE, can be found in Martin Loiperdinger and Ludwig Vogl-Bienek, *Lichtspiele und Soziale Frage: Screening the Poor 1888–1914* (München: Film & Kunst Edition Filmmuseum, 2011), 2 DVDs.

3. The Dutch version of this film preserved at the EYE-Institute is called KERSTGEDAGHTEN, which can be translated as "Christmas thoughts". However from a film description published by the German production company Deutsche Mutoskop- und Biograph-Gesellschaft, which I found in the German trade paper *Der Kinematograph*, I believe that the original German title was WEIHNACHTSTRÄNEN ("Christmas tears"). See *Der Kinematograph*, no. 202 (9 November 1910).

4. See for example Ludwig Vogl-Bienek, "Projektionskunst und soziale Frage: Der Einsatz visueller Medien in der Armenfürsorge um 1900", in Jörg Requate (ed.), *Das 19. Jahrhundert als Mediengesellschaft* (München: Oldenbourg, 2009), or Martin Loiperdinger and Ludwig Vogl-Bienek, "Lichtspiele und Soziale Frage", in Marie-Paule Jungblut and Claude Wey (eds), *Armes Luxemburg? Pauvre Luxembourg?* (Luxembourg/München: Musée Belleville/Verlag Farin, 2011).

5. George R. Sims, "In the workhouse: Christmas Day", in Richard Crangle and Robert MacDonald (eds), *The Illustrated Bamforth Slide Catalogue* (London: Magic Lantern Society, 2009).

6. See Lydia Jakobs, *George R. Sims' viktorianische Armutsballaden im Medium der Projektionskunst* (Universität Trier: unpublished MA thesis, 2011), 33.

7. However, it should be noted that the film version of CHRISTMAS DAY IN THE WORKHOUSE as preserved at the British Film Institute is incomplete; approximately 30 seconds are missing.

8. See for example the slide set ORA PRO NOBIS (Bamforth & Co, 1897) where the poor child dies on her mother's grave. This set is reproduced in Loiperdinger and Vogl-Bienek, *Lichtspiele und Soziale Frage*, DVD 1.

9. André Gaudreault, *Film and Attraction* (Urbana, Illinois: University of Illinois Press, 2011), 10.

10. Gaudreault emphasises that the diverse practices associated with the cinematograph (as a technological device) should not be understood as historically continuous with the "cinema", which he defines as a set of relatively stable institutions and practices that had converged by 1915.

11. See Loiperdinger and Vogl-Bienek, *Lichtspiele und Soziale Frage*, DVD 1.

12. Tom Gunning, "Now You See It, Now You Don't: The Temporality of the Cinema of Attractions", *Velvet Light Trap*, 32 (Fall 1993), 3–12.

13. Joe Kember, *Marketing Modernity: Victorian Popular Shows and Early Cinema* (Exeter: University of Exeter Press, 2009), 151.

14. Jörg Schweinitz, *Film und Stereotyp. Eine Herausforderung für das Kino und die Filmtheorie* (Berlin: Akad.-Verlag, 2006), 71. Translated into English as Jörg Schweinitz (trans. Laura Schleussner), *Film and Stereotype: A Challenge for Cinema and Theory* (New York: Columbia University Press, 2011).

15. Gaudreault, *Film and Attraction*, 14.

16. André Gaudreault, *From Plato to Lumière* (Toronto: University of Toronto Press, 2009), 156.

PART II:

The Use of Lantern Shows, Photography and Early Films for Social Prevention by Charity Organisations

Preis 10 Pfg.

DIE WELT — FÜR GOTT

DER
KRIEGSRUF

Offizielles Organ der Heilsarmee für Deutschland

| № 3 | William Booth, General der Heilsarmee. | Telephon: Amt IX. Nr. 4194. Berlin, den 21. Januar 1905 S.W., Blücherplatz 1. | W. Elwin Oliphant, Kommandeur für Deutschland. | Band XIX |

Ein Fest für 1500 Arme in Berlin
im Konkordiasaal am 10. Januar 1905.

Einige glückliche Stunden bei der Heilsarmee.

Karen Eifler

Feeding and Entertaining the Poor: Salvation Army Lantern Exhibitions Combined with Food Distribution in Britain and Germany

"Well, the Emperor can't have enjoyed his meal more than us today!" said a poor man in praise of a feast the Salvation Army organised in 1906 in Spandau near Berlin. On the occasion of the imperial couple's silver wedding, 60 needy people were offered a meal and, among other items, the projection of lantern slides.[1]

The Salvation Army is the best-known among a wide range of British welfare organisations that, around the start of the 20th century, used projection media for poor relief.[2] While some events aimed at fund-raising, many were meant to directly help poor people, for instance lantern exhibitions within food distributions. This context is a particularly interesting example for direct poor relief measures because the multi-sensory experience of a lantern entertainment was complemented by a haptic impression – the sense of taste.

This article explores, in a broad sense, the *taste* of these events: How were they designed and experienced by their audiences? What were their implicit pur-poses? It will be useful to begin with a brief outline of the Salvation Army and the audience appeal of their lantern exhibitions.

The Salvation Army: a successful lantern exhibitor

Uniforms and musical bands are still typical features associated with the Salvation Army, which has been an independent religious community from its beginnings. Its success began over 130 years ago in Britain, where within four years of its foundation in 1878 it was the sixth largest religious community.[3] In the 1880s, with 5,000 meetings weekly, it attracted millions of people.[4] In Germany it also registered a considerable rise: by the First World War there

---

Facing page:
Cover of the German *Kriegsruf*, 21 January 1905, with photograph of a lantern exhibition with food distribution.

were 224 branches in almost 150 towns, and in 1910 alone one million people attended its meetings.[5] Its founders William and Catherine Booth aimed to struggle against mass poverty by a religious mission overtly driven by military structures and lay preaching.[6] During the 1880s the Army began to maintain such social facilities as night shelters for the homeless and accommodation for unemployed people, and to care for other groups like released prisoners, travelling workers and soldiers.[7]

The growing investment in projection media by the Salvation Army Trade Department reveals the increasing popularity of lantern exhibitions in missionary work. From 1893 onward, the Army Headquarters distributed lantern slides;[8] in 1894, the Trade Department began to manufacture "Real Salvation Army Lantern Slides", destined to be distributed throughout the organisation "at a special low price that will bring them within the reach of every Corps".[9] It also invested in film production, as well as the loan of commercial films suited to missionary work.[10] As the organisation expanded internationally and the branches were strongly bound to the London headquarters, the same slides were shown throughout the world.[11]

Reviews celebrated the success and popularity of Army events with lantern services: in Walthamstow "Many attended to the meeting; Citadel crowded", in Leeds lantern exhibitions "captivated the large and representative crowds" and in Cheltenham they "drew great crowds to the hall, which was packed both afternoon and night".[12] The German Army organ *Kriegsruf* reported that doors had to be unhinged to accommodate the many attendees at lantern services in Pfullingen and Pforzheim, while in Reutlingen "It would have been very useful to shift away a wall; but this was very difficult to realise ... the whole room was packed with people sitting and standing".[13] Several special events with lantern exhibitions attracted vast audiences: even before the "Limelight Memorial Service" on the fourth anniversary of Catherine Booth's death, the Army expected "thousands of visitors" and "crowded houses".[14] In April 1903, over 10,000 people assembled in London's Royal Albert Hall to welcome William Booth after his return from the United States. After songs and musical pieces, a procession and a speech of the General himself, the cinematograph took them on his trip by "throwing lots of moving pictures ... on an indescribably huge sheet".[15]

Reports on lantern and cinematograph exhibitions combined with food distribution in the *War Cry* and the *Kriegsruf* show that the use of projection media by welfare organisations was a mass phenomenon in Britain and Germany. For example, at Christmas 1905 1,020 poor children were offered sweets and a cinematograph exhibition at Northampton; in February 1906, 320 adults and 540 children from New Brompton were entertained to a free hot dinner, musical performances and moving pictures; and in 1907 1,200 Welsh children enjoyed a lantern and cinematograph show, along with tea and Christmas presents.[16] In Berlin, the Salvation Army received 1,500 adults and 150 children in January 1905 and in 1906 as many as 2,000 needy people.[17]

Welcome congregation for General Booth in London's Royal Albert Hall. *Kriegsruf*, 18 April 1903.

According to the reviews, these exhibitions were very successful and left lasting impressions. A free tea and lantern service in Hereford was directly described as "a grand success".[18] At a lantern service in Portsmouth, 1,050 children "thoroughly enjoyed themselves, and one was overheard to say 'Isn't it nice?'" After a Salvation Army entertainment in Berlin, a "little wifey with her children" expressed how much she had enjoyed it and that she wanted to give the commissioner's wife a nice bunch of flowers next time.[19] The free meals which offered the prospect of a normally unaffordable spectacle were in great demand in Germany as well:

> We had just arrived at our office in the morning of January 6, when the bell rang. It was a street vendor who had followed us and asked "Mr Captain" for a ticket to the feast of poor people. These tickets were so much in demand that to our sorrow they were already out-of-stock at noon and we had to refuse some of the applicants. All the seats in the big Concordia Hall and the Hall above were taken.[20]

The popularity of these non-commercial lantern exhibitions raises the question of *why* they were so successful. Was the attendance at a lantern exhibition just a kind of side-effect, due to the satisfaction of basic needs by these missionary organisations? Some reports suggest, however, that the lantern or cinematograph exhibitions were the very point of attraction. For example, while about 700 children were present at a free tea in Wood Green near London, almost one thousand attended the following cinematograph exhibition.[21] At another lantern exhibition with tea near the capital, "an additional crowd of youngsters" joined the 400 children who had already been present.[22]

Poor people in Cardiff were offered tickets of admission to lantern services *after* attending a Salvation Army feast.[23]

The questions of how and why the Salvation Army designed its lantern exhibitions within food distributions to arouse the enthusiasm of poor people will be examined in the following section. In order to do so, detailed analysis of exhibition practices will be gleaned from two newspaper reports. The first and main example from the *War Cry* deals with a children's treat in London at Christmas 1895. Second, as an example for Germany, is my opening example from the *Kriegsruf* about a feast and lantern exhibition in Spandau in 1906.

Emotions, community and taste: the design of Salvation Army lantern entertainments

In "mixing the popular with the deeply religious", the Salvation Army saw the "main force to touch the hearts especially of the common people".[24] This reveals that one of the purposes of events with lantern exhibitions for poor people was to create an emotional resonance. Reported reactions suggest as well that this was considered a very important point to convince poor people. "Hearts were moved, good desires aroused, and conviction produced", according to a report summarizing the successes of several lantern lectures in London.[25] A lantern service in Glasgow resulted in the conversion of a young man who had been deeply impressed: "[He] could not keep back the tears as he said, 'I've found in Him a Friend'".[26] Children in Berlin "sat there, with bright eyes and open mouths for wondering, watching the wonderful images conjured up on the big screen".[27]

A useful starting point for examining how the Army influenced the audience's mood is the harmonious programming of these events: They normally offered a kind of balance between recreational and instructive parts. However, analysis of my first example reveals that this not only served to provide variety to the 1,800 children who were entertained to tea, games and lantern slides.[28] The composition of the lantern views aimed at creating strong emotional effects which were closely related to the promotional intentions of the exhibition: during the prelude to the show, at the projection of the slogan "There is a better world they say", "the excitement grew almost breathless". At a first (unnamed) service of song which dealt with Temperance, the children "gazed in breathless silence", "carried by the vivid pictures". At the climax of the story, they reacted with "a gasp of delight". Then a "funny little image with the enquiry, Good evening! Have you read the 'Young Soldier'?" caused a "merry laugh". Views of the General, Mrs Booth and the Chief-Commander (Bramwell Booth) followed, "each calling forth a burst of affectionate greeting". Afterwards, "the first scene of the most touching story of all [LITTLE JAMIE] riveted every eye". The service was concluded by the projection of the Band of Love Pledge which "urged" the children, "fresh from the deep impressions just made", to join this organisation for young people. At the end of the event, they marched past the

Field Commissioner who offered each one a free copy of the "beautiful" *Young Soldier*, the Army organ for young people.

The arousing of emotions certainly was partly based on the story LITTLE JAMIE which offered several possibilities for identification: Jamie is a boy who tries to get his father to give up drinking, which has plunged whole the family into poverty, and founds with other street children the Cold Water Army, a Temperance group.[29] Poverty and broken homes would be well-known experiences for most of the young spectators. They also could take Jamie for a great example because he was an active, fighting and responsible hero. There was also a link between the story and the event: on Christmas Eve, the family father drinks away all the money saved for Christmas presents. The Salvation Army's treat also took place at Christmas, but unlike the story the children were presented with food, a day full of pleasure – and a free copy of the *Young Soldier*. A further resource of identification was the *Cold Water Army*, which was based on the street children's common hardship. From the story, the children learned that personal strength is achieved by belonging to the group. These different levels of identification certainly contributed to a positive image of the Salvation Army and aroused wishes of belonging.

I want to emphasise though that the emotional address to the whole crowd of

Feast for poor children with lantern exhibition in Berlin, 1906. *Kriegsruf*, 13 January 1906.

Die Kommandeure auf dem Kinderfest.

„Heute haben wir Kaffeefest!" rief mir ein kleines Mädchen am Montag nachmittag im Industriefestsaal zu und drückte mir ganz aufgeregt die Hand. Sie sah ordentlich stolz aus und machte wie die andern jungen und jüngsten Festteilnehmer kein Hehl aus ihrer Freude. Erwartungsvoll saßen sie da, aber die Erwartung vermochte doch nicht die kleinen Mündchen zu verschließen, und unaufhörlich waren sie am Schwatzen und Lachen. Daß sie die Kommandeure mit Eifer und Begeisterung begrüßten, bedarf kaum noch einer besonderen Erwähnung, ebenso daß sie dem Kakao und den belegten Brötchen, den Kuchen, Flammeri und Apfelsinen alle Ehre angedeihen ließen. Außerdem wurde ihnen so reichlich vorgesungen und gespielt, daß man fast meinen konnte, die kleinen Gäste würden gar nicht wissen, was sie zuerst tun sollten, ob essen oder hören. Aber ich denke, viele werden die Entdeckung gemacht haben, daß sich beides sehr wohl vereinigen ließ. Auch die „Jungen Soldaten" und die reizenden Kalender fanden reißenden Absatz, ja sogar die größeren Kinder von 14 bis 40 Jahren, die diesmal bescheiden in den Ecken des Saales stehen mußten, streckten verlangend die Hände danach aus. Großen Beifall fanden auch die kinematographischen Vorführungen. Ebenso ließen es sich die Kleinen nicht nehmen, verschiedene ihnen bekannte Lieder mit rhythmischen Taktschlägen gegen die Tassen zu begleiten, ein Verfahren, das unstreitig sehr einfach ist, aber trotzdem auf die Nerven der leidenden Mitmenschen eine geradezu verheerende Wirkung ausübt. Hoffentlich hatten aber alle ihre Nerven zu Hause gelassen.

Die Kommandeure ließen sich keine Mühe verdrießen, das kleine Volk recht gut zu unterhalten und

Report on a feast for poor children with lantern exhibition in Berlin, 1907 (extract). *Kriegsruf*, 26 January 1907.

children throughout this colourful programme was to intensify collective feelings. The interchange between fictional and advertising/documentary material linked imagination to reality with the effect that spectators did not sink into distant illusions. Such visions beyond fiction brought about feelings of self-confidence and community: the chance for self-fulfilment in life was associated with the Salvation Army, making membership very attractive. Andrea Haller and Martin Loiperdinger have commented that early cinema programmes "in a certain manner, not only the films but also the audience was programmed" which meant that "programmers undertook ... an 'arrangement of emotions'" in the choice and juxtaposition of films.[30] The authors attribute to the audience the role of a "medium in the strictest sense of the word" because the non-cinematic parts "made the programme, at least partially, a live event with a great amount of participation and action on the part of the audience".[31]

The Salvation Army also arranged its programmes to provoke different emotional responses and built upon the participation of the children. As the reading accompanying the slide set LITTLE JAMIE reveals, its exhibition was planned interactively. The spectators' participation was explicitly desired and even expected: "The audience should be supplied with books of words; and, if thought advisable, these could be used as tickets of admission".[32] Spectators were expected to join in three of the fourteen songs, which they obviously knew from religious services and prayer meetings.[33] By becoming thus involved in the creative act, the entire congregation experienced the confession of faith actively and even seemed to initiate it. The intersection of imaginative and real space intensified collective feelings.

On the visual level, this was intensified by the life model technique. According to Ludwig Vogl-Bienek, photographs of real actors created a strange realistic impression within the (fictional) depiction.[34] Telling a story, the slides clearly adhere to the world of fiction, but the life models gave them a particular credibility that made the shift between fiction and reality easier or even made audiences perceive it as entirely natural. However, the performative agents were the decisive go-betweens. According to the LITTLE JAMIE reading, it was "advisable to preserve the continuity of the service" which mainly meant smooth transitions between verbal and musical parts.[35] Corresponding to this, from the projection of the first (unnamed) slide set, verbal and musical elements were perfectly harmonised: "high above the sea of childish faces rose the ringing voices and the first picture appeared ... . Then, as the children gazed in breathless silence, from behind the screen rose a single, clear, child voice, singing". At the exhibition of LITTLE JAMIE, "after a few words of explanation, the chorus rose again from that little hidden voice". The acoustic accompaniment intensified the visual impressions, but the performers were physically present and therefore – at least the lecturer and the choir – perceived as participants of the community who clearly anchored the story in the here and now. It is interesting, though, to note that the review attributed exactly to the hidden solo singer, who probably created a kind of illusionary effect, this role of go-between: "Here the voice of Johnnie, behind the screen sings out, 'Kind words can never die,' which rivets another life-lesson on the impressionable minds of the gathered children".

As a result of these performances, this auspicious community was not perceived as a distant image, but as a concrete experience. "No more entertainment to please and arouse for a while, but real life lessons", the review ends, with the hope that the feeling of community, based on the fiction, could now be transported into reality. Last but not least, this positive experience of belonging was literally a *tasteful* one because the communal tea (and games) had aroused sympathies towards the Salvation Army. In a way, the opening address of the children as a whole body had been continued and intensified by the shared viewing of projections with the effect that membership of the *Band of Love* – and with this the Army and the Christian community – was made desirable.

Returning to my first example, the feast of 60 poor people in Spandau: like the children in London, they were offered a varied programme which included – besides the meal and the projection of slides – songs and speeches, the reading of Bible texts, verses and a prayer.

According to the review, the audience was involved in the performances as well: the "entire congregation" cheered when the imperial couple was seen on the screen, and joined in the song *Wir gehen voran* (*Marching Onward*) during the following projections of the "Kommandeure".[36] By the direct association of *actual* views of German's monarchy with leading personalities of the Salvation Army, the organisation appeared as sympathetic because it presented itself as highly modern. Firstly this was because these poor people were probably seldom offered a free lantern exhibition, so that they associated the Salvation Army with the exhibition of technical innovations. Secondly and more importantly, audiences were offered insight in and even a sort of contribution to up-to-date daily events, the feast being in celebration of the imperial couple's silver wedding. Thirdly and, in my opinion, crucially, the Army offered their audience participation in a modern, globally-active organisation via the collective feelings referring to the German nation. The spectators' enthusiastic reactions suggest that such appeals to the national conscience were an effective strategy to introduce the Army. The organisation took advantage of the patriotic mood in the German Empire at that moment to address audiences emotionally and inspire them for their aims. Similarly, the appeal to the national conscience created a kind of familiar ambience, as in the previous example in which the spectators were offered new information. During the direct succession of slide views, collective feelings of nationalism were blurred into those towards the Salvation Army. This emotional resonance meant that spectators concretely *experienced* being part of a community which stretched far beyond the exhibition venue. Prayers and group singing played an important role here because they gave the audience the occasion to participate and thus intensified collective feelings. Even the title of the song *Marching Onward* echoes the sense of modernity which was conveyed in this lantern exhibition, contributing to the image of the Army as a progressive organisation in the sense of improvement. Membership of this organisation would seem very *tasteful*.

Conclusion

Taste can be understood as a key notion to lantern exhibitions of the Salvation Army, combined with food distribution. In order to offer audiences something pleasant, the organisation designed whole events according to their tastes. Embedding lantern projections in food distribution was one recipe for success because the simultaneous appeal to the senses of sight, hearing *and* taste was especially persuasive. The Army literally wanted their audiences to acquire a *taste* for their missionary purposes: what people saw and heard, they also got to know, so to speak, as something both *tasty* and *tasteful*.

The Salvation Army considered lantern exhibitions as a powerful instrument for creating strong sensory experiences in order – via collective feelings – to convey positive self-images. Lantern exhibitions were the perfect medium for this because of their specific features: colourful, well-balanced programmes, that continuously reminded spectators of the welfare context (food distribution). Since the audiences' participation was immanent to these events, the sense of community could easily be intensified. A distant relationship towards the images – created by the permanent shifts of the programme parts, between what was to be seen on the screen and what happened in the hall of entertainment – still held possibilites to be close to audiences. The German examples show that the Army used lantern exhibitions to adapt their events to different of their audiences.

If poor people – who represented the vast majority of the population – were considered as a serious public in quantity and in their needs, this has important consequences for social and visual media history. To argue with Miriam Hansen's idea of "vernacular modernism",[37] I suggest that these organisations procured their audiences experiences of modernity, due to the sensory effects of lantern projections. Although Hansen is referring to classical Hollywood cinema which "could be imagined as a cultural practice on a par with the experience of modernity, as an industrially-produced, mass-based, vernacular modernism",[38] her arguments can be easily applied to this much earlier medium because it also

---

Ein Fest für Arme
in
Spandau.

Ein besonderer Tag für Korps Spandau war der 27. Februar. Aus Anlaß der Silberhochzeit des Kaiserpaares hatten wir ein Festessen für 60 arme und unbemittelte Leute veranstaltet. Nach Wochen von Gebet und Arbeit für dieses Unternehmen kam der schöne Tag und als die Feier begann, hatten sich die Festteilnehmer zahlreich eingefunden, sodaß alle Tische besetzt waren. Es war uns eine große Freude, den lieben Sozialsekretär Stabskapitän Stankuweit in unserer Mitte zu haben. Nach einem Lied aus dem Kriegsruf und Gebet, gab der Stabs-

kapitän die Speisekarte aus, welche mit viel Interesse aufgenommen wurde. Das Menü bestand aus: Fleischbrühe mit Brödchen, Gulasch, Kartoffeln und Pflaumen; Kaffee und Pfannkuchen und Apfelsinen. Die lieben Kameraden taten ihr Bestes, um die hungrigen Magen zu befriedigen. Ein Zeichen von der Vortrefflichkeit der Speisen war, daß am Schluß jemand sagte: „Nun, dem Kaiser kanns heute nicht besser geschmeckt haben, wie uns!" Auch fehlte es nicht an der Unterhaltung. Lieder und Ansprachen wechselten. Auch erfreute Leutnant Danielowsky die lieben Gäste durch Lichtbilder. Bei dem Bilde des Kaiserpaares brachte der Stabskapitän ein Hoch auf dasselbe aus, worin die ganze Versammlung mit einstimmte. Bei den Bildern unserer Kommandeure wurde der Chorus: „Wir gehn voran" gesungen, welches allgemein eine gute Stimmung hervorrief. Bei alledem vergingen die schönen Stunden zu schnell und wir mußten an den Schluß denken, aber nicht ohne daß der Stabskapitän einige Verse aus dem Worte Gottes mit auf den Weg gab. Noch das Schlußgebet und den schönen Schlußvers: „So nimm denn meine Hände und führe mich!" und die schöne Feier hatte ihr Ende erreicht.

Report on feast and lantern exhibition with Imperial and Salvation Army slides.

"opened up hitherto unperceived modes of sensory perception and experience".[39] Food distributions and lantern exhibitions were mutually complementary and intensifying elements in welfare entertainments which resulted in temporary, if not lasting, bonds with audiences. Against the backdrop of the massive distribution of the medium for welfare purposes even *before* the introduction of cinema, this special use of the lantern tremendously shaped projection media as a whole.

Notes

1. "Nachrichten von unseren Kampfplätzen. Ein Fest für Arme in Spandau", *Der Kriegsruf. Das offizielle Organ der Heilsarmee* XX, no. 11 (17 March 1906). Unless otherwise stated all translations are by the author.

2. Others included the UK Band of Hope, Church of England Temperance Society, Co-operative Movement, Sunday School Union and the Church Army. See Karen Eifler, "Between attraction and instruction: Lantern shows in British poor relief", *Early Popular Visual Culture* 8:4 (November 2010): 363–384. See also Richard Crangle and Mervyn Heard, "The Temperance Phantasmagoria", in Richard Crangle, Ine van Dooren and Mervyn Heard (eds), *Realms of Light: Uses and Perceptions of the Magic Lantern from the 17th to the 21st Century* (London: Magic Lantern Society, 2005); Torsten Gärtner, "The Sunday School Chronicle: Eine Quelle zur Nutzung der Laterna magica in englischen Sonntagsschulen", *KINtop* 14/15: 25–35; and Torsten Gärtner, "The church on wheels: Travelling Magic Lantern mission in late Victorian England", in Martin Loiperdinger (ed.), *Travelling Cinema in Europe: Sources and Perspectives*, (Frankfurt and Basel: Stroemfeld, 2008), 129–141.

3. Roland Robertson, *"The Salvation Army. The Persistence of Sectarianism"* in Bryan R. Wilson (ed.), *Patterns of Sectarianism: Organisation and Ideology in Social and Religious Movements* (London: Heinemann, 1967), 49–105, here 91 and 93. The Booths had founded the Hallelujah Band in 1861, which after several renamings became the Salvation Army in 1878. See Lilian Lewis Shiman, *Crusade against drink in Victorian England* (Basingstoke: Macmillan, 1988), 131–133.

4. Christoph Ribbat, *Religiöse Erregung. Protestantische Schwärmer im Kaiserreich* (Frankfurt/Main and New York: Campus, 1996), 36.

5. Ribbat, *Religiöse Erregung*, 37. Nevertheless its influence in Germany, in both religion and welfare, was not comparable to that in Britain. See Dirk Gnewekow and Thomas Hermsen, *Die Geschichte der Heilsarmee: Das Abenteuer der Seelenrettung; eine sozialgeschichtliche Darstellung* (Opladen: Leske und Budrich, 1993), 82.

6. Gnewekow and Hermsen, *Geschichte der Heilsarmee*, 65.

7. Gnewekow and Hermsen, *Geschichte der Heilsarmee*, 134–140.

8. "Magic Lanterns" (advertisement), in *The Officer* (March 1893): 84–85.

9. "Lantern Lessons and Book Blessings" (advertisement), *The War Cry* (14 August 1894): 15.

10. *Selected List of Films available for Renting Purposes* (London: Salvation Army, 1906); "Army Cinematographs", *The Field Officer* (October 1906): 383.

11. Not much is known about the establishment of regular lantern exhibitions by the Salvation Army in Britain and even less in Germany. More information is available about its film activities. See Dean Rapp, "The British Salvation Army, The Early Film Industry and Urban Working-Class Adolescents, 1897–1918", in *Twentieth Century British History* no. 7 (1996, 2): 157–188, or Elizabeth Hartrick, *Consuming Illusions: The Magic Lantern in Australia and Aotearoa/New Zealand 1850–1910* (PhD dissertation, University of Melbourne, 2008). In 1910, the Australian Limelight Department was closed and the use of films throughout the Salvation Army forbidden. The use of lantern slides was allowed, with restrictions – see "Lanterns and Cinematographs", in *Orders and Regulations for Field Officers of The Salvation Army* (Salvation Army, 1917), 568–569.

12. "Walthamstow Mothers", *War Cry* (13 October 1906): 6.; "Com. & Mrs. Booth-Tucker. Successful Gatherings in Leeds", *War Cry* (20 October 1906): 11; "Cheltenham I", *War Cry* (23 November 1907): 7.

13. "Oberst Bullard hält gute Versammlungen im Süden", *Kriegsruf* XXIV, no. 8 (19 February 1910):

10; "Ueberall überfüllte Lokale", *Kriegsruf* XXIV, no. 9 (26 February 1910): 8. "Der Kinematograph in Reutlingen", *Kriegsruf* XXI, no. 10 (9 March 1907): 8.

14. *War Cry* (30 June 1894): page number illegible.

15. "Des Generals Willkommen in der Albert-Halle, London", *Kriegsruf* XVII, No. 16 (18 April 1903): 10. The audience may be exaggerated: the Albert Hall, built in 1871, today holds approximately 5,000–7,000 spectators.

16. "Watch-Night! Glorious Finish to the Old Year. Hundreds begin 1906 with New Hearts. Striking Captures of Drunks, Gamblers and ex-Prisoners", *War Cry* (6 January 1906): 6. "Guests of The Army. 860 Poor Entertained at New Brompton", *War Cry* (10 February 1906): 10. "Barry Dock children", *War Cry* (4 January 1908): 6.

17. "Ein Fest für 1500 Arme in Berlin im Konkordia-Saal am 10. Januar 1905. Einige glückliche Stunden bei der Heilsarmee", *Kriegsruf* XIX, no. 3 (21 January 1905): 1-2. "Kommandeur und Frau Oliphant leiten die großen Festessen für Arme und Kinder in Berlin", *Kriegsruf* XX, no. 2 (13 January 1906): 7.

18. "Children cheered. Hereford", *War Cry* (10 January 1903): 10.

19. "Die Kommandeure auf dem Kinderfest", *Kriegsruf* XXI, no. 4 (26 January 1907): 7.

20. "Festklänge in Berlin. Speisung 1600 Armer. Die Kommandeure auf dem Soldatenfest", *Kriegsruf* XXII, no. 3 (18 January 1908): 7.

21. "Wood Green", *War Cry* (7 January 1905): 7. It is not very clear whether this exhibition took place after the feast or as an independent local event the same evening.

22. "Converts of all sorts. Hounslow", *War Cry* (20 January 1912): 7.

23. "Cardiff Division", *War Cry* (13 January 1900): 13.

24. "Ein Fest für 1500 Arme in Berlin", *Kriegsruf* XIX, no. 3 (21 January 1905): 2.

25. "Colonel Higgins at Bexley Heath", *War Cry* (3 October 1906): 6.

26. "Latest by Wire. Glasgow City Hall", *War Cry* (21 April 1906): 7.

27. "Der Kommandeur feiert Weihnachten in Berlin. Unser Leiter, begleitet von Oberbefehlshaber Schoch und Gauntlett, leitet gesegnete Versammlungen", *Kriegsruf* XXI, No. 1 (5 January 1907): 7.

28. "A Practical Christmas Lesson and A Delightful Treat for London's Juniors", *War Cry* (6 January 1895): 6. All the following citations are from this source.

29. For content details and images, see *Lucerna, the Magic Lantern Web Resource*, www.slides.uni-trier.de

30. Andrea Haller and Martin Loiperdinger, "Stimulating the Audience: Early Cinema's Short Film Programme Format 1906 to 1912", in Martin Loiperdinger (ed.), *Early Cinema Today: the Art of Programming and Live Performance* (New Barnet, Herts.: John Libbey, 2011): 7–24, here 13.

31. Haller and Loiperdinger, "Stimulating the Audience", 16.

32. Thomas E. Hallsworth (compiler), *Little Jamie: A Service of Sacred Song* (London and Manchester: S.W. Partridge & Co. and John Heywood, 1894), front endpapers.

33. *Thy Faithfulness, Lord* at the beginning, *Blessed Words of Jesus* at the end and *Rescue the Perishing* at one of the story's turning points.

34. For this manufacturing method, used from the late 1870s onwards, real actors posed in front of mostly painted backdrops. While projected, the photographic images had a particularly naturalistic effect. See Ludwig Vogl-Bienek's article in this volume.

35. Hallsworth, *Little Jamie*.

36. "Nachrichten von unseren Kampfplätzen", *Kriegsruf* XX, No. 11 (17 March 1906): 8. The Salvation Army is divided into 50 Territories, led by Commanders; this rank is second after the General, the international leader of the organisation.

37. Miriam Bratu Hansen, "The Mass Production of the Senses: Classical Cinema as Vernacular Modernism", in *Modernism/Modernity* no 6.2 (1999): 59–77.

38. Hansen, "Mass Production", 65.

39. Hansen, "Mass Production", 72.

Band of Hope Union Dissolving Views.

Several new Lectures have been added to the List, while many of the others have been improved by the addition of fresh Views. No expense has been spared. The first Artists have been engaged to paint the Views, which will be shown by means of the Oxy-hydrogen apparatus.

LIST OF LECTURES.

LECTURE I.—LONDON : in the Olden Time.
   ,,   II.—LONDON : Striking Events in its History.
   ,,   III.—INCIDENTS OF PERIL AND HEROISM.
   ,,   IV.—WONDERS OF THE MICROSCOPE.
   ,,   V.—THE BOOK AND ITS STORY : or, Passages in the History of the Bible.
   ,,   VI.—LIGHTS OF THE WORLD : or Passages in the Histories of Eminent Men.
   ,,   VII.—WONDERS OF NATURE.
   ,, VIII.—NOTES OF A TOUR TO MONT BLANC AND THE GREAT ST. BERNARD.
   ,,   IX.—A TOUR TO THE OBERLAND ALPS, VIA BELGIUM AND THE RHINE.
   ,,   X.—THE BOTTLE.
   ,,   XI.—BRITISH SCENERY AND ITS ASSOCIATIONS.
   ,,   XII.—PILGRIM'S PROGRESS.
   ,, XIII.—THE ARCTIC REGIONS, AND THE FATE OF FRANKLIN.
   ,,   XIV.—THE VILLAGE.
   ,,   XV.—THE GORILLA AND HIS COUNTRY.

Each Entertainment comprises from 30 to 40 Views, including a variety of Miscellaneous Views, Chromatropes, &c.

The Views measure Twelve Feet on the Canvas.

MAGIC LANTERN EXHIBITIONS,

Accompanied by Descriptive Lectures, can also be obtained to illustrate the following Lectures:—PILGRIM'S PROGRESS ; WONDERS OF NATURE ; NATURAL HISTORY ; THE BOTTLE ; DICK WHITTINGTON ; and COUSIN ALICE, or the TRIALS OF A DRUNKARD'S CHILD.

TERMS TO LONDON SOCIETIES.

For the DISSOLVING VIEWS.—For each Exhibition, £1 5s., if the place of exhibition be within four miles of the General Post Office. This charge includes Exhibition, Lecturer's Expenses, Cab-hire, and all expenses incurred by the Union. A deduction of 5s. is made to Affiliated Societies. Provincial Societies may best avail themselves of the Views, by those in neighbouring towns and villages arranging about the same week or so.

For the MAGIC LANTERN.—For each Lecture, Half-a-Guinea, and Travelling Expenses. A MUSICAL ACCOMPANIMENT, with a Performer, provided on payment of an extra 3s. 6d.

All Applications to be made to the Secretaries of the Union, 37 Queen Square, Bloomsbury, London, W.C.

Annemarie McAllister

"To assist in the pictorial teaching of Temperance": the use of the Magic Lantern in the Band of Hope

---

This article will explore the way in which two major developments of the 19th century intersected with and supported each other at a key period. From the 1860s until 1914, the magic lantern benefited from leaps in the technologies of production, distribution and performance. This was also the high point of the massive cultural, social and political force that was the teetotal temperance movement, and I shall argue that each, without the other, would not have been as significant and successful. This will be seen in a case study of the Band of Hope, the children's temperance society which claimed over three million members by the second half of the period in question, endured for over 140 years, and was a major distributor of slide sets designed to persuade millions of people in the 19th and 20th centuries to improve their lives.

Before 1832, the term "Temperance" bore its original meaning in discussions about alcohol, with societies devoted to temperance in the US and the UK advocating moderation, or abstinence only from "ardent spirits" such as gin, whisky or brandy. The perception of the threat to individuals and the social order from such spirit drinking, for example, lies behind Hogarth's engravings of *Gin Lane* and *Beer Street* (1751). There was widespread concern about the availability and consumption of spirits, after government encouragement of gin production since 1689, and Hogarth emphasises the prosperity and happiness of Beer Street, where folks drink the traditional English beverage. However, the dangers of this promotion of beer were evident when the Beerhouse Act of 1830 allowed any rate-payer to open a beer shop on payment of two guineas, radically decreasing regulation on the sale of beer and cider so that "by 1834, for a population of 15 million in England and Wales, there were now one million places at which one could obtain a drink, and almost half of those were under no public control".[1] The crowded industrial regions were particularly

Joseph Livesey, one of the original seven men of Preston, became revered as the father of teetotalism. This slide is from the UKBI IU series TEMPERANCE FIGURES.

well (or ill) served: the immediate effect of the Beer Act was that "in Liverpool alone there opened more than fifty additional beer shops every day for several weeks". And this in turn led to the creation of a new kind of temperance society: in 1832 seven working men from Preston, in the heartland of the industrial northwest of England, signed a pledge to abstain from *all* intoxicating liquors, whether ale, porter, wine or ardent spirits. The existing temperance societies, often organised by middle class philanthropists, were overwhelmed by the largely working-class total abstinence movement which "moved triumphantly south from Preston".[2]

"Teetotalism", as it became known, was the basis for many new societies, and the word temperance came to signify complete abstinence. As a simple, clear, creed it lent itself to dramatic – or even melodramatic – conversions and discourse, and, like religious conversion, could be more easily sustained by creating an alternative social and cultural life with like-minded people. Temperance hotels, bars, music halls and billiard halls reinforced the message, as well as many public affirmations of the temperance community such as processions, concerts and galas, and of course there were many temperance organisations to which people could feel a sense of belonging.

One of the most powerful and influential of these was the Band of Hope, the group formed in 1847 which became the most comprehensive and influential children's temperance organisation, still existing today under the name of Hope UK.[3] It may seem paradoxical that children were seen as needing propaganda against alcohol, but in fact there were several reasons why this group provided a prime target. Obviously children were victims of the poverty and violence which could follow parental indulgence in alcohol. But children themselves were at risk from drink, and were often targeted by publicans, or indeed child workers were paid in pubs, and it was only in 1908 that children under 14 were banned from licensed premises in the UK. The Band of Hope was thus founded to warn children of the perils of easily-obtainable drink, but it had another agenda which became predominant. This was to empower children as agents, rather than victims, to bring about social reform. Children over seven signed the pledge never to drink alcohol, and attended weekly meetings where they were instructed and entertained to reinforce this message. Such instruction frequently suggested arguments which children could use to adults, and stories and images featured enterprising, confident, children per-suading adults to forswear drink. The Band of Hope was often linked with churches or Sunday Schools, but retained its non-denominational approach, and indeed its mission not to provide merely negative teaching, but to entertain, inform and educate, for over 100 years, and this privileging of the child's power must have been one aspect of its appeal. Joseph Livesey had advised temperance proselytisers to bear in mind John Bunyan's metaphor of "Eyegate" and "Eargate" as conduits to the mind and heart, and the magic lantern show as mass visual communication became central to Band of Hope work – originally as a special event, but becoming much more available during this key period so that by 1914 most of the almost 28,000 Bands of Hope throughout the UK possessed their own equipment and some slides. Lantern shows or illustrated lectures were also used in adult temperance meetings, but given the varied age, literacy and attention-span profile of the Band of Hope meetings, they were used with far more frequency for children. The technology and the social reforming group had each had met its perfect partner.

One of the key features of the Band of Hope which is very relevant here was its organisational structure, enabling communication and liaison in both direc-tions. An individual Band, numbering up to 300 children, would be linked with other local groups in a district organisation, then these districts formed a regional union, often county-based, and a national UK Band of Hope Union oversaw the whole. The districts and regions could influence policy, but also benefit from economies of scale in production and distribution of material (including lantern slides), which in turn ensured some control over a coherent message, nationally. Much of my data comes from the annual reports of this national organisation, which was founded in 1855, at a period when photographic glass slides were presenting a major development for the magic lantern. The magic lantern features in the first national annual report, in 1856. Stephen Shirley, the chairman

> having kindly placed at the disposal of the Union his magic lantern and about fifty slides illustrative of scenery and natural history, with other instructive and amusing subjects, and Mr Haynes having recently granted the Union the use of eight slides, representing Mr G. Cruikshank's plates of "The Bottle, or the Drunkard's Progress", several meetings have been held [twelve shows were given in total] … it is believed that much benefit has accrued from this mode of attracting and interesting audiences chiefly of young people in reference to the Temperance Cause.[4]

The Bottle, George Cruikshank's 1847 series of engravings, was a mainstay of temperance propaganda, selling over 100,000 copies in the first few days and influencing most subsequent narratives by its "Road to Ruin" message.[5] It was also produced as a series of slides. The seventh image from the series of eight illustrates the melodramatic nature and graphic power of the narrative, which thus lent itself well to lantern presentation.

By the next year the report was emphasising:

> From the formation of the Union, the Committee have been fully alive to the importance of furnishing the means of amusement, combined with instruction, to young people in connection with Bands of Hope, and have freely made use of

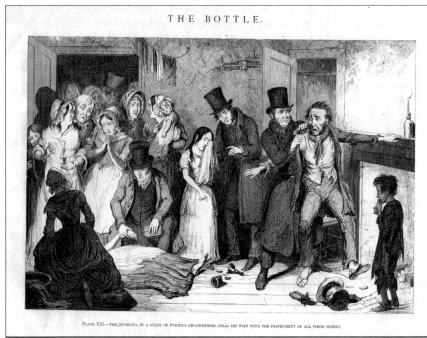

THE BOTTLE.

PLATE VII.—THE HUSBAND, IN A STATE OF FURIOUS DRUNKENNESS, KILLS HIS WIFE WITH THE INSTRUMENT OF ALL THEIR MISERY.

"The Husband, in a State of Furious Drunkenness, Kills His Wife with the Instrument of All Their Misery" – Cruikshank's own title for Plate 7 of *The Bottle*.

the magic lantern for this purpose. In the autumn of last year … a first-class apparatus was purchased and brought into use; the light used is oxy-hydrogen, producing a very brilliant effect. The views have been prepared by skilful artists, and embrace Natural Phenomena, Human Physiology, Natural History, Scenes in Switzerland, and Mr George Cruikshank's plates of "The Bottle, or the Drunkard's Progress". These have been shewn in about fifty halls, schools and chapels, in town and country, and have been found very valuable auxiliaries in carrying out the objects of the Union.[6]

By 1862 there was regular appreciation of lantern slides, which, it was re-marked, "make it easy for the conductors of local Bands of Hope to give their members a pleasant entertainment".[7] *Entertainment* was constantly emphasised. The growth in activity over the six years since the first mention of twelve shows, in 1856, is striking: during the year 1861–62 there were 64 Dissolving View Exhibitions in London, 63 around the country, and another 22 Magic Lantern Exhibitions, giving a total of 149. The endpaper of the 1862 report also contained the full page advertisement shown at the start of this article.

There are two points of interest here. At this stage, the lantern seems to have been seen as a scarce and possibly complex technology, and control was firmly in the hands of the national organisation which sent out the apparatus and slides, with approved lecturers. The programme of dissolving views offered varies little from the original selection of 1856, with improving topics such as history, topography and natural history joined by THE BOTTLE once again. But the list of lantern slide lectures includes COUSIN ALICE, OR THE TRIALS OF A DRUNKARD'S CHILD, showing that the Band of Hope had begun its role as a commissioner of specialist temperance lantern slides, which was to become a key aspect of its activity, important for the spread of both lantern shows and the temperance movement.

By 1866, ten years after the national organisation was founded, 20 slide set lectures were available, 144 illustrated lectures were given, and in the next year more apparatus was purchased so that four lecturers/operators could be sent out to fulfil engagements on the same evening. It is important to consider the context in which such shows were given: in the 1860s they were still a relative novelty and tended to be given to large audiences, for example a Band of Hope public lecture in 1868 on "The Noble Army of Martyrs",

> for the illustration of which a new series of dissolving views were expressly prepared. Six hundred children, trained by Mr Frederick Smith, sang before and after the lecture. The execution of the piece, "Father, come home", will it is believed, be remembered for years by those who were present. It was sung in so pathetic and beautiful a style as to move many to tears.[8]

The way in which visual and aural elements were combined here was charac-teristic of Band of Hope work, as was indeed the privileging of sentiment in such presentations: this is probably the most challenging aspect for modern reader trying to understand such performances. The 1870s saw the mass production of lantern slides expand, and this coincided with an expansion of Band of Hope lantern work – and a very significant change. Until 1875 the

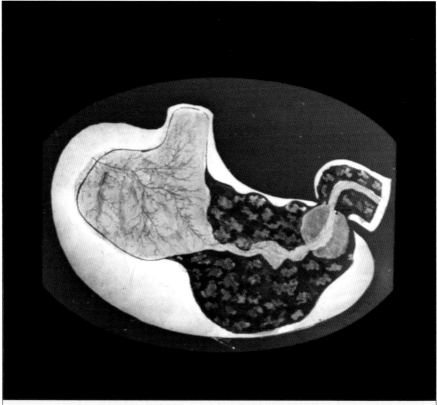

This view of "The cankerous stomach of a heavy drinker" is from the slide set THE STOMACH.

norm was that an agent of the society visited locations, and thus kept control of the performance and material. However, demand was now such that arrangements were made to lend the slides to Unions possessing an apparatus of their own, and also "a first-class Magic Lantern, lent with slides and photographed hymns" – this was a package including a sheet for projecting upon, an oil lamp with supply of oil or a lamp for burning common gas, and all other requisites, with a reading lamp, and notes of the lecture.[9] The slide selection for this package was – inevitably – Cruikshank's THE BOTTLE, joined by JESSICA'S FIRST PRAYER, miscellaneous views, and humorous and mechanical slides, with four melodies to be sung from the sheet. This new policy was to result in a vastly expanded use of the lantern, and make it almost universal within the Band of Hope. Numbers of slides hired and performances given showed a vast increase, year on year, until 1915. The organisation possessed 1,200 slides by 1892, but made multiple loans in that year of more than 37,000 slides; in subsequent years slide numbers are not given, as reports focus on performances. From 983 performances in 1891-92, numbers had doubled by the beginning of the next century, and reached 2,221 in 1914–15. Each of these shows might potentially reach, as my earlier examples show, hundreds or even thousands of audience members. Regularly the annual report speaks of adding *another hundred* slides to the stock, with new sets such as OUR FOUR-FOOTED AND FEATHERED FRIENDS which was added in 1879, and engaged no less than 34 times in its first nine weeks. In the 1880s, the Schools Scientific Temperance Teaching Scheme developed to deliver temperance teaching – and the lantern became central to this endeavour, too, with slides of diseased organs and chemical experiments as well as sporting heroes stressing the link between health and temperance.

As the report for 1887 remarked, "In a movement, the chief aim of which is to secure the adhesion of young people, it is necessary to provide the teaching in a very attractive form, and also to provide entertainments for festivals and other occasions".[10] By the end of the 1880s the Band of Hope Trading Department, which supplied adult temperance organisations as well as Sunday Schools, was turning over £4,000 annually, up to £5,000 by 1893, and much of this trade was in lanterns, dissolving views and slides, whether for sale or hire. Catalogues also featured several guides to using the lantern in temperance work, encouraging meetings to use this technology. They added a powerful triple lantern, and now had up to six sets of lime-light apparatus to hire in 1892, with two new lecture sets, A TEMPERANCE JOURNEY ROUND THE WORLD and DEEDS OF DARING AND DEVOTION. The former became one of the most popular Band of Hope slide sets ever. The commission and distribution of material was not confined to the UK: in 1892 "Slides and apparatus were dispatched to the Australian Colonies, India, Finland, Norway, Switzerland, and other places".[11] In successive years popular sets such as THE TEMPERANCE PICTURE GALLERY (40 slides), ALCOHOL AND THE HUMAN BODY (12 slides), joined later by ABSTINENCE AND HARD WORK, THE TEMPERANCE SKETCH BOOK, and THE TEMPERANCE PICTURE BOOK were commissioned and produced. These were mainstays of Band of Hope work. Many meetings now owned their own apparatus, and one example of how central it was to their work comes from 1895 – the small but populous district of Newton Heath in Manchester, which numbered 10 societies and just under 2,000 members, reported having a "very good open air meeting with the lime-light lantern, at which between 400 and 500 people were present".[12]

As the Band of Hope began the 20th century it was stronger than ever, claiming well over three million members and continuing to make extensive use of the lantern. A list of customers for slides and lanterns in 1905–06 included users in Finland, Sweden, New Zealand, Switzerland, the New Hebrides, and India. The business was responsive to trends which would interest their young audiences: when oriental bazaars and tales became the fashion, "To assist in the pictorial teaching of Temperance, new Lantern slides were prepared illustrating six Eastern Fairy Tales, besides a number of pictures bearing short sentences of a striking character", in 1906–07. By now "in view of the fact that many societies possess lanterns of their own, the chief method employed was

This image is from the UKBHU annual report for 1923, page 12, and manages to show both a side view of the lantern and audience, and the slide image projected onto the screen – here a well-known temperance slogan, "where there's drink there's danger".

the letting on hire of slides on easy terms. By this means temperance truth was attractively placed before 2,053 audiences."[13]

As the lantern trade faced growing competition from film, the Band of Hope faced the First World War; each threat was to eventually prove near-fatal. In 1913–14 "in the use of the Optical Lantern there was no falling off, notwithstanding the popularity of "Moving Pictures", but soon there were "great numbers of the workers absent on national service and many meetings suspended on account of the darkened streets and other causes".[14] Nevertheless, in 1915–16 slides were hired for some 1,600 meetings and in 1917–18

> The use of the Optical Lantern was maintained to a larger extent than could have been expected, considering how many workers capable of operating had been called to the colours, and also that the use of Oxygen and other illuminants had been seriously restricted by military requirements.[15]

The magic lantern had clearly become a staple part of temperance teaching in the Band of Hope. Post-war, the slide stock had to be built up again, and although in 1920-21 sales and loans were described as vigorous, there were no details given, and most focus was on the School Lecture Scheme and the use of lanterns in charitable institutions.

In 1924, for the first time, there was no mention of dissolving views, slides, or lanterns in the Trading Department section of the annual report. From time to time they resurfaced, however, with a tribute in 1925 to the Union's

DON BRADMAN,

The World-famous Cricketer, says :

" Total abstinence from all alcoholic beverages is a big factor in success. The most refreshing beverage of all I find is a cup of tea. Alcohol must necessarily interfere with one's condition, thereby reducing one's power in every direction ; so

My advice to boys is to leave strong drink alone at all times."

* * * *

This advice is good for girls also.

The Australian cricketer Don Bradman, from the slide set TEMPERANCE FIGURES.

full-time lanternist, Mr C.T. Hedgcombe, who had been employed for forty years in this role, or the claim in 1926 that "The supply of lantern apparatus and slides continued active, several new Temperance lectures being added, including two showing the improvement effected by Prohibition in the condition of child-life", and in the next year that lantern slides were "still drawn upon for the entertainment and instruction of numerous meetings".[16] In 1927 the 80th birthday of the Band of Hope was celebrated, and the juvenile temperance movement as a whole was still asserted to be over three million, with 15,000 Bands of Hope and "an army of children which cannot number less than a million-and-a-half, and probably approximates more closely to two millions", but from then on the only mentions in national reports of lantern performances were in charitable institutions such as orphanages, training ships and poor schools, the last such being in 1931–32.[17]

I have focused on the use of lanterns, rather than the content of Band of Hope slide sets, but as programmes were usually a mix of the serious and the more amusing, the improving and the entertaining, and the sentimental and the

133

practical, the slides produced, distributed and used reflected this. Children were often presented as heroic agents of change, such as in THE DUSTMAN'S DARLING where a girl not only reforms her father, but escorts him past temptation each evening.[18] But children were also shown the results of drunkenness in a less overtly sentimental way, for example in the set SLUM LIFE. Well-known nursery rhymes or songs were adapted to a temperance message, and children's heroes were featured.

To explore the content of the slide sets fully would take another article, which in due course I hope will be written, but further examples of temperance slides can be seen in the *Lucerna* web resource or books such as *To Catch a Sunbeam*.[19] Here I have explored and, I hope, highlighted the promotion of the magic lantern by the Band of Hope, and the prolific, varied and comprehensive use it made of this technology in its enlistment of children in the war on alcohol.

Notes

1. J. O'Connor, *The Young Drinkers: a Cross-National Study of Social and Cultural Influences* (London: Tavistock, 1978), 44.

2. Brian Harrison, "Drink and Sobriety in England 1815-1872: A Critical Bibliography", *International Review of Social History,* 12 (1967): 219.

3. See Annemarie McAllister, "'The Lives and the Souls of the Children': the Band of Hope in the North West", *Manchester Region History Review,* 22 (2011): 1–18; and Annemarie McAllister, "Rational Recreation and Leisure for Children: The Band of Hope in the Twentieth Century" in *Recording Leisure Lives: Everyday Leisure in 20th Century Britain* (Brighton: Leisure Studies Association, 2012), 113–129.

4. *UK Band of Hope Union annual report* (London: UKBHU, 1856), 10.

5. A very informative account of the series' popularity can be found at blogs.princeton.edu/graphi-carts/2011/04/the_bottle.html (accessed June 2013).

6. *UK Band of Hope Union annual report* (London: UKBHU, 1857), 6.

7. *UK Band of Hope Union annual report* (London: UKBHU, 1862), 9.

8. *UK Band of Hope Union annual report* (London: UKBHU, 1868), 9.

9. *UK Band of Hope Union annual report* (London: UKBHU, 1875), 19.

10. *UK Band of Hope Union annual report* (London: UKBHU, 1887), 19.

11. *UK Band of Hope Union annual report* (London: UKBHU, 1892), 15.

12. *UK Band of Hope Union annual report* (London: UKBHU, 1895), 50.

13. *UK Band of Hope Union annual report* (London: UKBHU, 1907), 19.

14. *UK Band of Hope Union annual report* (London: UKBHU, 1913), 18; and (London: UKBHU, 1916), 14.

15. *UK Band of Hope Union annual report* (London: UKBHU, 1918), 7.

16. *UK Band of Hope Union annual report* (London: UKBHU, 1926), 50; and (London: UKBHU, 1927), 24.

17. Numbers from *UK Band of Hope Union annual report* (London, 1927), 6. Filmstrips and films came to be used, but never as much as lantern technology. Undoubtedly some traditional lanterns continued to be used: I have interviewed a Band of Hope worker who used one in the 1980s.

18. The slide set THE DUSTMAN'S DARLING (Bamforth, 9 slides, 1894) is reconstructed with slide images and audio recitation in the DVD-ROM *Lichtspiele und Soziale Frage: Screening the Poor 1888–1914* (München: Film & Kunst, 2011).

19. *Lucerna: the Magic Lantern Web Resource*, www.slides.uni-trier.de; G.A. Household and L.M.H. Smith (eds), *To Catch a Sunbeam: Victorian Reality through the Magic Lantern* (London: Michael Joseph, 1979).

Marina Dahlquist

Health Entrepreneurs: American Screen Practices in the 1910s

"Pure milk, pure water, sanitary sewerage, and good food are better than moonlit nooks, golf links, tango teas, or boardwalks".[1]
Dr Charles Bolduan

Bureau of Public Health Education

Public health discourses in relation to cinema are particularly rewarding to study during the Progressive Era of the early 20th century, especially as it played out in major American cities. In the variegated metropolitan civic fabric, cinema became a tool for health instruction as an intertwined aspect of Americanisation and civic learning. Moving pictures were used for raising awareness about the link between sanitary and civic conduct in efforts to reshape behaviour. Cultural integration, Americanisation, and body politics at large were thus correlated with images of citizens keeping their bodies clean and healthy. These didactic initiatives during the first decades of the 20th century brought together a cross-section of civic movements and organisations in lieu of government leadership at the federal as well as municipal level.

Moving pictures provided reformers and agencies with a tool to reach a mass audience and grab their attention. Irrespective of the medium's tainted reputation in many quarters during the transitional period, health educators nevertheless considered it unrivaled for attracting large audiences for educative entertainment in a way other visual media could not. The posited persuasiveness of the moving image was indisputable, for betterment or corruption, especially for uneducated and "primitive" audiences. Around 1910, moving pictures were taken up as a pedagogical tool for campaign work in different contexts across the United States on a more regular basis, signalling, for some, that the medium finally had found its true mission. Knowledge and insights earlier restricted to a select few, often professionals, could now potentially reach everyone when adapted for the screen. In the process cinema became both a power tool and a democratic instrument. Notions and conceptions

Facing page: Advertisement for Excelsior Slide Company, *Moving Picture World* 12, no. 5 (6 May 1912): 442.

Advertisement for Feature Film Company, *Moving Picture World* 12, no. 5 (6 May 1912): 457.

bearing on class, race, and gender are of course key to how this work was orchestrated.

Notwithstanding the success of instructive cinema, a slew of visual media continued to be used in the wider context of health instruction/social activism in 1910s and 20s, often together with moving images. These included: lantern slides, models, cartoons, photographs, posters, billboards, signs and so on: anything to catch audience attention and reach the masses. In this article I will mainly explore the interrelated use of lantern slides and film in public health instruction in the US circa 1910.

Lantern slides did not disappear with the emergence of moving pictures and later nickelodeons, even though slide exhibition was partly dethroned as a visual medium in its own right. From the first years of moving pictures, still projected images were, according to Charles Musser, employed in shared screen practice for several reasons: as a relief to the eyes from the "flicker" and "shakiness" of the moving image; as a contrast effect between static and moving photographs; as easily accessible due to the larger supply of photographic slides on the market; and finally due to the high costs of buying or renting films. According to Musser, the different media emphasised different pro-filmic elements: film/theatrical re-enactment versus slides/non-theatrical actualities.[2] In certain states in the US there were also regulations up until 1914 of the maximum time film could continuously be shown. In Massachusetts, for example, the limit was 20 minutes, after which the media or entertainment form had to be changed. The combined use of lantern slides and short films implied a varied programme in a sweep of media and at times also including live acts. Most moving picture theatres even had special stereopticon projectors or projectors with dual capacity.[3] This transitional exhibition practice is how-ever seldom mentioned in the advertisements of the programmes, or if so only in passing.

Examples of lantern slides shown at moving picture theatres in the United States in the early 20th century.

In the 1910s, illustrated lectures still relied mainly on lantern slides, but at times a mixture of films and slides were offered to elucidate the complexities of unique events, such as the sinking of the *Titanic* in 1912.[4] Lantern slides and moving pictures were for a long time closely interrelated in moving picture theatres. Between films and reels, song slides and announcement slides for upcoming films were shown,[5] as well as suggestions for proper behaviour: to refrain from profane language or information about where to turn if assaulted by another person in the audience. Even the sanitary status of the venue was sometimes announced with slides indicating how often the theatre was ventilated or disinfected in addition to orders from the Board of Health with texts such as: "No smoking or spitting allowed".

As well as advertisements and announcements, slides also provided a different mode between reels. At times they were even utilised to garner support in local elections (as Jan Olsson has shown for Chicago in 1907, when theatre proprietors were pressured to show slides encouraging the audience to vote for the Mayor Edward Dunne, of the Democratic party – to no avail, as he lost to the Republican candidate.[6] But most importantly in our context, moving picture theatres also became an important *venue* for lantern slides announcing health campaigns such as the Red Cross Seals campaigns from 1907 onwards.

Lantern slides had at least one advantage over film. It was possible to make them yourself without a production company. It was therefore possible for a motion picture theatre or a private organisation to produce their own slides by hand or with a typewriter, and also to reuse them after cleaning.[7] These

139

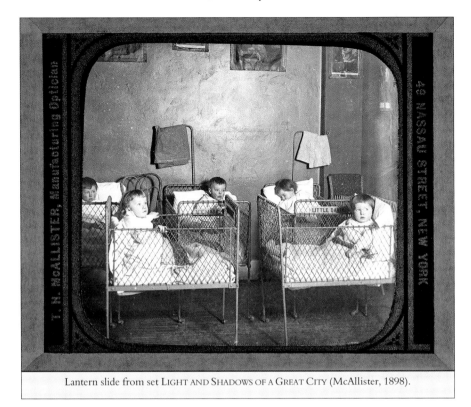

Lantern slide from set LIGHT AND SHADOWS OF A GREAT CITY (McAllister, 1898).

campaign slides are difficult to get hold of, to say the least. Most of them seem to have disappeared and slides in general are not accessible in the archives in the same way as films. And even when they exist, there are rarely records of where and when the slides were produced or used.

In health contexts, photographs were displayed in many formats, as illustrations in books and folders, enlarged for exhibitions, as slides and so on. The Department of Health in New York City, for example, does not specify in what format their photographs were displayed, even though they describe each and every photograph used. Still photographs were even used in films: an image of a Southern family treated for hookworm disease was used both as slide and photograph by Rockefeller Foundation in their Hookworm Campaign in the Southern States of the U.S., and the same still image is also to be found in Rockefeller's campaign film *Unhooking the Hookworm* from 1920. Even though this health film was produced for global distribution in health campaigns orchestrated by the International Health Board, as late as the mid-1920s lantern slides, charts, and other visual material were considered to give as good results as film in "backward" countries where the moving picture theatre had not yet been developed on a commercial basis.[8]

Lantern slide sets were produced to attract attention to the darker sides of city life, before the "discovery" of moving pictures' pre-eminence for this type of

Lantern slide from set STREET SCENES IN NEW YORK (S.C. Long, date unknown).

campaigning. "Lights and Shadows of a Great City" was for example the topic of stereopticon lectures in several cities during the first years of the 20th century.[9] Seemingly influenced by *Darkness and Daylight; or, Lights and Shadow of New York Life* written by the missionary and philanthropist Helen Campbell, the journalist Thomas Wallace Knox, and Thomas Byrnes, the Chief of N.Y. Police and Detectives. The book, published in 1892, describes New York from three different perspectives and is illustrated with engravings based on photographs by Jacob A. Riis amongst others. Children in distress was a recurring motif.

As early as 1894, Dr Herman M. Biggs, appointed by the Department of Health in New York City, initiated a programme for the Health Department concerning tuberculosis control, by means of newspaper publicity, leaflets and public lectures illustrated with lantern slides.[10] From 1906 onwards, free stereopticon exhibitions on health issues were given on a large scale by the Department in twenty-three of Manhattan's public parks during the summer, to teach citizens how to deal with the consumption of Tuberculosis.[11] The Health Department's innovative initiative to use the parks as venues to reach a big audience was described in *The New York Times* as "Vaudeville Methods" and considered "purely experimental". I have not been able to locate the slides used for this exhibition experiment, but the performance and images are vividly described

> ## THEATRE HEALTH LECTURES
>
> ### Illustrated Talk on Tuberculosis, In the Moving Picture Houses Meets With Success.
>
> A unique plan of presenting to the public information about health and the prevention of disease is being used by the Boston Association for the Relief and Control of Tuberculosis, in cooperation with the motion picture theatres The association has a trained lecturer, who gives a 7-minute talk, illustrated by 31 colored slides The plan has been successful and applications have been received from managers in other New England cities to have the lecture at their houses
>
> This lecture has already been produced 235 times in 22 theatres and has been listened to by more than 35,000 persons. In addition to this more than 22,000 health circulars have been given out at the exits of the theatres. The lectures have been unusually well received by the audience.

Boston Daily Globe (23 July 1912): 9.

in the *Times* article. It started in Battery Park on 30 July where a white screen was erected. After dusk the park was gradually filled by workers and "strange tongues from distant land" were heard. The one-hour show was well attended and "every available inch of space was occupied by an interested observer".[12] The images supposedly transfixed the audience despite many pictures being purely scientific. Slides showed sanatoria and hospitals for the treatment of tuberculosis, and interiors of old-law tenement houses were exhibited, vividly illustrating the unsanitary conditions.[13] As a counterpoint, views of new-law tenements followed, "with light, airy rooms, scrupulously clean, and under the watchful care of the Department of Health". According to the writer, the audience gazed longingly at the new-law pictures and some even considered the old tenements shown to be in better condition than their own.[14]

According to Dr B.H. Waters, from the Department of Health, in charge of the exhibitions, the campaign had two key missions: firstly to aid in preventing the extension of pulmonary tuberculosis; secondly to promote the recovery of those already stricken with the disease, partly by informing about patent medicine which in most cases consisted of pure alcohol. According to Waters:

> I feel that the novelty of this new means of education will appeal to that class which so much needs assistance. Even those who can neither read nor write will be materially benefited by the free exhibitions. The pictures tell the story, and their warning without words undoubtedly will exert a beneficial influence over the poor, whose ranks furnish so many victims to this disease.[15]

Popular education was considered the only viable option to halt the inroads of tuberculosis – the most widespread and fatal disease in the city. To be understood by everybody, the teaching had to be simplified and popularised. Therefore simple text slides in both English and Yiddish were used with written advice such as: "The trouble is that people don't let air enough or sunlight enough into their homes", and "Fresh air – night and day – Summer and Winter".[16]

Text slides such as "Don't waste time and money on patent medicines or 'consumption cures.' They don't cure", were commonly used despite the fact that a large percentage of the audience was illiterate, the contents were thus also probably read aloud. To make the exhibition more entertaining the Department presented a combination of amusement and instruction. Between the health slides other pictures were shown featuring public figures, funny kidnapping, burglar and fire-fighting scenes together with an occasional song from a quartette.[17]

After the successful Battery event, the exhibitions were to be given in all parks in the city, three evenings a week, working gradually from downtown up to Colonia Park on 145th Street where the last lecture was to be given in the first week of October. Moving pictures were planned to be shown later on in the campaign in order to keep up the interest.

The annual lantern slide exhibitions in New York parks attracted large audiences and the programmes were adapted to various language communities. In 1908, for example, the stereopticon exhibits in the public parks of the Boroughs of Manhattan and Brooklyn were in English, Italian, and Yiddish.[18] In July 1911, these exhibitions were hosted in public parks and on recreational piers of Manhattan, Bronx and Brooklyn and consisted of 125 coloured lantern slides, describing the essential facts about the disease – its causes, symptoms, methods of infection, and treatment, as well as the work of the Department to stamp out the disease by way of prevention and instruction to the public. In that year the Committee on the Prevention of Tuberculosis of the Charity Organization Society, with which the department recurrently collaborated, provided lecturers to explain the pictures and answer questions that the audience might have.[19]

In the content of the slides, population density was a recurring topic, especially in New York City with its horrendous slums and ethnic colonies. Alongside Chicago, with its overpopulated working class wards, New York City enjoyed a prominent position when it came to city-sponsored health campaigns.[20] Even though health education in a modern sense has a history from at least the mid-19th century, when a Bureau of Health Education was formally established in New York City in 1914, under the reform administration of Mayor John Purroy Mitchel, it was considered to be the first such bureau in the world to be affiliated with a public health agency.[21] And when the newly formed Bureau made its first attempt to educate the public about health issues, the officers turned their efforts to exhibitions at moving picture theatres. The Motion

Picture Exhibitors' Association, controlling 800 theatres, volunteered to show slides dealing with health topics free of charge on Saturday mornings in connection with a large clean-up effort under the name of Clean-Up Week.

Once again the lantern slides came with texts in English, Italian and Yiddish, with statements including "Dirt Breeds Flies", "Flies Carry Disease", "Disease Means Doctors' Bills", "Avoid Disease and Doctors' Bills by Cleaning Up". Shortly after this campaign, novel sets of slides addressed other aspects of health instruction – typhoid fever, and how to care for the baby for the upcoming Baby Week.[22]

The Department of Health also arranged free moving picture exhibitions labelled "health films" outdoors in New York City from 1912 onwards.[23] In June 1913, *Moving Picture News* devoted editorial space to this "new" method in the work of fighting tuberculosis by cinematically educating the public. From 16 June until 24 July an almost daily schedule was presented. At 8.00 p.m., in a mixed sweep of park locations and recreation piers in Manhattan as well as the Bronx, moving pictures were shown. The screenings were arranged by the Department of Health, assisted by the Committee on the Prevention of Tuberculosis.[24] The year before, 1912, the attendance was estimated at one hundred thousand, and according to *Moving Picture News* an even higher number was expected for 1913.[25]

The event was obviously a success as almost 20,000 people attended the open-air moving picture shows during the first week in 1914. This year the programme included titles such as THE STORY OF A CONSUMPTIVE, THE PRODUCTION AND HANDLING OF MILK, THE CITY BEAUTIFUL and THE LITTLE CRIPPLE.[26] Between the films a large number of instructive lantern slides were shown.[27] Health films and lantern slides were also presented at a large number of meetings in Brooklyn during the summer of 1914.[28] The audience consisted primarily of those who could not afford the regular shows at the theatres. These public health campaign films were considered to be popular with the public at large, but especially amongst children and immigrants. As Ernest Dench tersely summed up these efforts: New York's large percentage of immigrants understood neither printed nor spoken English, while motion pictures worked.[29] These outdoor screenings featuring health films continued throughout the 1910s with the exception of 1916 due to the polio epidemic.

Parallel to the health screenings, the baby-care work continued. In 1915, health reels were shown in moving picture theatres in connection with Staten Island Baby Week, and also loaned to schools, settlement houses etc.[30] In 1916 ten films were shown in large moving picture theatres throughout the city on baby subjects. And in August 1916, 400 lantern slides with references to the different phases of infant diet, hygiene and care were distributed to moving picture theatres in the sections of the city with the highest infant mortality.[31]

Health talks were also delivered in moving picture theatres in Boston; here by the Boston Association for the Relief and Control of Tuberculosis. The talk

Lantern slide "A Happy Home" from set LIGHT AND SHADOWS OF A GREAT CITY (McAllister, 1898).

was delivered by a trained lecturer giving a seven-minute talk, illustrated by 31 coloured slides. According to the *Boston Globe*, the successful campaign was well received by the audience and theatre managers alike and had already reached an audience of 97,000.[33]

When the Civic Department of the Women's Club ran a clean-up campaign in Gardner, Massachusetts, in April 1912, the manager of a local moving picture theatre got involved, which led to a multimedia performance typical of its time. According to *Moving Picture World* he distributed 4,000 booklets, advising residents to clean up their yards, and explaining how contagious diseases were carried by flies. He also screened the films FLY PEST (Urban, 1909) and THE AWAKENING OF JOHN BOND (Edison Company, 1911) besides several comedy slides at each performance, reading "Swat the Fly", "Kill Flies and Save Lives" and so on. A whimsical advertisement in the local newspaper claimed that "a Fly had escaped from the Gardner Theatre during the past week, if you see it kill it quick", and offered four movie tickets for every 200 dead flies brought to the box office.[33] This was not an uncommon ploy.

Most of the educational moving pictures were shown outside the regular commercial moving picture theatres. Still, moving picture theatres had turned into the most important venue for showing lantern slides announcing health

145

and civic campaigns. This co-operation between the exhibitors and authorities also gave the moving picture business good press, and favourable comments from the public and the city officials, which was highly welcome for a medium often in the critical crosshairs.[34]

In 1915 a national stereopticon loan library, according to *Los Angeles Times* the first of its kind in a government department, was established within the public health service. Thousands of slides had been collected showing various activities for safeguarding the health of the country.[35] The lecturers of the Department of Health in New York regularly used the materials, and in addition provided slides for the library illustrating their own public health initiatives.[36] Still, moving pictures were considered *the* most effective and popular means of disseminating health information, to usher in and secure what was pointedly illustrated as "A Happy Home".

According to Michael E. Teller, writing on the tuberculosis campaigns, lantern slides could be used to attract a crowd or educate a lecture audience but their impact paled in comparison with the motion picture. Films were first used in the tuberculosis crusade in 1910, when the Edison studio in co-operation with the NASPT (National Association for the Study and Prevention of Tuberculosis) produced THE RED CROSS SEAL.[37] This was the first film in a series to be made each year in cooperation with the American Red Cross campaign.

As late as 1923, Don Carlos Ellis and Laura Thornborough write on the subject of stereopticon images used as a complement to motion pictures in education: "Stereopticon slides will serve as valuable complements to motion pictures and will introduce a pleasant variation, particularly if the slides are colored".[38] While the slide gave the opportunity to study a static detail, motion pictures were more favourable if a detail in action or operation were to be studied. Obviously, moving pictures had a much higher degree of poignancy and visual impact for disseminating educative entertainment. Irrespective of this, the broader context for visual culture continued to be mobilised across the contexts for civic education. As the articles in this book demonstrate, this is a field that previously has been severely under-researched, not least due to the precarious archival situation of lantern slides and the ephemeral chronicling of their viewing contexts.

Notes

1. Dr Charles Bolduan, quoted in "To Head Health Teachers: Dr Bolduan Put in Charge of New Bureau of Education", *New York Times* (29 May 1914): 11.

2. Charles Musser, *Before the Nickelodeon: Edwin S. Porter and the Edison Manufacturing Company* (Berkeley/Los Angeles/Oxford: University of California Press, 1991), 123.

3. "Stereopticon" is the generic American term for a magic lantern projector; it does not imply stereographic image projection.

4. Advertisement for Carnegie Alaska-Siberia Pictures, *Moving Picture World* 12, no. 1 (6 April 1912): cover. In the same volume of *MPW* we find advertisements for sets of slides including photographs of the ship and its captain (Excelsior Slide Company, *MPW* 12, no. 5 (6 May 1912): 442) and for the possibility to order slides and films together or separately (Feature Film Company, *MPW* 12, no. 5 (6 May 1912): 457).

5. See Epes Winthrop Sargent, "Advertising for Exhibitors", *MPW* 12, no. 1 (6 April 1912): 35.

6. Jan Olsson, "Penny and Nickel Crusades in Chicago and Their Contexts", paper presented at the Annual Meeting of the American Studies Association, San Juan, 2012.

7. See F.H. Richardson (ed.) "Projection Department", *MPW* 12, no. 12 (22 June 1912): 1131.

8. "Unhooking the Hookworm", Memo, RF, RG 1: 100, box 5, folder 40, Rockefeller Archive Center.

9. "Stereopticon Lecture", *Atlanta Constitution* (17 May 1905): 10. "New Hampshire Conference: Concord District Manchester District", *Zion's Herald* (7 Dec 1902): 51.

10. Arthur Bushel, *Chronology of New York City Department of Health (and its Predecessor Agencies) 1655–1966* (New York: Department of Health, 1966), 9. One way of reaching different classes of the population was to print circulars in different languages. See *Annual Report of the Board of Health of the City of New York for the Year Ending December 31, 1908* (New York: Board of Health, 1909) – hereafter referred to as *ARBH*.

11. Bushel, *Chronology*, 14. For a discussion on the Department of Health in New York City and their use of lantern slides and moving pictures during the 1910s see Marina Dahlquist, "Health Instruction on Screen: The Department of Health in New York City, 1909–1917", in Marta Braun et al. (eds), *Beyond the Screen: Institutions, Networks and Publics* (New Barnet, Herts: John Libbey, 2012), 107–116.

12. "Vaudeville Methods to Teach the Masses How to Deal with Consumption", *New York Times* (5 August 1906), SM6.

13. *ARBH 1908*, 558.

14. "Vaudeville Methods".

15. Quoted in "Vaudeville Methods".

16. "Vaudeville Methods".

17. "White Plague. On Slides. New York Department of Health Will Educate People in Consumption Matters", *Los Angeles Times* (22 July 1906): 15.

18. *ARBH 1908*, 558, 565.

19. "Public Exhibitions on Prevention of Tuberculosis", *Monthly Bulletin of the Department of Health of the City of New York* I, no. 7 (July, 1911): 168–169 – hereafter referred to as *Monthly Bulletin*.

20. For example see *Monthly Bulletin* II, No. 3 (March 1912): 68–73.

21. Bushel, *Chronology*, 20.

22. "Movies Teach Health Work", *Weekly Bulletin of the Department of Health, City of New York* III, no. 19 (16 May 1914): 153. Florence Margolies, "Promoting Public Health", *MPW*, 22, no. 10 (5 December 1914): 1359.

23. Ernest A. Dench, *Motion Picture Education* (Cincinnati: Standard Publishing Company, 1917), 192–193. "Health in Moving Pictures", *New York Times* (21 June 1912): 10.

24. "For Free Moving Pictures", *Evening Post*, New York (23 June 1914): 4.

25. "Films Will Show How to Fight Tuberculosis", *Moving Picture News* VII, no. 26, (28 June 1913): 31.

26. Dench, 193; Margolies, "Promoting Public Health"; *Annual Report of the Department of Health of the City of New York for the Calendar Year, 1916* (New York: Department of Health, 1917), 58 – hereafter referred to as *ARDH*.

27. "Free Movies have begun", *Weekly Bulletin of the Department of Health* III, no. 26 (4 July 1914): 213–214.

28. "Moving Picture Activities", *ARDH 1914* (New York: Department of Health, 1915), 96.

29. Dench, 196. For a description of how a Clean-Up campaign was organised in the city of New Britain, where 80 % of the population were foreign born, see Herbert A. Jump, "A Municipal Spring House-Cleaning", *Independent* (27 April 1911): 884–888.

30. "Moving Picture Activities", *ARDH 1915* (New York: Department of Health, 1916), 110.

31. "Bureau of Child Hygiene", *ARDH 1916*, 49.

32. "Theatre Health Lectures: Illustrated Talk on Tuberculosis in the Moving Picture Houses Meets With Success", *Boston Daily Globe* (23 July 1912): 9.

33. Epes Winthrop Sargent, "Advertising for Exhibitors", *MPW* 12, no. 7 (18 May 1912), 623. For a discussion on anti-fly campaigns in the U.S. see Marina Dahlquist, "'Swat the Fly': Educational Films and Health Campaigns 1909-1914", in Corinna Müller and Harro Segeberg (eds) *Kinoöffentlichkeit/Cinema's Public Sphere* (Marburg: Schüren Verlag, 2008), 211–225.

34. "Moving Picture Educator", *MPW* 20, no. 5 (2 May 1914), 661. "Exhibitors News", *MPW* 20, no. 5 (2 May 1914), 687.

35. "Stereopticon Loan Library", *Los Angeles Times* (13 April 1915), II 9.

36. *ARDH 1919* (New York: Department of Health, 1920), 236.

37. Michael E. Teller, *The Tuberculosis Movement: A Public Health Campaign in the Progressive Era* (New York: Greenwood Press, 1988), 61.

38. Don Carlos Ellis and Laura Thornborough, *Motion Pictures in Education: A Practical Handbook for Users of Visual Aids* (New York: Thomas Y. Crowell Company, 1923), 168.

Judith Thissen

Education or Entertainment?: Early Cinema as a Social Force in New York's Immigrant Jewish Community

A t the turn of the 20th century America went through a deep societal crisis. Industrialisation, rapid urbanisation and the mass arrival of poor immigrants from southern and eastern Europe were profoundly transforming the nation's social, cultural and political landscape, challenging established norms and values. Stock market panics and severe economic depressions provided a context for violent labour disputes and created a breeding ground for left-wing radicalism. New commercial leisure forms and the emergence of an urban mass consumer culture cut across existing class, gender and ethnic boundaries. The rise of an immigrant proletariat and concomitant growth of poverty-stricken tenement districts demonstrated that the balance between "labour" and "capital" had been profoundly disturbed.

More than any other American city, New York symbolized for many the apparent breakdown of the social order and the excesses of the modern era. Indeed, nowhere seemed solutions to "the social question" more urgent than in Manhattan, where 47.4 per cent of the population was foreign born and 35.1 per cent first generation Americans, according to the 1910 census. The circumstances in which these recent immigrants worked and lived were often appalling. The tenements with their narrow doors and windows and small air shafts lacked direct daylight and decent sanitation. Long hours, small wages, unhealthy sweatshops and unsafe factory work were no exception. Many residential buildings and factories were death-traps in case of fire; so were many entertainment venues. In 1890, Jacob Riis' landmark publication *How the Other Half Lives: Studies among the Tenements of New York* exposed the New York slums to America's middle and upper classes. Over the next decades, dozens of reports were published on the city's social problems, ranging from child labour and poor living conditions to diseases, alcohol abuse, crime and the allegedly corrupting influence of cheap amusements.

This article examines how progressive forces in New York used the cinema to address the social question and encourage social or political activism among eastern European Jews. Jewish immigrants are singled out not only because they constituted the largest immigrant group in the city (about 25 per cent of the total population) but also because they were widely acknowledged as fervent fans of moving pictures. Considering this enthusiasm for the cinema, one might expect that the film medium was widely embraced in the Jewish immigrant milieu, either for educational purposes and uplift efforts by social reformers and other Americanizing agencies, or by the Jewish labour movement and Yiddish socialists to address the injustices of industrial capitalism. However, a close examination of the use of cinematography in non-commercial contexts reveals a more complex configuration. Settlement houses and other civic institutions repeatedly integrated moving pictures into their educational programmes and informational campaigns. Progressive Jewish leaders, on the other hand, failed to see cinema's potential as an instrument to raise awareness of social evils among Jewish workers.

First, I will discuss how two prominent Americanising agencies – the University Settlement House and the Educational Alliance – approached the film medium, whereby each example represents a particular strategy to make use of moving pictures to advance the project of Progressive social reform. Then I will address the question why moving pictures were not considered a constructive social force by Jewish socialist intellectuals and the leaders of the Jewish labour movement.

University Settlement House: Moving Pictures as a "Drawing Card"

Right from the first screenings of the cinematograph, the new film medium had been hailed as a universal language that could reach audiences across national, cultural and social boundaries. The metaphor of film as a universal language was especially powerful in the United States because a large part of the urban population was foreign-born. Institutions concerned with Americanising these newcomers favoured visual media over the written word because they typically considered the newcomers a poorly-educated lot whose "undeveloped" minds could be easily impressed by images. In *The Art of the Moving Picture* (1915), the poet Vachel Lindsay elaborated the notion of the movies as "American hieroglyphics" and stressed cinema's democratic nature and civilising potential:

> The invention of the photoplay is as great a step as was the beginning of picture-writing in the stone age. And cave-men and women of our slums seem to be the people most affected by this novelty ... . The slums are an astonishing assembly of cavemen crawling out of their shelters to exhibit for the first time in history a common interest on a tremendous scale in an art form.[1]

Progressive reformers discussed in more friendly terms cinema's potential impact upon "the tired workers, overburdened men and women", who filled "the little halls throughout the city and throughout the land".[2] Influenced by the ideas of Matthew Arnold, they believed that education and reform were the answers to America's social question. More than any other civic movement,

Progressive reformers inscribed the cinema with a rhetoric of uplift. Their discourses abounded with clichés like "the poor men's elementary course in drama", "the academy of the working man", and "a grand social worker". "The nickelodeon is the thing", John Collier of the People's Institute argued as early as 1908 in an article that appeared in *Charities and Commons, a publication for social workers*:

> All the settlements and churches combined do not reach daily a tithe of the simple and impressionable fold that the nickelodeons reach and vitally impress every day. Here is a new social force, perhaps the beginning of a true theater of the people, and an instrument whose power can only be realized when social workers begin to use it.[3]

Progressive reformers took special interest in immigrant Jews, who they believed conformed to such native Protestant values as a drive for education, seriousness, industry, and temperance. In its 1907 yearbook, the University Settlement Society described the "Lower East Side Dwellers" as follows:

> The people are industrious, they go struggling on, and their children rise, frequently moving away, mingling with the general population, and living lives of less economic stress than their parents. That is the prosaic sequel of the story of the immigrant Jewish family of the Lower East Side.[4]

In the opening decade of the 20th century, the downtown Jewish quarter, east of the Bowery and below East Fourteenth Street, was the home of over half a million immigrant Jews. It counted several settlement houses, where men and women with college degrees lived and worked among the immigrant population and sought with their scientific knowledge to improve the living and working conditions in the neighbourhood by offering education, advice and psychological assistance.[5]

With its clubs and classes, gymnasium, kindergarten, roof garden and public baths, the University Settlement at 184 Eldridge Street, strategically located opposite a public school and next door to a branch of the New York Public Library, was among the best-frequented institutions of its kind on the Lower East Side. It offered evening classes on a wide range of subjects, from cooking and sewing to city history, progressive literature and drawing. Most of its social clubs aimed at the immigrant youth. Programmes for children typically combined "little talks on the most elementary civics" with "amusing stories, songs and recitations". The ambition was to teach them what "the little citizens *should and should not do* out of regard for his neighbourhood". In 1907, the social workers decided to integrate moving pictures into their summer programme to lure more children to their indoor activities. As they put it, the summer clubs needed a "drawing card" that "would make the children eager to come and to come regularly". The Miles Brothers cordially furnished the settlement with a projector and fresh films every week. The plan worked out in so far as the movies increased the attendance, but the head worker admitted in his annual report that "most children who came had little idea that they were coming to anything but the 'moving picture show' ... . Very few expressed a desire for a club membership card". Eventually many joined the indoor summer programme but "the indoctrination of the children with Settlement ideals" remained a difficult task, he concluded.[6]

Manifestly, the University Settlement initially did not consider the film medium as an educational tool in itself but as a means to a different end: the moving pictures were primarily used to lure children *to* the Settlement House. However, as nickelodeons opened up everywhere in the Jewish quarter, the discourse of social workers on the cinema changed fundamentally. The new rhetoric centred on the potential moral and physical dangers of the five cent shows and the need to lure the immigrant youth *away* from the nickelodeons. Obviously, this was merely a renewed version of an older hegemonic discourse on low-brow entertainment that had emerged in the 19th century and now aligned the moving pictures with other forms of cheap commercial amusement that were considered harmful.[7]

Educational Alliance: Fighting fire with fire

"Too much emphasis cannot be laid upon the necessity for providing abundant, wholesome recreation and for the separation of recreation and vice", the Committee of Fourteen concluded in its 1910 report *The Social Evil in New York City: A Study of Law Enforcement*. To avoid recent immigrants being "contaminated" by the evils of the public dance halls or falling "a prey to the vicious tendencies of cheap drama, appealing to them on all sides",[8] settlement houses and other uplift institutions took on the task to organise counterattractions, typically in the form of a "wholesome" variant of the commercial original. The head worker of the College Settlement on Rivington Street articulated this strategy as follows: "our close study of the dance halls, moving picture shows, and the allurements of the nearby avenues, had taught us that we must renew our efforts to provide greater attractions within our doors".[9] Thus, when the Yiddish music halls gained widespread popularity, some workers of the East Side Settlement tried to establish a model German Bier-Garten and concert hall.[10] At the height of the dance craze, others advocated a large model dance hall in the Jewish quarter. Both the College Settlement and the University Settlement regularly organised large dances on their premises as well as smaller dancing classes on Saturday evenings. Altogether, however, most of the counterattractions organised by settlement houses on the East Side remained relatively modest initiatives.

Of an entire different kind were the entertainments offered by the Educational Alliance, a large uplift institution on East Broadway that was set up in 1889 with the financial support of the German Jewish elite, to facilitate the rapid assimilation of the eastern European Jews into American society. In the words of the uptown *Jewish Messenger*, the eastern European Jews had to "be Americanised in spite of themselves, in the mode prescribed by their friends and benefactors".[11] In the realm of leisure, this meant that the newcomers should not pass their evenings at the five cent moving picture shows, in Yiddish music halls or watching 10-20-30 cent English melodrama, but favour more elevating cultural occupations.

As William Uricchio and Roberta Pearson point out, "the alliance's literary clubs, English literature classes, theatrical performances, and free lectures constitute one of the most extensive arrays of counterattractions in New York City".[12] As the cinema became a structural part of Jewish life on the Lower East Side, moving pictures also gained prominence on the entertainment programme of the Educational Alliance. Considering the low-brow reputation of the movies, this strategy to integrate the cinema into its cultural programming practice and uplift strategy needed some explanation. A note clarified to the Alliance's uptown sponsors that "the 'moving picture show' is to the East-side what an uptown matinee is for those living on Riverside Drive".[13] "Because the 'moving picture show' is the East-Side child's theatre we 'fight fire with fire' by giving a *better* show for the *same* price". In addition, for those "who have no nickel", every Sunday the Alliance offered a free show for 750 children.

The moving picture shows at the Alliance "consisted of dramatic stories, sometimes based on historical themes; comic stories and industrial and scenic pictures".[14] About half of the films were "of educational nature".[15] For instance, a 1910 programme featured WHALE FISHING, THE MOUNTAINS FROM HONG KONG, GLIMPSES OF YELLOWSTONE PARK, OLIVER TWIST, A TRUE PATRIOT, SNOW WHITE AND ROSE RED, HIS LAST ILLUSION GONE and THE KING'S PROTÉGÉ.[16] Quality films with high cultural references figured prominently on the bill. For instance in May 1912 a "special moving picture exhibition of operas" was scheduled for Sunday evenings, with the films "preceded by short and appropriate talks on the biographies of the respective composers".[17] However the attendance was below expectation: only 271 persons attended the show in the 750-seat auditorium. In fact, finding the right balance between education and entertainment remained a difficult task, as the Board of Directors openly acknowledged:

> While not wishing to fall behind in the educational results, the idea has been to make the programs of the moving pictures so varied that everyone will find in them something to his taste and that the contrast between pictures will show all of them in a better light. Every effort is being made to increase the attractiveness of the educational features.[18]

At the same time, comments and explanations were also provided with the fiction films to enhance their educational value and to "minimize any harmful suggestions in the pictures".[19] The entertainment committee repeatedly expressed its intention to increase the number of "purely educational films" on the programme, but typically with the proviso that this should be done "as far as it proves possible to do so and still keep our audience".[20] If we look at the attendance figures, it is clear that the counterattraction strategy was only moderately successful. Only on the Saturday night did the moving picture shows fill the auditorium at full capacity. The average attendance was around 400, and with two to four shows per week the Alliance did not even equal the box-office figures of a single nickelodeon in a neighbourhood that counted over 30 such venues with a seating capacity of 300 each.

In this respect, it should be emphasised that the "civilizing" activities organised by the Educational Alliance and settlement houses met quite some resistance and suspicion. As one contemporary observer noted "the Jew does not readily avail himself of opportunities whose sources appear to him as of a charitable nature, no matter how well meant, or how democratically managed such efforts to benefit him may be".[21] In particular, many East Siders resented the Educational Alliance because it was financed by the wealthy "uptown" German Jewish community. In the garment industry, where many immigrant Jews were employed, German Jews were among the leading manufacturers and they controlled most of the downtown factories and sweatshops where many immigrant Jews toiled under oppressive working conditions. There was little doubt that the well-established German Jews provided much-needed material aid on the East Side, but at the same time, many "downtown Jews", especially those engaged in the labour movement, argued that philanthropic undertakings would not be needed if the bosses would pay better wages and keep workers employed during the slack season.

The *Jewish Daily Forward*: Theatre versus Moving Pictures

The uplift efforts of Progressive reformers and their German Jewish allies were paralleled by the efforts of Jewish socialists and labour leaders, who devoted much of their time and energy to improving the conditions of the Jewish working classes. Within the progressive immigrant milieu, the main media platform to address the social question was the Yiddish-language labour press, in particular the *Jewish Daily Forward (Forvertz)*. Under the editorship of Abraham Cahan, this newspaper had developed into one of the most influential institutions in the immigrant Jewish community, with a reach far beyond the organized working class. The *Forward* not only served as a platform for labour activism but also operated as a cultural force. Thus it offers the historian a keen insight into the ways in which entertainment was used as an instrument for social change.

The socialist position towards commercial entertainment should be understood as part of a broader effort by the Russian-Jewish intelligentsia of newspaper editors, writers, labour activists and other left-wing "radicals" to raise the cultural standard of the "uneducated" Jewish masses.[22] From the 1890s onwards, this cultural elite sought to transform the Yiddish legitimate theatre from a lowbrow entertainment into a highbrow institution for cosmopolitan art and enlightenment. As Yiddish theatre historian Nina Warnke points out, they condemned melodrama and historical operettas as stupid and stupefying amusement, and demanded the elimination of this *shund* (trash) from the Yiddish stage. At the same time, they "postulated realist plays and natural acting style as true art and exhorted both actors and audience to embrace their artistic values".[23] Drama with realist character development and psychologically motivated action was to make working-class audiences aware of social ills and thus would reinforce the revolutionary demand for change. Well into the 1910s, the Yiddish labour press targeted theatrical entrepreneurs, actors, and audiences for giving preference to spectacle and attractions rather than to content and drama as art.

How then did the *Jewish Daily Forward* respond to the cinema, a commercial entertainment based on visual spectacle? Somewhat surprisingly, Cahan and his staff initially took a neutral stand towards the *muving piktshurs* as they were called in Yiddish. This attitude stood in sharp contrast with their reception of Yiddish vaudeville entertainment, which was condemned as the wrong kind of Americanisation as soon as the first Yiddish music halls opened their doors.[24] For several years, *Forward* railed against the "*shmuts*" on the vaudeville stage and warned "respectable" workers to stay away from the Yiddish music halls. There was no such reaction when the first nickelodeons opened in the Jewish quarter. The *Forward*'s first article on the nickelodeon boom, published in March 1908, simply commented:

> Popular entertainment renews itself time and again, and art is becoming less and less expensive, not more than a *groshn*, to fit the taste and purse of small children and the poor, uneducated big children who are their parents. And once again the goyim start with it and the Jews get carried away.[25]

The *Forward* explained that the nickelodeons did not show any offensive fare. In the past, "scenes of the secret relations between the sexes" and "scenes of prize fights" had been "feature hits" in Bowery arcades and Coney Island saloons. Now one could now "sit through an entire program in a moving picture gallery without a blush of shame". Even so, the reporter still showed some concern about the effects of movie-going on children:

> The moving picture galleries are managed by ignorant and reckless people who are only interested in business. These people never consider whether or not a particular show is dangerous for children. And because children are very impressionable, they let the picture turn their heads and their fantasy, thoughts and character take a turn which the parents do not want at all.[26]

The *Forward* reassured its readers, however, that "the moving pictures are not a bad thing as long as they are in qualified hands". To make his point, the reporter gave the example of the picture shows presented at the University Settlement.

Although cinema's influence upon child audiences and uneducated workers was one of the most recurring obsessions of the period, the subject was not further developed by the *Forward*. The popularity of movie-going in the Jewish quarter was primarily discussed in terms of cinema's economic impact on the Yiddish legitimate theatre and the Yiddish vaudeville business. It seems as if the Jewish socialists were unable to articulate their ideas about the new film medium other than in terms of the vested discourse on the Yiddish stage or as a general critique of commercial entertainment. Thus, when the East Side mourned the casualties of a balcony collapse in a five cent theatre on Rivington

Street, Cahan addressed the unsafe conditions of the nickelodeons as a result of capitalist greed and social inequality more generally:

> The masses that are squeezed together in the tenements do not know where to go during the cold evenings. In the gloomy buildings where they sleep and have their sacred homes, there is no space to live. They are forced to go outside. They cannot afford real amusement, so they pass their time for five cents in a moving picture show. This business is booming thanks to the sorrowful life of the masses. These places are crammed like the rooms where they live. Who cares when this human merchandise is crushed? One more person squeezed inside, one more nickel earned.[27]

The moral impact of movies on Jewish workers was not an issue at all. This is striking considering that the *Forward*'s reports about the audiences of East Side picture shows frequently underscored how spellbound Jewish immigrants were by what they saw on the silver screen. It is clear that Jewish socialists and labour leaders did not consider the cinema as an agency for class struggle, unlike for instance the American Federation of Labor, which realized early on that labour-friendly movies could help the cause of the unions and that anti-labour films did not help the cause of the organised labour. Thus in 1910, AFL delegates urged local unions to "use all legitimate means ... to discourage the exhibition of such moving pictures that falsely pretend to represent instances in connection with our movement".[28] I found no such calls in the *Forward*.

By 1910, however, the Jewish socialist appreciation of the cinema had fundamentally changed. As the cinema became a serious rival to the Yiddish stage and thus undermined its influence as an institution for enlightenment, we witness a clear shift in the discourse from a neutral stance towards straightforward denunciation. The turning point came in September 1909, when the 2,000-seat Grand Street Theater, a major venue for Yiddish literary drama, fell into the hands of Marcus Loew and Adolph Zukor and reopened as a small-time vaudeville house. In the aftermath of the takeover by these future Hollywood moguls, the *Forward* relegated the cinema to the bottom end of the cultural hierarchy, a position previously occupied by Yiddish vaudeville entertainment. Henceforth, the paper repeatedly wrote about the moral dangers that the nickelodeons held for young people, especially young women. In addition to highly sensational front page stories, which associated movie-going with the sex trade, short back page news items with titles such as "break into a home because of moving pictures" and "movies turn children into gangsters" depicted local movie houses as schools of crime where murder, shoplifting, robbery and holdups were illustrated. Admittedly, such articles highlighting the moral dangers of movie-going were commonplace in the English-language newspapers too. Yet, in the mainstream press, cinema's critics often used these stories to illustrate the need for regulation and censorship. Many argued that if immoral movies could turn children into criminals, moral subjects might just as well turn them into good citizens. This type of reform discourse was absent in the comments of the *Forward*.

But there is more to it than criminalisation alone. In the aftermath of the takeover of the Grand Street Theater, the entire Yiddish press – left and right – redefined the cinema as a fundamentally *goyish* (gentile) entertainment and a *Fremdkörper* (foreign body) to Jewish culture. Thus across the political spectrum, cinema's potential as an educational instrument and a vehicle to address social evils was blocked. For the Jewish socialist intellectuals as well as the Orthodox leadership the cinema was simply not compatible with a continued Jewish identity. This idiosyncratic response should be understood within the context of ongoing power struggles within the immigrant Jewish community, in which the community's self-appointed elites sought to maintain their authority over the "uneducated" masses.[29]

Finally, it should be emphasised that there is no indication that Jewish immigrant workers shared the denunciation of the cinema as a *Fremdkörper* to Jewish culture. On the contrary: in the public mind, the cinema was synonymous with Jewish upward social mobility. Movie moguls like Loew and Zukor – already powerful entrepreneurs before their rise as captains of the American film industry – were role models for many Jewish workers. Accounts of their entrepreneurial success "from rags to riches" functioned as Horatio Alger stories within the immigrant Jewish community, and their names were a shorthand for the Jewish pursuit of the American Dream. This too may have made the moving picture medium a rather unlikely candidate to address the social question.

Notes

1. Vachel Lindsay, *The Art of the Moving Picture* [1915] (New York: The Modern Library, 2000), 116 and 139.

2. Mary Heaton Vorse, "Some Picture Show Audiences", *The Outlook* (24 June 1911): 445.

3. John Collier, "Cheap Amusements", *Charities and Commons* (11 April 1908): 76.

4. Charles S. Bernheimer, "Lower East Side Dwellers", *Yearbook of the University Settlement Society of New York* (1907): 32; see also David Blaustein, "The Inherent Cultural Forces of the Lower East Side", *Yearbook of the University Settlement Society of New York* (1901): 20–25.

5. For the range of activities see Robert A. Woods and Albert J. Kennedy, *Handbook of Settlements* (New York: Russell Sage Foundation, 1911).

6. "The Inside Summer Work at the University Settlement", *Yearbook of the University Settlement Society of New York* (1907): 17–20.

7. See Lawrence W. Levine, *Highbrow Lowbrow: The Emergence of Cultural Hierarchy in America* (Cambridge, Mass.: Harvard University Press, 1988).

8. *Thirteenth Annual Report of the President and Board of Directors of the Educational Alliance* (1905): 52, quoted in William Uricchio and Roberta E. Pearson, *Reframing Culture: The Case of the Vitagraph Films* (Princeton: Princeton University Press, 1993), 37.

9. Elizabeth S. Williams, "Report of the Head Worker", *Twenty-first Annual Report of the College Settlement* (1909–1910): 7.

10. *University Settlement Studies Quarterly* (1906): 23.

11. *Jewish Messenger* (25 September 1891): 4.

12. Uricchio and Pearson, *Reframing Culture*, 37.

13. "East Side Cameo", May 1912. Records of the Educational Alliance. YIVO Institute for Jewish Research, New York, reference R.G. 312.23.

14. Meeting of the Board of Directors of the Educational Alliance, 13 March 1911, YIVO RG 312.2. All dates have the same YIVO reference.

15. Ibid., 13 May 1912.

16. Ibid., 10 June 1910.

17. Ibid., 13 May 1912.

18. Ibid., 8 May 1911.

19. Ibid.

20. Ibid. See also the meeting of 13 May 1912.

21. Blaustein, "Inherent Cultural Forces", 21.

22. See Judith Thissen, "Reconsidering the Decline of New York's Yiddish Theater in the Early 1900s", *Theatre Survey* 44.2 (2003): 173–197.

23. Nina Warnke, "Reforming the New York Yiddish Theater: The Cultural Politics of Immigrant Intellectuals and the Yiddish Press, 1887–1910", Ph.D. Dissertation, Columbia University (2001), 63.

24. Nina Warnke, "Immigrant Popular Culture as Contested Sphere: Yiddish Music Halls, the Yiddish Press, and the Processes of Americanization, 1900–1910", *Theatre Journal* 48 (1996): 321–335.

25. "Di muving piktshur geleris", *Jewish Daily Forward* (4 March 1908).

26. Ibid.

27. "Der unglik oyf Rivington Strit", editorial, *Jewish Daily Forward* (15 December 1908).

28. Quoted in Steven J. Ross, "The Revolt of the Audience: Reconsidering Audiences and Reception during the Silent Era", in Melvin Stokes and Richard Maltby (eds), *American Movie Audiences: From the Turn of the Century to the Early Sound Era* (London: BFI Publishing, 1999), 96.

29. For a detailed analysis, see Judith Thissen, "Next Year at the Moving Pictures: Cinema and Social Change in the Jewish Immigrant Community", in Richard Maltby and Melvin Stokes (eds), *Hollywood and the Social Experience of Cinema* (Exeter: University of Exeter Press, 2007), 113–129.

State Thomas Asylum for Orphan and Destitute Indian Children,
Iroquois, N. Y.

KINDERGARTEN   NURSERY-CHILDRENS DORMITORY

Michelle Lamunière

Sentiment and Science in Harvard University's Social Museum

In the second half of the 19th century, widespread industrialisation, immigration, and urbanisation resulted in the fundamental transformation of American society. For Francis Greenwood Peabody (1847-1936), Harvard University's Plummer Professor of Christian Morals and the founder of its Social Museum, the key to the question of how to address problems that arose from these dramatic societal changes was the relationship between ethics and economics: "Sentiment without science is like steam unapplied to its proper work", he wrote in 1887. "It seethes and boils and threatens its tumultuous vitality until it is compressed in its proper engine. Science without sentiment", he continued, "is mechanism without steam, ingenious and complete, but without the dynamic which gives it motion and power".[1] Succumbing to pure emotion weakened one's ability to reason, Peabody believed, but an over-emphasis on fact deadened the capacity to feel. Positioning reform as a modern agenda, he held that economic principles based in scientific method supplied the mechanism, but that a sense of moral purpose – defined by the rubric of "sentiment" – provided the motivating power.

The widespread adoption of photography as a tool for social reform is indicative of a crucial and transformative shift in ways of thinking at the end of the 19th century, associated with the changing relationship between sentiment and science. In the 1880s when reformer and activist Jacob Riis (1849-1914), a pioneer in the use of social reform photography, was lecturing on the desperate living and working conditions associated with slum life in New York, sentiment *connoted* an overly emotional reaction to social problems that focused on the needs of the individual rather than the common good. Rather than eliciting sympathy by imagining oneself in the place of those in need, sentimental and

Facing page:
Upper: Races, Indians: United States. New York. Iroquois. Thomas Asylum for Orphan and Destitute Indian Children, c.1903. Gelatin silver prints and printed label mounted to board, black ink, 35.5 x 55.9 cm.
Lower: Display Room, Social Museum, Emerson Hall, Harvard University, c.1910. Gelatin silver print, 11.6 x 16.8 cm.

stereotypical images of the poor prevalent in news sources and in the literary and visual arts fed excessive emotion. Riis's dramatic lantern slide lectures, which presented scenes of urban strife that contributed to the image of the city as a moral blight and social menace, drew on popular forms of entertainment and spectacle to evoke an emotional reaction and appealed to his audiences' guilt as a way of soliciting support for reform efforts.[2]

Peabody's understanding of sentiment was rooted in the 18th-century belief that emotion creates sympathy for others and that the feeling of gratification that comes from helping those less fortunate is an important aspect of living a moral life. At the same time, a scientific spirit was changing approaches to the study of society in both reform and academic circles. In the 19th century, the reform movement was dominated by religiously-motivated charitable efforts to help the poor and disadvantaged overcome the moral weaknesses that were viewed as the causes of social problems. With the embrace of scientific method as the 20th century opened, reformers began to accept environmental conditions – overcrowded housing, unsanitary living conditions, unemployment, etc. – as possible causes, and to promote conclusions, such as tenement legislation, based on unsentimental empirical research.

This article addresses the varied ways in which sentiment was strategically mobilised in social reform photography, specifically in the Social Museum – a collection of empirical data in the form of photographs and related graphic and text-based materials compiled for the comparative study of social problems and solutions in Europe and America. The Social Museum was established to "promote investigations of modern social conditions and to direct the amelioration of industrial and social life".[3] While Peabody used sentiment as a moral catalyst, the vast majority of the photographs in the Social Museum served a didactic purpose, portraying reform initiatives and institutions that he viewed as the only solutions to social problems. As such, sensationalist imagery was rejected in favour of pictures portraying effective systems of reform that elicited a different kind of an emotional response – one of sympathy rather than pity – and that inspired a larger recognition of a collective responsibility for the good of humanity.[4] By appealing to an 18th-century definition of sentiment as a means of maintaining social order, while also grounding the institution in a scientific framework, what becomes evident is that the Social Museum was not intended to be simply a collection of facts or data, but an archive of ideological persuasion.

As an influential educator, religious leader, and advocate for reform for over thirty years, Francis Greenwood Peabody believed that social problems had taken the country by surprise and that students being educated at Harvard University were ill-equipped to deal with the realities of their age.[5] To prepare his students for these challenges, Peabody began in the early 1880s to teach courses on social ethics, which emphasised personal responsibility and civic action as ways to effect change.[6] In 1903 Peabody founded the Social Museum as a visual complement to his classes. By the 1920s the collection consisted of more than 10,000 photographs, publications, albums, diagrams, booklets, handwritten matter and hand-crafted objects. Materials were organised using a classification system based on social reform topics, such as charity, improved housing and health. The idea was to "lay before the student the total experience of the world in various forms of social service ... to impress him with the scope of the Social Question and to send him back to his own work with a sense of background, enlargement, and hope".[7] Although the establishment of similar collections was being explored worldwide, Peabody's Social Museum was distinguished by its association with academic life and its primary concern with the instruction of university students.[8]

The Social Museum comprised two display rooms, a Social Ethics Library, a small seminar room, a study for Peabody, and a lecture room with a lantern stand for displaying slides. For the museum's exhibition materials Peabody adopted the system of display that had become prominent at world's fairs' social economy exhibitions. Photographs and other graphic material were mounted onto 14 x 22 inch (and some 22 x 28 inch) grey exhibition boards. Titles were printed on thin paper, matching the finish of the cards, and then adhered above the photographs; captions were hand-lettered below. Most of the exhibition boards were stored in portfolios or cabinets where students could flip through them as one looks through a card catalogue. Others were shown in large wing frames – hinged at one side and attached to a central post – in which three boards could be displayed on each side and slipped in and out with ease for changing exhibitions. Many statistical charts and diagrams also hung on the museum's walls.

Early social reform photography relied upon well-known discourses of senti-ment, referencing familiar cultural symbols and prejudices in order to motivate and manipulate viewers. One common method for distributing sentimental images of the urban poor was through travelling lantern slide shows, in part because the technology for printing photographic imagery during this period was limited. Although not widely used for reform purposes at first, moralistic tales such as THE ROAD TO RUIN and temperance stories like THE BOTTLE were particularly popular in the 1870s and 1880s. Social reformers like Jacob Riis took advantage of the performative aspect of such presentations to exploit emotional, and frequently overwrought, reactions. But with the turn of the 20th century, reformers like Peabody began to present photographs as graphic records in conjunction with data reflecting a shift toward the objectivity of scientific method as a more productive way to affect radical change in society.[9]

While continuing to be popular vehicles for entertainment, lantern slides also began to play more of an educational role, facilitated in part by the use of photographic images (as opposed to earlier hand-painted slides). Commer-cially produced slide sets depicting popular subjects like travel, science, and religion were widely marketed by companies such as the Stereopticon & Film Exchange; Moore, Bond & Company; and Chicago Projecting Company. They often included lecture scripts so that anyone could present the material. As

Display Room, Social Museum, Emerson Hall, Harvard University, c.1910. Gelatin silver print, 11.6 x 16.8 cm.

technical advances made the production of slides easier, social and professional organisations, clubs, and schools began producing lantern slides of their activities as a way to record and publicise their efforts as a means of soliciting additional support and drawing attention to their cause. Many had exchange schemes and circulating libraries of lantern slides of a variety of social subjects, which supported their institutional missions and countered the more moralising, commercially-produced lantern slide sets, which continued to be popular into the first decades of the 20th century.

One organisation that utilised photographs – particularly in the lantern slide format – for this purpose was the League for Social Service in New York. The League served as a resource, and ultimately a competitor, to Peabody's Social Museum. Social Gospel leader Josiah Strong believed that social problems reflected the need for a period of readjustment to the resulting environmental changes. In 1898 Strong and William Howe Tolman, a social engineer formerly affiliated with the New York Association for Improving the Condition of the Poor, founded the League for Social Service to facilitate this process: "The League gathers from all civilized countries facts of every kind which bear on this great problem of readjustment, interprets them, and then in many ways disseminates them so as to educate public opinion".[10] In 1902, the League was expanded and renamed the American Institute of Social Service (AISS). It comprised eleven departments, including a Bureau of Information, a library of books, pamphlets, annual reports, magazines, and newspapers; an Illustration Department, including photographs, lantern slides, and other graphic material;

and a Lecture Bureau, which sponsored lectures by Tolman and Strong in addition to experts in the field, and a corps of "lantern lecturers" who could speak to individual groups across the country. Additional services included consultation and investigation by trained staff for special inquiries on any number of reform topics, as well as its publishing arm *Social Service*.

It was the visual material collected by the AISS that most interested Peabody, and he and Tolman corresponded about duplicating photographic prints in the collection for the Social Museum. By 1902, they had available for purchase 3,000 lantern slides and 4,000 photographs that could be made into slides. The AISS also provided the necessary equipment for viewing the slides, as well as skilled lantern operators. "An ounce of picture is worth a ton of words", wrote Tolman. "By means of this illustrated material, women's clubs, labor unions, charity organization societies, and the young peoples' societies in the various churches, can show their respective committees how they may be made better places to live in".[11] A list of available subjects from 1900 included services provided by the Children's Aid Society in New York, municipal activities such as sewage works in Glasgow, educational activities at the Hampton Normal and Agricultural Institute in Virginia, and services provided by Salvation Army organisations across the United States.[12] These and many other subjects reflect the type of relief and betterment efforts also included in the Social Museum.[13]

The model Riis had popularised was still embraced, however, and at least one local reformer encouraged Peabody to follow it. In 1908 Walter E. Kruesi, Secretary of the Boston Association for the Relief and Control of Tuberculosis, wrote to Peabody:

> No doubt you have considered the ultimate addition of material showing the negative side – terrific congestion in cities, slums in villages, the menace of the saloon and brothel, the drainage and sewer problems, unclean food, lack of public comfort stations, degeneracy of eastern rural life, and the taxation incidence and proportion to whole income.[14]

As photographs of poor living and working conditions became more ubiquitous, the shock value of Riis's night-time scenes began to wear off. As his collection of lantern slides demonstrates, ultimately even he sought to emphasise social progress rather than social failure.[15]

Photography complemented the new scientific approach to reform because of its perceived authenticity and its usefulness as an educational and psychological tool. At the same time, the power of images to evoke an emotional response competed with and complicated the idea of a photographic record. In a 1910 survey of 50 charity organisation annual reports, the author Margaret Byington notes that photographs can be effective, describing "an excellent photograph of a typical family", where "the photographer has caught wonderfully the spirit behind the faces which reveal the tragedy and the beauty of these people ... . Such studies", she concludes, "cannot fail to make givers understand how real and human the tragedies which a charitable society meets".[16] Clearly a photograph's ability to make an emotional connection between subject and

Display Room, Social Museum, Emerson Hall, Harvard University, c.1910. Gelatin silver print, 11.6 x 16.8 cm.

viewer was perceived by reformers as an important key to engaging potential supporters.

The emerging field of sociology, however, viewed statistical charts and graphs based on empirical research as holding more scientific and intellectual authority than photographs. Their aversion to photography stemmed from the concern that a viewer's first response was more likely to be based on an emotional, rather than an intellectual or rational, reaction. As Clarice Stasz observed in her study of the development of visual sociology, "The pictures scream 'We are real! We live'! – tugging on sentiments and emotions".[17] Science relied on practical methods of observation and the analyses of facts; emotions were irrational, uncontrollable, and unpredictable and therefore could not be reliably considered as data.

Peabody's use of photography as the primary source material for the Social Museum indicates his awareness of the persuasive power of visual imagery to engage viewers on both an intellectual and an emotional level. In terms of his teaching, he recognised photography's value as a visual device that could teach students more effectively than lectures. "Not the ear, but the eye", he wrote in the introductory essay to a classified index of the Social Museum collection, "is the primary organ of scientific knowledge".[18] While examples of specific images employed by Peabody for teaching purposes are not known, classes came to the Social Museum to study specific subjects, such as charity and crime, or to view temporary exhibits on such topics as the prevention of accidents; the correlation of alcohol abuse with crime, illness, and death; the development of social surveys; welfare work or employee benefits; and the causes and prevention of "defectiveness". Exhibition boards were also taken into, and hung in, the classroom to illustrate larger social issues. Peabody presented photographs and graphic illustrations as "facts of social life", equating them with specimens found in natural history museums and thus corroborating his belief in their scientific objectivity. He wanted the photographs to provide pictorial evidence to assist his students in their study of social ethics in the same way that the laboratory was employed for inquiries related to chemistry or biology. At the same time, he hoped that his students would experience an emotional engagement with the subjects that would inspire compassion and heighten awareness of their moral responsibility to society.

The Social Museum photographs, however idealistic, attempted to break down social barriers by presenting the poor and immigrant classes in ways that projected their path toward successful assimilation. A shift in the use of sentiment signifies an evolving ideological position whereby approaches to social reform under Peabody are informed and influenced by the viewer's emotional engagement and identification with the photographs' subjects. This way of thinking, however, reflects the limits of Peabody's approach. Although rooted in Christian ethics and empowered by moral sentiment, ultimately Peabody's students were privileged individuals with little exposure to true social hardships. Moreover, their views were guided and shaped under the protective authority of equally privileged Harvard faculty and by the scientific method that dominated instruction at the university during this period.[19]

While mounted onto exhibition boards and presented as data, the subjects of the photographs are also intended to generate an emotional response. To elicit sympathy and compassion, the photographs needed to create a feeling of identification between subject and viewer, a result more easily achieved when the person depicted looks and acts like "us". Yet, as museum objects, could the photographs be successful in motivating students if they were intended to be observed purely as scientific data? That the subjects are both human and specimen, individual and institutional, supports Peabody's contention that in order to be effective, the photographs in the Social Museum needed to reflect aspects of *both* sentiment and science. Whether staged or spontaneous, the photographs are intended – both through emotional appeal and as objective evidence – to persuade the viewer of the ameliorative power of social reform programs and to instil in the viewers a higher purpose of service to humanity.

This duality is demonstrated in a portrait of a mother and her twins, who are the recipients of a milk distribution programme sponsored by the Starr Centre Association, a social settlement that served the South Central district of Philadelphia, Pennsylvania. Pasteurised milk was made available for infants because of its nutritional value and because milk-borne diseases were prevalent. Alluding to the long visual tradition of the Madonna and Child in Western art, the mother holds the children on her lap, wrapping a protective arm around

Social Settlements: United States, Pennsylvania, Philadelphia. Starr Centre Association, "Twins when they began to take modified milk", c.1907. Gelatin silver print, 23.5 x 19 cm.

each one. The subjects are positioned in the centre of the composition and the mother's knees are pressed against the picture plane. This effect, in addition to her direct gaze, ensures her candid and sincere engagement with the photograph's viewers, who are meant to connect with the determination and perseverance conveyed in her expression. The caption describing the photograph – "Twins when they began to be fed modified milk" – is somewhat ambiguous, placing the infants in an uneasy space between before and after. The alertness in their faces suggests that they have begun to consume the modified or sterilised milk, but their continuing lack of nourishment is apparent in the fragile thinness of their arms and legs. In addition, the twin at the right is smaller than his sibling, and the amount of catching up he needs to do is evident in his disproportionately large bare feet. The room in which the family sits is cramped and disorganised, suggesting a lack of domestic order. The threadbare furniture is practically touching, and the presence of swaths of fabric and a sewing machine on a small table behind the subjects suggest that this is also a workspace. Clothes lie upon every surface and hang from the wall, and an old newspaper is stuck behind the sewing machine. The woman's white blouse and delicate earrings show her efforts to look presentable, but the dirt on her skirt betrays the struggles of raising children, working, and maintaining a home under difficult circumstances.

In the context of the Social Museum, the photograph of the mother and her twins was intended to humanise its subjects, enabling viewers to sympathise with them through feelings of identification. Whereas Jacob Riis, capitalising on the 19th-century evocation of sentiment as emotionally excessive and self-serving, used photographic images to protect his audiences from having to engage with their fellow man, this portrait embodied Peabody's definition of sentiment in the way it evoked feelings of compassion that created and nurtured a sense of social duty in the minds of reform-oriented viewers. Yet, while the Social Museum photographs may have been intended to traverse cultural and racial boundaries, as with Riis's illustrated lectures, the ultimate effect was to reinforce binary divisions, in this case between the reform programme recipients they depicted and the privileged Harvard students who viewed them from a distance. Thus, even though such photographs were part of a standardisation of imagery and increasingly regarded as "data" in the larger reform movement, within the context of the Social Museum, they never fully made the transition from sentiment to science.

A longer version of this article appeared as Michelle Lamunière, "Sentiment as Moral Motivator: From Jacob Riis's Lantern Slide Presentations to Harvard University's Social Museum", *History of Photography* 36, no. 2 (Spring 2012): 137–155.

Notes

1. Francis Greenwood Peabody, "The Philosophy of the Social Questions", *The Andover Review* 8, no. 48 (1887): 564.

2. For more on Riis's lantern slide lectures, see Bonnie Yochelson's article in this volume.

3. Francis Greenwood Peabody, *The Social Museum as an Instrument of University Teaching* (Cambridge, Mass.: Harvard University, 1911), 2. Established as the cornerstone of the newly founded Department of Social Ethics, the Social Museum opened in 1907; it was available to students and scholars until at least the 1930s when the Department of Social Ethics was absorbed into the newly formed Department of Sociology. For a public announcement of the Social Museum, see David Camp Rogers, "A Social Museum in a University", *Charities and the Commons* 18, no. 3 (1907): 653–656.

4. Surprisingly, even though Riis and Peabody shared a similar moral and religious foundation, there is no evidence of contact between the two men, and there are no photographs by Riis in the Social Museum.

5. For more on Peabody's background and impetus for founding the Social Museum, see Michelle

Lamunière, "Sentiment and Science: Francis Greenwood Peabody and the Social Museum in Context", in Deborah Martin Kao and Michelle Lamunière (eds), *Instituting Reform: The Social Museum of Harvard University, 1903-1931* (Cambridge, Mass.: Harvard Art Museums, 2012), 39–55.

6.   While Peabody's direct influence is difficult to determine, by 1902 almost 400 Harvard students were engaged in some kind of volunteer social work in the Boston and Cambridge communities. See David B. Potts, "Social Ethics at Harvard, 1881–1931", in Paul Buck (ed.), *Social Sciences at Harvard, 1860-1920: From Inculcation to the Open Mind* (Cambridge, Mass.: Harvard University Press, 1965), 96.

7.   Francis G. Peabody, *The Approach to the Social Question: An Introduction to the Study of Social Ethics* (New York: Macmillan, 1909), 31.

8.   For more on the Paris Musée Social, which was the primary inspiration for the Social Museum, as well as other models, including social economy exhibitions, which demonstrated international efforts to create better living and working environments through a range of reform initiatives, see Michelle Lamunière, "A Great Social Encyclopedia: Social Economy Exhibitions and the Creation of Museums for their Permanent Display", in Ilja Van Den Broek, Christianne Smit and Dirk Jan Wolffram (eds), *Imagination and Commitment: Representations of the Social Question* (Leuven: Peeters, 2010), 121–142; and Julie K. Brown, "Making 'Social Facts' Visible", in Kao and Lamunière, *Instituting Reform*, 93-109.

9.   An early scientific use of lantern slides to draw attention to social conditions in the United States occurred in February 1879 when New York Metropolitan Board of Health President Charles F. Chandler gave a lecture on the history of tenement house construction that included pictures of decrepit buildings. This account is described in Bonnie Yochelson and Daniel J. Czitrom, *Rediscovering Jacob Riis: Exposure Journalism and Photography in Turn-of-the-Century New York* (New York: New Press, 2008), 44–45.

10.   Josiah Strong, "Why the League for Social Service", *Social Service* 6, no. 3 (September 1902): 43.

11.   William Howe Tolman, "The League for Social Service", *The Arena* 21, no. 4 (April 1899): 476.

12.   "A Descriptive List of Lantern Slides Illustrating Movements for Social and Industrial Betterment", *Social Service* 2, no. 1 (January 1900): 4–15.

13.   For an example of the extensive use of lantern slides by a commercial enterprise, see Elspeth H. Brown, "Labor, Management, and Photography as 'Social Hieroglyphic': the National Cash Register Company and the Social Museum Collection", in Kao and Lamunière, *Instituting Reform*, 201–219.

14.   Harvard University, Social Ethics Museum Records. Letter from Walter E. Kruesi to Francis Greenwood Peabody, 6 April 1908. UAV 800.157, Harvard University Archives. Kruesi's letter offers other "friendly and suggestive criticisms" like including more descriptive literature and beefing up the tuberculosis section. Unfortunately, Peabody's response has not survived.

15.   The Museum of the City of New York houses the Jacob A. Riis Collection of lantern slides, glass negatives, and prints.

16.   Margaret Byington, "Fifty Annual Reports", *The Survey* 23, no. 6 (1910): 972. This article is cited in Peter Bacon Hales, *Silver Cities: Photographing American Urbanization, 1839–1939* (Albuquerque: University of New Mexico Press, 2006), 383.

17.   Clarice Stasz, "The Early History of Visual Sociology", in Jon Wagner (ed.), *Images of Information: Still Photography in the Social Sciences* (Beverly Hills: Sage Publications, 1979), 134.

18.   Peabody, *The Social Museum*, 1.

19.   See Jon H. Roberts and James Turner, *The Sacred and the Secular University* (Princeton: Princeton University Press, 2000), on the development of social science instruction at Harvard University.

PART III:

Approaches to the Hidden History of Screen Culture

Frank Gray

Engaging with the Magic Lantern's History

In 2001, reporting on an influential symposium held at the British Academy, Ian Christie asked, "Could it [the magic lantern] be considered a "medium" with its own distinctive culture and history?"[1] The answer is an unequivocal "yes". The magic lantern as a medium and as a cultural phenomenon represents a distinct screen practice that has developed from its origins in the 17th century to the present day. As a technology and as a cultural form it was dedicated to sharing projected images on a screen with an audience. Lanternists first used glass slides as a surface for hand-drawn and photographic imagery and, in the 20th century, glass was replaced by 35mm film transparencies. It continues today in a digital iteration, through the combination of digital pictures, picture organisation and presentation software (e.g. Microsoft's PowerPoint and Apple's Keynote) and viewing hardware (data projectors and computer screens).

The late 19th century marks the moment when the lantern had its greatest cultural capital. Embedded into all aspects of the late Victorian world, contemporary newspapers of that era from Europe and North America reveal its ubiquitous nature. Lanterns and lanternists were found in theatres, music halls, churches, schools, universities, hospitals, department stores, piers, aquaria and private homes. Slides were made either commercially or by lanternists themselves, and were used within entertainments and lectures designed for the purposes of pleasure, education, instruction, religion, charitable work and the spread of news. Professional lantern lecturers went on tours with highly structured programmes that featured slides, narration and music. Chemists' shops (pharmacies), photographers and opticians offered lanterns, slides and handbooks for sale, and slides and readings could also be ordered by mail for purchase and hire from manufacturers' and dealers' catalogues. An understanding of the magic lantern's history makes clear this diversity of use and its cultural presence.

As a cultural phenomenon, what are the lantern's distinctive characteristics? What makes it different from film, that other dominant screen practice? The

Facing page:
Brighton Aquarium and sea front, from a Photochrom postcard, c.1890.

history of the lantern is often represented by an aesthetic appreciation of either a particular slide or set of slides, such as a chromatrope (a rackwork-driven slide that produced kaleidoscopic patterns through the rotation of two hand-painted glass discs) or a set of dissolving views (images which would dissolve or fade from one to the other in order to represent a slow and seamless passage of time such as from day to night). However this fascination with the lantern's "magical" and very beautiful past is both a simplification and a distortion of the lantern's actual history. To study and to know lantern history is to appreciate an understanding of its rich complexity.

One lantern show, for example, represents an historically-specific synthesis of one or more lecturers and/or showpeople, a set of slides on a transparent medium, a projection device for their display, its illuminant, a screen on which to view the enlarged imagery, a screen presentation (a programme, the selection and organisation of the slides, narration, performance and music), an audience seated in the dark, and a venue. This holistic perspective combines technology with a multi-media performance and an audience within an event space; an iterative practice that was designed for the visualisation and narrativisation of sets of related images, enlarged and projected on a screen for an audience facing that screen. As a screen practice, we need to understand its distinctive audio-visual and performative nature and to engage not only with what was seen on screen but also with what was heard and experienced in a particular immersive environment.

From this understanding, what therefore would constitute a discipline of "lantern studies"? It would first need to plot the lantern's evolution as a technology and as a cultural form (this history is far from static as it is one that displays the lantern's malleable and mutable character). As many lantern histories and historians have revealed, the Victorian world witnessed its phenomenal development. It saw the development of different slide types and slide subjects, different kinds and patterns of manufacturing and retailing and a very wide range of performance practices and styles. What is obvious and crucial to an analysis of this history is that each slide and each show/performance had a very distinctive context. It had an inter-textual and inter-medial relationship with a wide, complex set of ideas, discourses, events, other lantern shows, other vision technologies and practices (such as photography, painting, graphics, and panoramas) and other cultural practices such as theatre and literature. To unlock the lantern's history therefore requires the generation of historically-informed description and analysis that positions lantern practice and culture within a defined ideological context and locates it within a particular moment of production and consumption.

The study of the lantern is obviously informed by image reading practices (as found in art history) in terms of addressing the slides and their characteristics (subject, composition, masking, colouring, sign-type and iconography) as well as authorship, use and meaning. Origination is also an issue, as often slides were derived from engravings, paintings and photographs that had their own history and context. However what defines the lantern and distinguishes it from the histories of painting and photography is the fact that the slides were always part of a sequence and a programme. Unlike a two-dimensional still image, slides are still only for a moment as they also move and change. It is this temporal character which defines both the nature and use of lantern slides.

The slides functioned as a visual element within a performed text that was shaped by a narrative that functioned as a structuring device. It is this fact that requires, as does film studies with its allied interest in the meanings of shots and sequences within a particular whole, very careful consideration of the role of narrative in shaping and organising a magic lantern performance. What is the nature of the narrative to be performed and what therefore are the paradigmatic (what to select) and syntagmatic (what to combine) logics at work in the presentation of a distinct series of slides and their place within a lantern show? This was a process of selection, combination and organisation for a *live* public presentation. It is this aspect that also connects the lantern to the history of performance in general and to staged audio-visual productions in particular.

To investigate a lantern show as a signifying practice is therefore an essential activity, as this analytical work can begin to reveal how a production represents the world through a linear sequence of slides on screen with spoken narration. However, one of the challenging aspects for contemporary lantern historians is that rarely will all of the artefacts be in place for such an analysis (e.g. slides, readings, performance notes/script, reports and reviews as well as contextual detail on the lanternist and the production). Instead there will just be fragments, but when supported by a strong conceptual model these can provide genuine insight into particular productions and their meanings. Theatre historians and early film historians inhabit a very similar space when investigating plays and films that can never be seen. The challenge for the lantern historian is to be excited and intrigued by a history that is ephemeral in its nature but was sufficiently extensive in terms of its cultural use and is well supported by a rich range of surviving fragments.

BRIGHTON AQUARIUM.

COMFORTABLE AND WARM.   SPECIMENS FED AT 12 AND 5.

Admission Every Evening after 6 o'clock, 3d. Tickets, including Admission & Entertainment, 6d, 1/, 1/6, & 2/.

No Sixpenny Seat Tickets sold at the Turnstiles at Wednesday and Saturday Matinées.

THIS DAY (SATURDAY), at 3.45 and 8, LAST TWO PERFORMANCES of
MR. ALFRED SELWYN'S COMPANY in the Sparkling Burlesque,

"ALADDIN, or the Scamp and the Lamp."

MONDAY NEXT, March 9th, and During the Week. Each Evening at 8; Matinées, Monday, Wednesday, and Saturday, at 2.30, Mr ROY E. REDGRAVE AND COMPANY in the Great Laughable Farcical Comedy,

"THE BETTER HALF."

MONDAY, March 16th, and During the Week, Re-Engagement of Mr G. ALBERT SMITH.

GRAND DIORAMIC ENTERTAINMENTS.

"The Glories of the Heavens," "Our Glorious Empire," and "Twenty Thousand Leagues under the Sea."

Advertisement for Smith's "Grand Dioramic Entertainments" at Brighton Aquarium. *Brighton Herald* 7 March 1896.

Fragments of Lantern History: A Brighton Illustration

My own research into lantern history focuses on Brighton in the 19th century, as this English seaside town provides a very good paradigm for the study of late Victorian visual culture in general and the rise of photography, the lantern and film in particular. As a modern new town, it was dedicated to leisure and tourism and entertained millions each year. For the lanternist, it offered many opportunities as it had many new theatres (including one on the West Pier and at the Aquarium), music halls and ready-made audiences. My lantern research has relied upon contemporary newspaper reports, the dedicated trade publication *The Optical Magic Lantern Journal and Photographic Enlarger*, slides from various collections and the extensive historical work on the lantern in this period undertaken by members of the Magic Lantern Society and others.[2]

Lantern lectures were a regular and distinctive part of Brighton's public culture. Around 1890, there were lectures with such titles as A JOURNEY TO ROME AND BACK, A VISIT TO SPAIN; OR A PILGRIMAGE TO THE LAND OF THE CID, A HOLIDAY TOUR IN SCOTLAND and CHINA AND THE CHINESE.[3] Many were didactic in nature, presented by travellers, missionaries and the representatives of organisations and charities. One of the great professional lanternists of the era was Benjamin J. Malden (1838–1933), known as "Professor Malden". He was recognised for his use of the triunial lantern (a lantern with three lenses allowing dissolving between images) and he regularly visited Brighton from 1890 to 1895, performing at both the West Pier Pavilion and the Aquarium. His "Dioramic Excursions", as he referred to them, took audiences on lantern journeys around the world. His show for 1895 was particularly praised by the *Brighton Herald*:

> Professor Malden, who, by, means of a powerful lantern and a number of fine photographic and dioramic slides, has taken his audiences in imagination for tours in Switzerland, Norway, and last night ... through 'Our Glorious Colonies' ... This afternoon the Professor will 'travel through space,' or, in other words, exhibit the glories of the Heavens by means of new photographs taken by the help of the great Lick telescope.[4]

There is a great correspondence between the subject matter of these shows and the first series of public lantern lectures by George Albert Smith (1864–1959). Smith had been a stage mesmerist in Brighton in the 1880s and in the 1890s first turned to the lantern and then to the new technology of the cinematograph. He is now recognised as a significant early film pioneer. His lantern shows at the Brighton Aquarium in 1896 and 1897 are well documented by the local press and indicate that by this date, he had acquired a good understanding of how to produce a popular lantern entertainment. Smith's first publicly advertised lecture was delivered as an afternoon show at the beginning of January 1896 for the holiday season. It was described as

> The Glories of the Heavens, or A Tour Through Space. A Grand Astronomical Entertainment of the most fascinating description. By means of Dissolving Views and Dioramic Effects, Earth, Sun, Moon, Planets, &c., in actual motion. Beautiful

photographs of the distant scenery of the Universe, taken through the Great Lick Telescope.[5]

The *Brighton Herald* was particularly complimentary on Smith's performance:

> The word 'fascinating', which has long been adopted by the lecturer, is scarcely too strong an adjective with which to designate the astronomical entertainments which are now being given at the Aquarium ... quality is well marked in the series of very fine views and mechanical apparatus with which something of those glories is illustrated, and by the easy and genial flow of explanatory comment from the lecturer with which the views are accompanied.[6]

What this lecture introduces us to is Smith's serious interest in astronomy. This was recognised professionally in February 1896 when he was elected a Fellow of the Royal Astronomical Society. As an FRAS, he may have used either lantern slides or photographs from the Society within his own lantern lectures.[7]

Smith was re-engaged by the Aquarium as the sole performer for the afternoons and evenings of the week starting 16 March 1896. On this occasion he offered the January lecture as well as two new ones. Each one was performed four times, making a total of twelve separate performances during the course of the week. The lecture titles were: THE GLORIES OF THE HEAVENS; OR, A TOUR THROUGH SPACE, TWENTY THOUSAND LEAGUES UNDER THE SEA; A ROMANTIC AND STARTLING TRIP WITH JULES VERNE and OUR GLORIOUS EMPIRE; A PICTORIAL AND DIORAMIC TOUR THROUGH JOHN BULL'S DOMINIONS.[8] The lectures were devised as three distinct journey narratives across air, sea and land. They exploited Malden's subject matter and, in part, addressed the aquatic context. The *Sussex Daily News*, in its positive review of THE GLORIES OF THE HEAVENS, now introduced him as a Fellow of the Royal Astronomical Society.[9]

Smith's lecture TWENTY THOUSAND LEAGUES UNDER THE SEA, and the words "with Jules Verne", also foregrounded his interest in contemporary science fantasy and his own pleasure in assuming an imaginary role. The lecture was described as "illustrative of Jules Verne's well known story".[10] This evidence situates Smith within that particular readership in the 1890s which was inspired by Verne's fictional journeys as found in *Five Weeks in a Balloon* (1863), *A Journey to the Centre of the Earth* (1864), *From the Earth to the Moon* (1866), *Twenty Thousand Leagues Under the Sea* (1870) and *Around the World in Eighty Days* (1873). It also places Smith as an entertainer who was aware of the high profile of Verne's fantastic adventures and the commercial value of aligning his lantern lectures with this famous author.

Smith's third lecture, OUR GLORIOUS EMPIRE, also declared his allegiance to contemporary patriotism and imperialism. In its review entitled "Around the World with a Magic Lantern", the Brighton Herald stated

> Among many cities and many people Mr Smith passes with his pictures with a few well-chosen words about each, and always with a well-timed and much-applauded recognition of the loyalty of those brethren of ours across the seas, the Colonists who when the clouds seemed to be gathering were prompt to avow themselves as

loyal sons of the old country. This tour round the world has been received with great favour.[11]

For the week starting Monday, 29 March 1897, Smith returned to the Aquarium to present the same set of lantern lectures as mounted at the venue in March 1896, but with a significant difference. "Animated photographs" were now presented at the conclusion of each lecture. This was Smith's first public engagement at which he had exhibited his own "animated photographs" and the first time that film had been incorporated into a lantern lecture in Brighton. As it had in the previous year, the *Brighton Herald* was particularly complimentary of Smith's performance and his choice of topical subject matter.

> It was positively inspiriting to hear at the Aquarium on Monday night a series of rounds of applause such as had not been evoked there for some time past. The occasion was a dioramic entertainment by Mr G. Albert Smith, F.R.A.S., illustrative of "Our Glorious Empire". Several causes combined to awaken the interest of the audience. On the eve of the Record Reign celebrations [the Diamond Jubilee of 1897], such an exhibition has a peculiar fitness to the spirit of the times, and these pictorial suggestions of the magnificence of the British Empire make a direct and moving appeal to our sentiments of patriotism and 'Rule Britanniaism'. Moreover the photographic pictures that yield such interesting glimpses of our possessions in all quarters of the globe are of special excellence; and Mr Smith makes a most agreeable guide. ... The dioramic effects include the discharge of a torpedo and the blowing up of a vessel, moonlight effects on water that looks positively liquid, the spray of Niagara, and the illumination of, and display of fireworks from, the great Canadian Ice Palace.[12]

Smith had transformed himself from being a popular mesmerist into a professional lanternist with special interests in journey narratives, modern Britain and natural phenomena. Besides the influence of Malden, it is also very likely that the structure and content of Smith's lectures were informed by the moving panorama entertainments designed and presented by the Poole Brothers. Their "pictorial tours", known by the name of "Myriorama" ("to view many scenes and objects"), travelled across Britain in the 1880s and 1890s and frequently visited Brighton and Hove.

Nurturing Lantern Studies

As these examples show, there is material available for wide-ranging research on lantern topics: contemporary references, the possibility of locating slides and other artefacts, supporting texts, and identifiable individuals who are known in this and other contexts. The histories of the lantern, as embodied by objects (e.g. slides, projectors, catalogues), the practices of lanternists and the meanings of their performances are eminently available for discovery and analysis. Significant research on the lantern has been and is being undertaken by a few scholars and the Magic Lantern Society has served as a valuable cluster for this work. This present publication is evidence too of the important research on the lantern being undertaken at various institutions.

But these studies are found at the margins of academic work within Film Studies, the histories of Art and Visual Culture and Victorian Studies. Why is this? What has kept the lantern on the fringes of scholarship? Is it because there still persists the notion that it was only a precursor of a more significant phenomenon – the arrival of film and the cinema? From this perspective, the lantern usually serves Film Studies as a proto-cinematic phenomenon, an anterior, primitive form. Without a doubt the other issue has been one of resources. The key obstacle that has thwarted research into the lantern has been very limited scholarly access to the surviving primary resources. So what can now be done to invigorate lantern studies?

I would suggest that two interventions can be made. One is conceptual, pedagogical and of relevance to contemporary archival practice. It is about advocating for the adoption of "Screen Studies" or "Screen History" as a subject discipline. I find this concept very enabling because it places the lantern within a particular historical framework that addresses the wider perspectives that are brought into focus when we see, from a longitudinal position, the relationships between the lantern, film, television and the networked and interactive digital practices of the present. Screen Studies addresses four centuries of screen practice. This is a history where the magic lantern and film are positioned as equivalences and play equal parts in a history that is shaped by a series of innovations, continuations and transformations. As Charles Musser emphasised as long ago as 1984, in his important article "Toward a History of Screen Practice", "Screen practice always has a technological component, a repertoire of representational strategies and a cultural function – all of which are undergoing constant interrelated change".[13]

Screen Studies therefore addresses each screen practice and the dynamic inter-connectedness between them. Its mission, as I interpret it, is to understand this history both diachronically (across time) and synchronically (at a moment in time) and to address how we have expressed our lives, ideas and stories through particular screen media and their means of representation. Screen Studies and the practice of writing screen history is therefore not about privileging particular media, practices and practitioners and not about conceiving this history as a set of phases or stages that are linear and successive (one practice / medium following another). It is about engaging with a plurality of histories, discourses and meanings within each medium and between the media.

In my own professional life and with colleagues at the University of Brighton, we've taken two steps to embrace this philosophy of Screen Studies. Our publicly-funded regional archive was known, when it was launched in 1992 as the South East Film and Video Archive. In 2006 we changed our name to Screen Archive South East. This reflected the archive's shift from being solely focussed on the moving image (film and video) to having a wider interest in screen technologies, histories and practices from the lantern to personal mobile devices in the early 21st century. The second step was to create an undergraduate degree dedicated to Screen Studies. This University's BA Screen Studies started in 2008 and has proved to be very successful with lecturers and students.

The other intervention is beginning to be made by Lucerna. Based at Universität Trier and in conjunction with the Kent Museum of the Moving Image, the Magic Lantern Society and colleagues at the Universities of Brighton, Indiana and Utrecht, the Lucerna project is building a free online resource that will underpin research into all aspects of the history of the magic lantern, and ultimately offer a repository for new work. Its database presents information on slides drawn from a wide range of public and private collections including titles, dates, production and commercial data and accompanying readings. Illustrated by digital versions of each slide, it is developing into a unique resource dedicated to lantern's history and character. Critical to its conception was the realisation that we can only begin to "scientifically" analyse the lantern's history when we can begin to see and share surviving slides and other documents. The conceptualisation of the lantern which this article offers has been shaped by my participation within the Lucerna project.

Notes

1. Ian Christie, "Through a Glass Brightly: the Magic Lantern in History", *British Academy Review* (February 2002): 22.

2. See for example: Richard Crangle, Mervyn Heard and Ine van Dooren (eds), *Realms of Light: Uses and Perceptions of the Magic Lantern from the 17th to the 21st Century* (London: Magic Lantern Society, 2005); Deac Rossell, *Laterna Magica / Magic Lantern Vol. 1* (Stuttgart: Füsslin, 2008); Laurent Mannoni, *The Great Art of Light and Shadow: Archaeology of the Cinema* (Exeter: University of Exeter Press, 2000); and Barbara Maria Stafford and Frances Terpak, *Devices of Wonder: From the World in a Box to Images on a Screen* (Los Angeles: Getty Research Institute, 2001).

3. Advertisements, *Brighton & Hove Guardian*, respectively (9 January 1889): 5; (27 February 1889): 4; (13 March 1889): 4; (3 April 1889): 4.

4. "The West Pier Entertainments", *Brighton Herald* (6 April 1895): 5.

5. Advertisement for the Brighton Aquarium, *Brighton Herald* (4 January 1896): 4. The Lick Observatory, on Mount Hamilton, California, was founded in 1888 and photographs of views from its telescope were turned into lantern slides, stereo views and publications.

6. "Up Among the Stars at the Brighton Aquarium", *Brighton Herald* (11 January 1896): 5.

7. *Monthly Notices of the Royal Astronomical Society*, vol. 56, no. 5 (14 February 1896): 174. "George Albert Smith, St Ann's Gardens, Brighton" and six others "were balloted for and duly elected Fellows of the Society".

8. Advertisement for the Brighton Aquarium, *Brighton Herald* (14 March 1896): 4.

9. "Brighton Aquarium", *Sussex Daily News* (17 March 1896): 2.

10. "Brighton Aquarium", *Sussex Daily News* (17 March 1896): 2. It is interesting to note that in Smith's cash book (1897 section, held at the BFI, London) there is an entry dated 27 March 1897 for "Whiskers & spirit gum". Given that Jules Verne had a full beard and moustache, were these items required by Smith so that he could alter his facial appearance to play the role of Verne at his Aquarium lantern lecture?

11. "Around the World with a Magic Lantern", *Brighton Herald* (21 March 1896): 5.

12. "The Brighton Aquarium", *Brighton Herald* (3 April 1897): 5.

13. Charles Musser, "Toward a History of Screen Practice", *Quarterly Review of Film Studies* 9:1 (Winter 1984): 60.

Ine van Dooren

Our Magic Lantern Heritage: Archiving a Past Medium that Nearly Never Was

In the 21st century digital image technology has firmly imposed itself on the world map; its "screens" take many forms and are multiple and common-place. It is rapidly changing the frameworks for technology, culture and perceived histories. Or as the British photographer Eamonn McCabe puts it, "we enter a new 'memory land'; a new way of capturing and remembering means a new way of looking at ourselves and the world around us".[1]

Analogue image technology is becoming obsolete. The celluloid film medium is lingering on the brink of extinction. Archivists, artists and historians do in many ways hail the "digital revolution", yet also ask ourselves: what do we lose? Especially in this time of marked transition relentlessly pushing us forward there is a need for reflection. What exactly are the archival and cultural legacies of screen practices, and how can we safeguard them from fading away to become unfamiliar and uncharted realms?

The analogue film medium was once so universally present, we might think it immune to disappearing from our knowledge of the past. But there is an instructive example for us in that other versatile mass screen medium that has practically vanished from view. How could it happen that the magic lantern was so easily forgotten? It is illuminating that in the present time of transition from analogue film to digital file there is a growing interest in re-visiting, re-assessing and re-interpreting magic lantern history.

My personal encounter with the magic lantern began in the 1980s. Repre-senting the Netherlands Film Museum, I was able to participate in a two-day extravaganza of presentations and shows organised by the Magic Lantern Society. I was enthralled and hooked, and wanted to find out more about this fascinating medium of which I had no knowledge. However that turned out to be more easily wished than done. In academia, lantern screen practice was (and in many ways still is) a "hidden history". Most books I was reading as a student presented the magic lantern as a form of "pre-cinema": magical and pretty, but a rather primitive precursor to film, meriting only a few introduc-tory pages, a mere footnote.

Facing page: Church Army Lantern Department slide carrying box, used to send slides by post or rail transport, c.1900.

In the world of museums and archives a similar lack of knowledge exists, with the result that much of the lantern's long and versatile history is unrecognised or misunderstood. Where institutions own lanterns or slides (and a great many of them do), frequently incidental pieces of apparatus and some beautiful hand-coloured pictures are put on display with little context or as a preface to other histories. Many collections of the more typical standard-size slides are put into cupboards, without an understanding of what they are or they mean.[2]

Of course there are various reasons why lantern history has been marginalised, but one important inherent feature of the medium itself may have a lot to do with it: namely the magic lantern's distinctive chameleonic trait. Practically from the time of its invention in the mid 17th century the lantern medium was a constantly changing and widening set of practices, instead of becoming more and more specific in what it was and what it was not. Over the centuries it did what it has always been extremely good at: it incorporated, amalgamated and adapted. Its uses were enormously diverse and its appropriation of other media through re-production, re-editing and re-presentation can be said to be the lantern's strength.

The lantern was and is a medium of re-use and re-shuffling. There are distinctly defined slide series and sets that can be traced through makers' catalogues and contemporary advertisements. But lanternists could also choose their own mixture of serial imagery to suit their particular sequential projections. Some images were added, others dismissed (or lost or broken) and some were given a different place. Some were unique, only ever available to one individual showperson. The travelling showpeople of the 18th century, carrying their trade on their back from place to place, were of course limited in their choice of pictures but could add actuality or change their shows to play to their varying audiences. Lecturers in general may have kept to available scripted texts or known information, but live delivery always allowed for improvisation. The 19th century saw an increase in standardisation through market manufacturing and regulated distribution systems, but choices in the grouping of sets and differences in presentation continued to influence what people got to see and how. The lantern was, in short, a performance medium which was just as ephemeral as any other.

However the practitioners of the medium itself never seemed bothered by its largely populist appeal or its "Jack of all trades" status: on the contrary it became a mass medium precisely because of these features. Commercial producers of lantern slides, far from craving the unique, were always on the hunt to re-distribute their own sets or find cheaper means to repackage in slide form what was already available in print, photography or painting.

Maybe this chameleon trait and range of possibilities have also played a part in the lantern's academic abstruseness. Its diversity of uses, as well as its re-use of representations from other media, make it difficult to define as a discipline. It is interesting that, in small but encouraging ways, lantern research is mainly beginning to find academic fruition in deliberately interdisciplinary contexts like this present volume.

So one problem with lantern research is that there are so many histories, approachable from as diverse a range of interests. And the way into these histories through empirical research is often not straightforward. Until now only a small amount of slides, apparatus and ephemera have been easily available for researchers, in piecemeal and unsystematic ways. A large part of the lantern's heritage is in private collections; meanwhile many of the artefacts in public museums and archives have not been fully catalogued and are not readily accessible. Lantern history can be traced in an extremely wide variety of primary and secondary printed texts (books, newspapers, parish records, magazines, club minutes etc.). But much of the information is buried amongst other histories and again not easily retrievable.

The lantern's somewhat doomed association with the film medium has also hampered an understanding of its historical significance. While relegated to the status of "pre-cinema" it was not researched under its own terms. This is especially relevant considering that the lantern medium is a combination of (optical) representation and live performance in ways that the commercial cinema is not; the subordinate role in cinema history tends to mask this important feature. The diversity in reception, narrativisation and perform-ability are crucial in the understanding of lantern history.

The misconception that the arrival of cinema more or less instantaneously swept away the outdated lantern medium is one of the myths that needs to be rectified. When editing *Realms of Light*[3] in 2005 it became yet again very clear that the lantern did not disappear overnight, nor even over a period of ten years. Throughout the period before World War II and even into the 1950s, the "traditional" optical lantern with standard glass slides was used in schools, in small village halls, by institutions such as the Church Army and by amateur photographic clubs.

Just as important was the development of another associated screen practice: the "modern" slide projector of the 1950s, whose only real difference from the "traditional" lantern (until the appearance of magazine-type projectors like the Kodak Carousel) was in using a smaller image format. The first period still saw the use of glass slides, but in the 1960s to 1980s a standardisation of the 35mm celluloid slide format in plastic or cardboard mounts led to a massive use in education as well as in the home. Artists working with the medium staged enchanting and complex installations, in certain ways reminiscent of the phantasmagoria and dissolving view shows of the now "long gone" magic lantern.

Recently I attended an event described as a "Festival of Light" and was pleasantly surprised to see a rather magical presentation using a 1960s slide projector.[4] The artist used hand-drawn images to create well-known lantern favourites such as panoramic movement and image superimposition, dissolv-ing from one image to the next to create a beautiful and enigmatic screen display. When talking to the artist it was in a sad way no surprise that he was unfamiliar with the history of the lantern, but nonetheless it was pleasing to see that the "magic" lives on.

And even in the digital age we are familiar with PowerPoint, Keynote and other applications that use the presentation format of serial image projection accompanied by speech or sound. They apply the same technical principles of lens system, light source and screen to entertain and educate their audiences.

To rediscover the magic lantern as screen practice we need to address the diversity as well as the specificity of the medium. This implies an interdisciplinary approach enhanced by a strategic academic and archival institutional recognition. But this only becomes practical, in any structured and sustainable way, if it is based on better ways of gathering and sharing information about the medium and its uses, and on some standardisation of terms and best practice.

A good case in point, based on my experience as the Archivist for Screen Archive South East, University of Brighton, has been the acquisition by that institution of the Hecht Collection.[5] This extensive collection of slides and equipment was shaped by an accidental rescue and a long-standing educational interest. One day in the 1960s Hermann Hecht, an art teacher, was passing the premises of the Church Army on Edgware Road in north-west London.[6] The CA had been an avid user of the magic lantern in their propaganda, but the glass slides were now deemed impractical (35mm celluloid slides were the way forward) and their entire stock was being dumped into a skip in the street. Hermann was horrified and was given a few hours to arrange a van and rescue the bulk of the collection.

One tendency detected when establishing a collection's provenance is "migration". Lantern slides have always easily changed hands, from producer to distributor to exhibitor and back. Hire libraries and individually purchased collections reshuffled what was on offer. Exchanges and re-issuing occurred repeatedly, not to mention the attributive ownership that creates collections when collectors purchase artefacts related to their specific interest, and the deliberate and un-deliberate acquisitions by archives and museums. Over the years the Church Army collection had grown and diminished according to demand. They produced some of the slides themselves but also used sets from other manufacturers. For practical purposes images were sometimes renumbered, making provenance even more difficult to ascertain.

When in many respects lantern history faded into obscurity there were always people like Hermann and Ann Hecht who kept the lights burning. Private collectors, often wonderfully obsessive enthusiasts, have amassed a vast quantity of lantern heritage objects. The magic lantern medium as a live (theatrical) practice has found a continuation in the variety of presentations and performances still delivered every year by collectors and showpeople.[7] Organisations like the international Magic Lantern Societies[8] have played a pivotal role in producing and assembling research on a wide range of the lantern's history, publishing regular journals and a number of books and playing an instrumental role in the development of the Lucerna web resource. But in all cases, whether done by individuals or organisations, these have been relatively small and self-contained activities and projects.

In 1998 Screen Archive South East took over the custodianship of the Hecht Collection. Since then additional material from the Church Army organisation has been obtained. In 2006 a significant amount of slides from this collection were digitised by Trier University, and these are now accessible to view through the *Lucerna* web resource.

Recently curatorial re-consideration linked to actual as well as virtual demands has led museums and archives to start rummaging around in their cupboards and re-addressing the medium's collection value. Hopefully this will lead to curation and preservation policies that place lantern artefacts within the specificity of their history as well as within an overall heritage of screen practices. The application of knowledge can help to avoid decisions informed by budget cuts leading to the de-accessioning of lantern materials, but this depends on that knowledge being easily and freely available.

This is broadly the purpose of the Lucerna magic lantern web resource.[9] In its most general form this is conceived as a platform for students, researchers and collectors as well as for curators and archivists. As a tool for finding information it can also be an effective opportunity for establishing professional connections. At present there is no widely shared and recognised network of professionals specialising in the lantern medium. Many museums and archives hold lantern artefacts, mostly amongst other (and often for them more important) collections, for example where film or photography is the dominant interest or in the context of local history. There are as yet few recognised conservation methods and techniques specifically developed for lantern or slide archival practice. Digitisation has started but the complexity of specific archival requirements and the expense of the required technological management puts a strain on institutional resources. There is a lack of shared expertise and this makes it difficult to make informed choices.

It is in the nature of museums and archives to care for "things" that can illuminate the past. The lure of the artefact may however bias us in our understanding of lantern practices. It is easy to get excited by beautifully hand-painted slides and mahogany biunial lanterns, but aesthetic criteria should not be the sole reason for deciding what is "better" or "more important". Millions of images were produced for the lantern, some unique and exquisite, others unremarkable and seemingly uninteresting. They all are part of this medium's history. They were all produced and screened for a reason. Of course we cannot, and would not wish to, collect *everything* but how do archives select what to collect and preserve? How do museums select what to display? And how can archives and museums determine collection selection criteria when, in this profession at least, still so little is known about the magic lantern?

Preservation demands and curatorial appraisals become more effective when guided by a well-informed and critical understanding of the medium's cultural and historical context. This is easier said then done. Archives and museums hold a rich and tangible part of the lantern's history. The physical evidence of slides, apparatus and texts has survived, but their context needs to be reconstructed and interpreted, especially in all the variations and amalgamations present in the elusiveness of a live performance medium.

Maybe here the digital can help to reinstate the analogue, through resources like the Lucerna web resource. Digital reproduction offers a wide and proficient accessibility to a vastly growing amount of imagery and information. But it is creating a different experience, more mental, less focused than the tangible original materials. And this in turn may feed a longing to revisit the specificity and tactility associated with the analogue audio-visual experience of the lantern medium. Here digitally generated knowledge and access can help to raise awareness to properly care for our analogue legacies – not to replace them or discard them as "old" but to rediscover their fascinating heritage, bringing them out of the stuffy cupboards of forgotten pasts into vibrant explorations in the brave new world of the future.

Through developments like Lucerna it should be possible to offer an authored environment that can be easily uploaded to and downloaded from, and which can consequently help to uncover the wealth of the lantern's marginalised and hidden history. Audio-visual and screen heritage has become a leading factor in establishing our memory bank. We should take good care of it.

Notes

1. BBC television news item, featuring the opening of the art installation *Film*, a "homage to the dying medium of analogue film" by Tacita Dean at the Tate Modern Turbine Hall, London, 10 October 2011.

2. The "standard" size slide (3.25 inches square in Britain and some other European countries, 3.25 by 4 inches in the USA) was mass-produced photographically in vast quantities from the 1870s to the 1950s, and it is perhaps this widespread and relatively commonplace nature that makes it so difficult to appreciate.

3. Richard Crangle, Mervyn Heard and Ine van Dooren (eds), *Realms of Light: Uses and Perceptions of the Magic Lantern from the 17th to the 21st Century* (London: Magic Lantern Society, 2005).

4. William Lindley, *Variable Editions*, exhibited at the *Final Light* event (a celebration of the winter solstice), Phoenix Brighton, 21 December 2012.

5. Hermann and Ann Hecht were keen collectors and presenters of the Lantern. They are the author and editor of the renowned work *Pre-Cinema History: an Encyclopedia and Annotated Bibliography of the Moving Image Before 1896* (London: Bowker Saur / BFI, 1993).

6. The Church Army was established by Wilson Carlile in 1882 to mobilise ordinary people to experience the word of the gospel. The organisation is still active.

7. These performances are often local events and not widely advertised. Many presentations are free interpretations of the "Victorian" lantern entertainment. Some are illustrated local history talks. There is also a small group of professionals who work with the television and film industry on re-enactments and who deliver shows in art venues.

8. The Magic Lantern Society (www.magiclantern.org.uk) was founded in the UK in 1976, and the Magic Lantern Society of the United States and Canada (www.magiclanternsociety.org) was formed a few years later. Both organisations have a worldwide membership and hold regular international conventions and other meetings.

9. Lucerna Magic Lantern Web Resource, www.slides.uni-trier.de. This project is discussed in more detail in the following article.

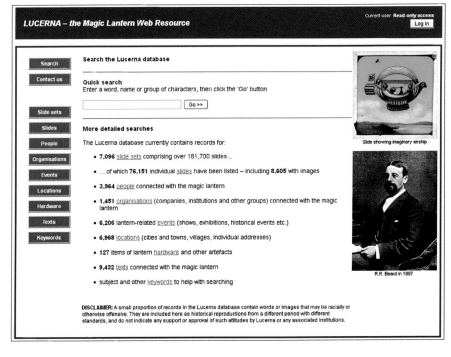

LUCERNA – the Magic Lantern Web Resource

Search the Lucerna database

Quick search
Enter a word, name or group of characters, then click the 'Go' button

Go >>

More detailed searches

The Lucerna database currently contains records for:

- **7,096** slide sets comprising over 181,700 slides...

- ... of which **76,151** individual slides have been listed – including **8,605** with images

- **3,964** people connected with the magic lantern

- **1,451** organisations (companies, institutions and other groups) connected with the magic lantern

- **6,206** lantern-related events (shows, exhibitions, historical events etc.)

- **6,968** locations (cities and towns, villages, individual addresses)

- **127** items of lantern hardware and other artefacts

- **9,432** texts connected with the magic lantern

- subject and other keywords to help with searching

Search

Contact us

Slide sets

Slides

People

Organisations

Events

Locations

Hardware

Texts

Keywords

Slide showing imaginary airship

R.R. Beard in 1897

DISCLAIMER: A small proportion of records in the Lucerna database contain words or images that may be racially or otherwise offensive. They are included here as historical reproductions from a different period with different standards, and do not indicate any support or approval of such attitudes by Lucerna or any associated institutions.

Richard Crangle

The Lucerna Magic Lantern Web Resource

This article offers an introduction to Lucerna, an ambitious and wide-ranging initiative to create an online resource with the aims of generating new interest and facilitating new work on the magic lantern in its social and historical contexts. This represents a revisiting of some points I raised in an essay published in 2000, discussing how lantern-based media have been neglected, or often misrepresented as "pre-cinema". One of my main arguments then was that "we need to make a more serious study of the nineteenth-century lantern trades, and we need to integrate our studies more closely".[1] I itemised a few aspects of this need:

- A clear and comprehensive picture of which companies operated when, their geographical and cultural spheres of influence, and the other companies they dealt with. [...]
- A reliable system of dating slides, based on careful analysis of manufacturers' catalogues and cross-referencing with other sources [which] implies some kind of database "union catalogue" of slide manufacture. [...]
- A reliable catalogue of published lantern lecture pamphlets and other "read-ings", cross-referenced to slide manufacture and to other sources of similar texts. [...]
- Some further work on development of lantern technology. [...]
- An understanding of the personalities of the trade, their backgrounds, and their ways into and out of the lantern business. [...]

But above all, what is important is coordination of this information. It is vital to be able to relate its various parts to each other; and to understand that complicated as it is, this is only part of an even larger picture which must also be considered.[2]

A lot of progress has been made, but it seems to me that the basic points of my 2000 argument remain valid.

Particularly in the later 19th century, the optical presentation of ideas permeated the great majority of areas of international culture, giving the basis for today's ubiquity of the screened image. The visual media of the 21st century, in their myriad forms, might seem fantastic to the practitioners of the 1890s and 1900s, yet might also remind them of a world they would recognise. This fundamental

---

Facing page: Lucerna online database, "Search" page with summary of database content.
www.slides.uni-trier.de/options.php

nature of the lantern image means that a clearer understanding of its develop-ment and uses would help us to grasp where we are now, culturally. Yet it remains an underappreciated area, at best peripheral to several established academic disciplines, at worst unknown. There are signs of a greater awareness among scholars that the projected image has a rich story to tell, but it remains difficult to approach in any systematic way.

One of the major problems is often (mis)understood to be a lack of primary resource material. There are certainly many portions of the 350-year history of the projected image for which there is a genuine lack of reliable material, forcing us to rely on hearsay and assumptions which may or may not be true – examples would be the "Savoyard" tradition of travelling entertainment of the 18th and early 19th centuries, or the extended role of projection in necro-mancy and magic (addressed by some excellent recent work on the phantas-magoria, but still an area where our current version of the story depends partly on myth).[3]

But for the richest portion of projected image history, the commercial heyday of the magic lantern – the five decades from the 1870s to the 1910s, with roots back to the 1820s – the problem is not lack of surviving material, but a combination of lack of awareness of the material that survives and lack of access to it. Partly as a result of those deficiencies, there is also a lack of accurate connections between the material that we do have and its historical and social contexts.

As the essays in this collection show, there is material to be found, and when looked at systematically and in context it forms a rich basis for research into areas stretching far beyond the conventional interests in development of moving pictures from technological, technical, artistic and commercial stand-points. Over those 350 years I suggest there have been no areas of human endeavour or parts of the physical world that were not touched by the use of projected images to portray them or contribute to their development and dissemination.

That suggests that what is needed, to investigate the history of the lantern image more fully, is twofold: some archaeology, in unearthing new sources of information and creative intelligent interpretation of what is found; but just as importantly a coherent scheme of resource discovery, making the discoveries available to all comers and, most important of all, making it possible to connect them together.

Private and public resources

Some of these problems arise because of the ways material and knowledge have been amassed over the past 50-60 years; this must be equally true of other popular media that have fallen from general currency and been relegated to the status of collectable antiques. Essentially there are two broad sources of material: private collections and public institutions. Each has strengths and weaknesses, and neither is particularly easily accessible, though many institu-

Lucerna record for slide set *Grizzie and Jim* (service of song: T.T. Wing, 22 slides, n.d.).
www.slides.uni-trier.de/set/index.php?id=3004232

tions are now making better efforts to describe their holdings and make them more available.

Private collectors – many of whom are very knowledgeable and committed – have been vital for the survival of much of the known material. Without individuals like John and Bill Barnes, Ron Morris and Janet Hill, David Henry, and Hermann and Ann Hecht, to name only a few, the inevitable process of collective forgetting and throwing-away of "old-fashioned" items would have eliminated a far greater proportion of the material. The societies into which these individuals have coalesced have proved vital for exchange and dissemination not only of the original materials, but more importantly ideas and discussions about their history.[4]

Yet private collectors, to generalise, have often been enthusiastic and comprehensive but not systematic. Neither have they always been objective about the significance of the material they collect: given a choice between something visually attractive or unusual, and something dull or routine, and with limited

Richard Crangle

Lucerna record for slide 4 of *Grizzie and Jim* (T.T. Wing, n.d.).
www.slides.uni-trier.de/slide/index.php?id=5020765

money to spend, the exotic will always take precedence. This is quite under-standable, but over time leads to a skewing of impressions of the original material. Magnified through a culture of buying, selling and collection-building for reasons other than historical completeness (including the desire to give attractive and entertaining shows to modern audiences), this leads to loss of context and scattering of related items far and wide. "Boring" photographic slides representing travelogues and social issues, or the many Bible stories and other religious subjects, have not been coveted by collectors in the same way as visually-stunning chromatropes and hand-painted dissolving views, and so are under-represented in private collections and works arising from them. Other professionally-based questions like conservation practice, in continuous tension with use of original material for performance, are often viewed with suspicion if not outright contempt.

Archives and museums have sometimes been more systematic than private collectors in their acquisitions and have given the material a more stable home, albeit one which may be a forgotten cupboard in the basement whose contents

Lucerna record for Nannie Preston (1873-1950), slide artist.
www.slides.uni-trier.de/person/index.php?id=6002334

were understood by a colleague who retired years ago. But these institutions tend to lack knowledge or interest in the material, and in harsh economic times the unpopular and unregarded materials are at greater risk of "de-accessioning" to save money. Some (particularly some of the better cinema museums) make more or less successful attempts to place lantern material in historical context and give an idea of its range, but this is frequently in a technological history rather than an examination of the social contexts of the projected image. A few examples of lantern hardware and some attractive slide images often have to represent the development of an entire visual medium over a lifetime longer than that of the steam engine.

There is also an underlying problem with institutional explanation of a performance medium. It is difficult to present thousands of slide images to capture

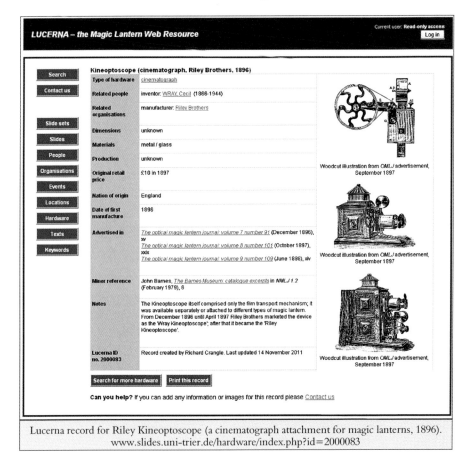

Lucerna record for Riley Kineoptoscope (a cinematograph attachment for magic lanterns, 1896).
www.slides.uni-trier.de/hardware/index.php?id=2000083

the essence of their original meanings, particularly for modern visitor-spectators who pass by them in a second or two. The original performance contexts were ephemeral in any case, and impossible to recreate in anything other than a historical pastiche, but this is an area where performance by private collectors has more to tell us than static institutional display.

A third type of resource

Recent technological developments – the falling cost of digital still and moving images, and widespread flexible distribution via the Internet – have opened up possibilities for a third approach to this hidden material. It has become possible to present masses of information and images in ways that are more accessible, can be searched for topics and themes, and can be updated easily and quickly. More importantly, it has become possible to do this outside large institutions: although this presents resourcing problems, it also permits individuals to contribute expertise and information which might otherwise be disregarded.

Leaving aside the important question of ensuring consistent image quality, in the last ten to fifteen years it has become straightforward to circulate digital

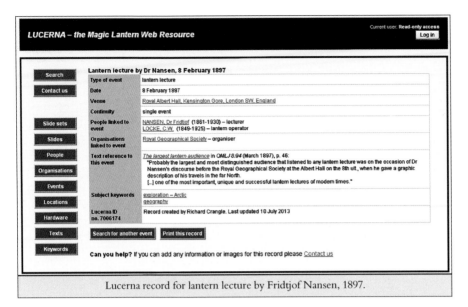

Lucerna record for lantern lecture by Fridtjof Nansen, 1897.

images of slides and artefacts which previously required a visit to a distant location, always assuming that their location was known in the first place. Of course digital reproductions do not give an accurate impression of the experience of (for example) viewing original slides projected by a lantern, with an audience. Placing digital images of a sequence of slides on an internet site, perhaps with accompanying written or audio text, may move us a little closer to the performed medium, but retains some of the problems of a static museum display. In short digitisation does not substitute for the experience of seeing, holding or using original artefacts, but it greatly simplifies and amplifies the distribution of awareness of them.

The implication of all this is that within recent years it has become possible to assemble just the sort of "union catalogue" towards which I was wishfully hinting in "What do those old slides mean?" The combination of open-access software for large-scale databases, easy creation of digital images, and internet distribution, has changed the "entry level" for the large resource that is implied by trying to increase access to such a wide-ranging medium. Whereas previously a large commitment would have been needed from one or more major institutions, which in a field which is still seen as a minority interest would be unlikely, it has now become possible for small groups of individuals (with, it has to be said, valuable technical and other support from sympathetic institutions) to begin to create resources that make a difference.

The Lucerna Database

In the autumn of 2006 some interested parties who had reached more or less the same conclusion, though from slightly different directions, convened at Universität Trier for a workshop to explore how possible this might be.[5]

Among the outcomes of this very fruitful week of discussions were an outline of some high-level concepts which we thought essential to developing a "magic lantern web resource", and a detailed relational database design which aimed to accommodate "everything" relating to the history of the magic lantern.

The database design collated this multi-faceted historical area into seven basic categories, each with a full set of descriptive data:

- **Slide sets**: most commercially-produced slides were published in identified sets, and this remains the most convenient way of identifying individual slides. This category also encompasses privately-produced or other unique sets, and single slides ("sets of one") as appropriate.
- **Slides**: the individual slides that make up each set are listed individually and linked to the sets to which they belong, with digital images where available.
- **People**: individuals connected with production of slides, hardware and related texts, also historical and other persons represented in slides.
- **Organisations**: businesses (from sole traders to long-lasting companies), societies, campaigning organisations, churches and other bodies which were involved in making, using or trading in lanterns or slides.
- **Events**: events (lectures, shows etc.) at which lanterns are known to have been used; also historical and other events (wars, expeditions, royal occasions, etc.) represented in slides.
- **Locations**: individual addresses where people or organisations were based, or which served as venues for lantern events; villages, towns and cities (which can be used for grouping events or people); nations or regions described by slide sets.
- **Hardware**: descriptive details of lanterns and accessories, with illustrations where appropriate.
- **Texts**: articles referring to lanterns and slides; "reading" pamphlets published to accompany slide sets; reference sources, histories and handbooks; websites, archives and other resources.

All these areas can be linked to others – so a typical "person" record carries biographical details and portraits where available, and links to: slide sets to which the person is known to have contributed (photographer, artist, model etc.); slides which show their image; organisations they were connected to; events they participated in; locations where they lived or worked; hardware they invented or designed; texts they authored or texts which refer to them. Equally a slide set, along with its dating and description, will potentially link to all its individual slides (with images); companies that produced and/or distributed it; people identified with its production; "reading" texts, with facsimiles where available; references to it in trade literature, advertisements etc.; collections known to hold examples; related slide sets (e.g. remakes or adaptations); and subject keywords and other metadata, including references to people, events and locations as subjects. The processes for entering data and linking it are relatively straightforward, with online editing forms available to authorised users via a password system.

To date most of the database content relates to British slides of the late 19th and early 20th centuries. This is a reflection of the main data sources incorporated so far, rather than an editorial decision – the overall aim is to create a data resource uniting information from all countries and historical periods. The first dataset added was a set of research findings listing around 6,000 lantern events in Britain in the later 19th century, drawn from mainly religious periodicals as part of the "Screen1900" research project at Universität Trier.[6] Several thousand slide images, and a large amount of data for individual slide titles, were drawn from the same research project. To this was added a database of around 3,500 slide sets, based on my research from manufacturers' catalogues, followed by the catalogue of the Magic Lantern Society's Slide Readings Library, comprising over 2,500 items. The dataset has continued to develop from similar sources, especially slide catalogues and the British trade paper *The Optical Magic Lantern Journal*.[7] At the time of writing the Lucerna database includes over 7,000 slide sets totalling over 180,000 individual slides (of which 75,000 have been listed individually and 8,500 include images), plus several thousand records in most of the other categories.

The real key to making this kind of resource creatively useful, though, lies less in the quantity of data than in the quality of indexing and cataloguing. At present in the Lucerna database this is at an early stage, but the structures for applying more sophisticated metadata have been built in from the start, and the current relatively basic level of indexing is simply a reflection of the amount of labour available. It is possible to search any of the categories above in several different ways, as appropriate for their descriptive data, and there is an overall "quick search" mechanism which searches all categories simultaneously for a string of text. In addition a system of subject **keywords** is used for cataloguing slide sets and texts – at present quite simple, but evolving towards adoption of one of the standard metadata systems, probably ICONCLASS.[8] The combination of subject keywords with several of the other categories (names of people as subjects of slide sets, for example) will allow the detailed indexing needed for flexible and reliable searching of the potentially vast body of data.

The wider Magic Lantern Web Resource

The database itself represents a key part of the overall project as conceived in the early workshop discussions, functioning as the foundation on which other resources can be based. The overall scope is much wider, with concepts including:

- **Internationality**: the lantern has always been an international medium, and its history is full of exports and imports of material, technology and personnel. To understand interactions between different national traditions and trades, we need a single resource which allows comparison and analysis across borders and time. Although most of the current content relates to C19[th]-20th British slide production, the design will support similar treatment of data in any language and from any background.

- **Open source software**: to avoid becoming tied to a single commercial format, the database and the web resource are built in freely-available standard web software (MySQL database with PHP web pages). This makes it relatively easy to develop and customise for different needs (including, potentially, custom views for inclusion in institutions' own web sites and online catalogues).

- **Public domain content**: the intention behind Lucerna is to broaden awareness of lanterns and slides for all comers; this implies that its content must be freely available to anyone, for any purpose compatible with the other aims of the project. We hope to avoid some of the issues of private "ownership" of images and data that can impede wider interest and research. Having said that, there are genuine issues of intellectual property, so the compromise is to include relatively low-resolution images, suitable for internet viewing but not good enough for projection or print publication.

- **Everything is (potentially) relevant**: no piece of information is too small or insignificant, everything has a place and potentially connects with anything else, and definitions of what is relevant are quite open-ended. In practice, of course, we have to make judgements about where we place our limited resources for best effect, but in principle any detail can be accommodated, and the fact of its inclusion in the database makes it available where previously it might have remained hidden. There are many tiny details in the existing body of data, apparently unconnected at present but possibly just needing the arrival of another detail to make them significant.

- **Work in progress**: many aspects of lantern history are quite imprecise, and it will never be possible to provide an absolutely definitive statement of what was made when, by whom, for whom and so on. Even in well-documented areas – like the slide manufacture of the turn of the 20th century, where relatively plentiful catalogue data survives – display a great deal of uncertainty and will always be subject to revision in the light of new evidence. This kind of flexibility is one strength of a database, of course, but it remains an important challenge to anyone involved in research in this area. However much data we record, and however convincing the conclusions we draw, the project will never be finished.

- **Collection management**: since so much of the source material is in private hands, in many cases without systematic cataloguing, there is great value in establishing a common cataloguing standard and using the same database to catalogue disparate collections. This has been designed into Lucerna, in the form of basic collection management functions. Some data (description and/or images of an artefact, details of related people or organisations, etc.) is shared publicly, some (location of specific examples, condition, provenance, notes relating to a given institution) can be kept private for internal use. The database benefits by gathering information and images that otherwise might not come to light; the collector or institution benefits by using a free resource and drawing on already-established metadata and links.

- **Collaboration**: because the materials are so widely distributed and potentially so numerous, it is essential that Lucerna should exist as a collaborative enterprise between institutions and individuals. This can take a number of different forms, such as material contributions like IT support; provision of staff time for resource development or data input; making images, datasets or research results available for inclusion; or simply allowing access to materials held. There is no particular financial commitment, although it would be useful for new partners to be able to contribute to project resources in some form or other. One primary aim is that the resource should become the natural repository for sharing data and other outcomes from research projects running independently of the Lucerna project itself; this might ultimately evolve into a moderated online journal, although that remains some distance away.

- **Multiple access points**: a common criticism of a relatively limited area of study like the lantern is that it only presents itself to the initiated and neglects the needs of those who encounter it for the first time, or as a peripheral aspect of their own main interest. The Lucerna concept is to offer multiple "gateways" which cater for different users' needs: for example an entry-level introduction to lanterns and slides; a more specific entry point for collectors or researchers of particular materials or subjects; a comparative entry point highlighting connections of this medium to others; and so on.

- **Performance**: as discussed earlier, static presentation of slides and other materials does not convey any sense of their use in performance practice. It is important, then, to include reproductions of lantern performances using digital video. Processes for creation and reproduction of performances, discussion of their degree of faithfulness to original practices, and non-technical issues like copyright and financing, remain to be worked out, but as a platform for their presentation the Lucerna resource, allowing linking to extensive metadata on slides shown and other details, would be ideal.

Resourcing the resource

For all the reductions in cost and simplifications of some of the technological processes, there remains a large and problematic question behind setting up a resource like Lucerna. The work so far has been generally voluntary and unfunded. There has been some very welcome support from some of the institutions concerned in funding workshops and meetings, and other minor project funding for some specific aspects of the development work, not to mention hosting the database on servers at Universität Trier. The project has got off the ground and reached a state where (for all the limitations around what the database does not yet contain, or the aspects of the larger vision which remain attractive ideas for the future) it is beginning to be used by researchers and others to find information about lanterns, slides and the peripheral aspects of their history. Yet the online database has so far been assembled and populated by a very small group of people working in spare time, with much of the work done by only one or two of them.

This has advantages and disadvantages, akin to those I mentioned earlier in discussing private and public collections and material sources. On one hand, being lean and fit means that it has been possible to avoid a lot of the internal obstacles to development which are inherent in an "institutional" approach to a new project. On the other hand, having a skeleton staff means that the project is potentially vulnerable to changes in interest or personal circumstances.

So the challenge for the Lucerna project in the coming few years is not only the vastness of the enterprise on which it has embarked, nor the scattered nature of the source material, but also the need to find an organisational structure that promotes permanence but preserves flexibility. The project also needs one or more "homes" in the sense of more formal relationships with institutions, or at least lasting communities of interested people who will be able to use and develop the resource in all the ways imagined. Implicit to all of these, of course, is some degree of reliable funding which will allow people to be involved on a more permanent and stable basis. The Lucerna Magic Lantern Web Resource has an important role to play, and its development and expansion have the potential to open up many new avenues in media history and other disciplines, and it would be worth the effort to find creative ways of enabling that to happen.

Notes

1. Richard Crangle, "What Do Those Old Slides Mean? or Why the Magic Lantern is Not an Important Part of Cinema History", in Simon Popple and Vanessa Toulmin (eds), *Visual Delights: Essays on the Popular and Projected Image in the 19th Century* (Trowbridge: Flicks Books, 2000), 16–24. This quotation is from p. 19.

2. Ibid., 19–20.

3. The "Savoyard" tradition is largely undocumented, and our impression of it based on contemporary prints and other indirect references; see Laurent Mannoni (ed. and trans Richard Crangle), *The Great Art of Light and Shadow: Archaeology of the Cinema* (Exeter: University of Exeter Press, 2000), chapter 4, and also Roger Gonin, "The Travelling Lantern of Auvergne" in *New Magic Lantern Journal [NMLJ]* 10:6 (Autumn 2010), 103–106. For recent work on the Phantasmagoria see Mannoni, op. cit., chapter 6 and Appendix B; Mervyn Heard, *Phantasmagoria: the Secret Life of the Magic Lantern* (Hastings: Projection Box, 2006); and David Annwn, "Returning to Fear: New Discoveries on Robertson's Fantasmagoria", in *NMLJ* 10:4 (Autumn 2008), 59–64.

4. The Magic Lantern Society (formed in the UK in 1976) and Magic Lantern Society of the United States and Canada (formed in 1978), whose memberships overlap slightly, have organised meetings, conventions and visits throughout their existence and produced books and journals to a high standard. See www.magiclantern.org.uk and www.magiclanternsociety.org for more information.

5. The original discussions were between Martin Loiperdinger, Ludwig Vogl-Bienek and Torsten Gärtner of Universität Trier; Mervyn Heard and Richard Crangle of the Magic Lantern Society; and Frank Gray and Ine van Dooren of Screen Archive South East, University of Brighton. Subsequently Joss Marsh and David Francis of Indiana University and the Kent Museum of the Moving Image, Sarah Dellmann of Utrecht University, and more colleagues at Trier, particularly Brigitte Braun, Karen Eifler and Lydia Jakobs, have joined the project. The name Lucerna was derived from *lucerna magica* ("magic light"), one of the earliest 17th-century Latin terms for the magic lantern.

6. For a short outline of the Screen1900 project, examining representations of poverty and other social issues in lantern slides and early film, see www.screen1900.uni-trier.de (accessed July 2013).

7. The *OMLJ*, published monthly between 1889 and 1903, is one of the major sources for this period of British lantern and cinematograph history. Its contents were listed in Lucerna in the course of preparation of a complete facsimile, including the advertising pages, published on DVD-ROM as *From Magic Lantern to Movies* (London: PhotoResearch, 2010).

8. ICONCLASS (www.iconclass.nl) was originally developed as a classification system for images in art and iconography, and is used for the description and retrieval of subjects represented in images by museums and art institutions around the world.

Ian Christie

Afterword:
How Does it Feel? Hidden Histories and the Elusive User Experience

This collection of essays began life with a three-day conference held at the elegant Bloomsbury Square premises of the German Historical Institute London, a short distance from the British Museum and from the Warburg Institute. For me, it proved to be a location conducive to thinking about the origins of "public enlightenment", many of which have their roots in this area of London. First developed in the late 17th century when the modern city's topography and institutions were taking shape, Bloomsbury Square would later house a generation of enlightened patrons, who included John Radcliffe, benefactor of Oxford's Radcliffe Library, and Hans Sloane, whose collection became the basis of the British Museum when this was launched just round the corner at Montagu House in 1759.

The current British Museum is one of London's – indeed the world's – great educational institutions, but how many of its millions of visitors realise that long before the Internet, much of its outreach work was carried on through loaning lantern slides for lectures?[1] In the case of the Warburg Institute, which came to London in 1933 to escape the Nazi regime that would have destroyed Aby Warburg's great collection, this included "thousands of slides" along with the books that are often regarded as its main resource.[2] How many today realise the revolutionary role played by photography and lantern slides in Warburg's work on "illustrating the processes by which the memory of the past affects a culture?"[3]

Is it fanciful to think of Bloomsbury, with its modern concentration of universities, museums and specialist institutes, as haunted by the ghosts of lanterns and slides that once were the principal means of disseminating visual information to audiences? Throughout the later 19th and early 20th centuries, these slides were 3¼ inch square glass, and projected by lanterns once called "magic" and later "optical", as the new educators and propagandists sought to throw off associations with the childish (or occult) history of the lantern. For a century, such lanterns and their associated slides held sway, until the rise of reversal film after the Second World War, and the adoption of 35mm slides during the 1950s, pushed lantern slides into obsolescence. As a Timeline on the history of visual resources in academia notes:

> 1952. All camera film is now triacetate based, paving the way for widespread adoption of 35mm film in both amateur and academic markets.
>
> 1952+. American faculty widely divided in their allegiances to lantern slides for their clarity or to 35mm slides for their ease of production and transport to class. Huge debates begin about whether 35mm color film is stable enough for adoption and whether the loss of clarity will ruin the teaching of art history. Younger faculty adopt 35mm film, while older faculty prefer lantern slides.[4]

The rise of 35mm slides combined with the pre-programming and speed of transition offered by the Kodak Carousel after 1964 quickly consigned not only the older large-format lantern, but even straight-tray 35mm projectors, to obsolescence.[5] For another 40 years the 35mm slide-show, with its increasingly sophisticated transitions and capacity to be automated, held sway, until displaced by data projectors and digital "slides" in the early years of the new millennium.

This progression is a familiar story for lantern scholars, ever keen to stress the continuity of projection practices, although I suspect it remains less widely recognised, even in academic circles that continue such practices. This may be mainly due to neither projection nor the slide-show being considered "media".[6] But I would suggest it also reflects an entrenched suspicion of technology in education, which persisted through much of the 20th century, in spite of mounting evidence of benefits from psychologists and progressive educationists. "Visual aids" were often looked down upon by traditionalists as benefiting only the less able, or in some ill-defined way "coming between" teacher and pupil. A report from Britain's National Education Association in 1909 which cast doubt on "the value of bioscope pictures in education" based its argument on describing how "a good teacher [...] regulates his pace and the fullness with which he treats his subject", adding that "this is possible when using pictures, diagrams *or even lantern slides*".[7] That "even" hints at a residual unease with the lantern, already widely used in education, which may stem from a still older iconoclastic tradition of doubting the image against the word.

Despite this, however, progressive thought about both evangelism and education had long recognised the power of images. As Annemarie McAllister notes, John Bunyan's view of the evangelistic advantage of "Eyegate" over "Eargate" was well known to Band of Hope activists.[8] The same recognition is present in John Locke's 1693 essay *Some Thoughts Concerning Education*, which became a cornerstone of subsequent educational theory and prescription. Discussing how to encourage children's early reading, Locke recommended Aesop's fables, noting that "if his Aesop has pictures in it, it will entertain him much the better".[9] Two centuries later, in the heyday of the lantern, John Ruskin would preach the doctrine of visual education in his own teaching and voluminous writings. Ruskin wanted to make art the core of a new regime of education and of morality. While his emphasis was on drawing as a tutelary discipline, supported by studying reproductions of great art-works, he also invoked the two most important optical instruments of the mid-century, the microscope and the lantern, as in this typically rhetorical passage:

> The vast extent of the advertising frescos of London, daily refreshed into brighter and larger fresco by its billstickers, cannot somehow sufficiently entertain the popular eyes [...] and I find my charitable friends inviting the children, whom the streets educate only into vicious misery, to entertainments of scientific vision, in microscope or magic lantern, thus giving them something to look at, such as it is – fleas mostly; and the stomachs of various vermin; and people with their heads cut off and set on again; – still *something* to look at.[10]

For Ruskin, even the knockabout imagery of the popular lantern show was preferable to the "corrupted modernity of the streets".[11] Clearly familiar with the magic lantern from childhood, he invokes it as a common experience in one of his stories for children, in which the moon is compared to "the biggest disk of light ever thrown by a magic lantern".[12]

Lanterns and slides were omnipresent at the time Ruskin was writing; and they would remain so until the rise of 35mm equipment pushed them first into basements, before finally making an inglorious exit to junk shops and dustbins. Their disappearance, and later resurrection as exotic objects of wonder, has perhaps created something of a mystique. The issue, however, is surely not the lantern apparatus so much as the many and varied uses to which it was put, in what Charles Musser identified as "screen practice". As I have argued elsewhere, the "hardware" of optical instruments certainly matters, and may tell us much about how various devices were conceived and perceived, but recognition of this runs the risk of fetishising apparatus and endowing it with mysterious properties held to constitute "the medium", which can only be properly understood as a set of practices which make use of technologies, but are not necessarily defined by them.[13] This collection makes a real contribution to shifting attention away from the apparatus *per se*, towards evoking a range of practices that reflected the moral and political concerns of the "long *fin de siècle*". These ranged from traditional children's entertainments and Christmas shows which, as Eifler and Henkes show, moved from slides to film during this period, to the popular balladry of George Sims revealed by Marsh and Francis, and the surprisingly extensive political uses of both slides and film by Britain's Conservative Party demonstrated by Bottomore. All of these are essentially social practices, which made use of available, as well as novel, presentation technologies.

Does this sound like heresy to anyone brought up on Marshall McLuhan's motto "the medium is the message", or on "apparatus theory" and the passionate debates about filmic specificity that first erupted in the 1920s and resurfaced in the 1960s and 70s?[14] Only if we regard the medium or the apparatus in either a reductively literal or an extravagantly analogical sense. Certainly there were affective and material qualities associated with large-scale lantern shows, just as there were with the mixed lantern and kinematograph shows that took place for at least 20 years from 1895 until the late 1910s, and with various stages of the evolution of the "all film" presentation. But rather than isolate some few characteristics of these as "defining the medium", which was a preoccupation of some periods in film and media theory, it would be more productive to locate what we know about such practices in the much larger "hidden history" of non-theatrical exhibition, which film scholars such as Gorham Kindem, Dan Streible and Greg Waller have been exploring for some time.[15] And what can be traced across many of the essays here is evidence of a welcome turn toward the de-centring of apparatus in media history, accompanied by a corresponding social or ethnographic turn.

In short, what matters is the overall communication context, whether this is the pre-1900 campaigning lantern shows of William Palmer in England and Jacob Riis in America, as discussed by Bottomore and Yochelson, or the large children's film shows staged by the Salvation Army revealed by Eifler, or the pioneering uses of film for health education and scientific communication documented by Dahlquist. Context, I would argue, is crucial, which involves trying to understand the expectations of presenters and audiences, as well as the material framing of the presentation. What was shown, in terms of identifiable slides or films, turns out to be of considerably less significance than a traditional history based on of a handful "landmark films" would suggest.

It has been claimed, with some justice, that the intensive study of early film that began in the 1980s helped bring about a major shift in the focus of film studies, challenging the dominance of an often ahistorical "theory" and reinstating interest in material and contextual factors within a wider historical framework. On the evidence of the essays in this collection, and the discussions that surrounded their first presentation, it could be argued that the direction of influence has now reversed. Scholarship trying to deal with the fast-changing contemporary profusion of multi-platform and mobile media focuses on convergence rather than difference between media, while calling into question any clear distinction between media based on their technology, and is above all concerned with the user experience.[16] What we *do* with contemporary media has made McLuhan's other famous claim about media as "extensions of ourselves" an obvious field of exploration – to text, to Google, to satnav is literally to extend our capabilities.

So the challenge to historians of the seismic media-accompanied communications revolution of *c.*1880–1914, through research initiatives like the Screen1900 project at Universität Trier (the driving force behind this volume and the conference which inspired it), is to take on board more fully these new insights into media *experience* rather than technology, or indeed what are often confusingly referred to as "media". Media ethnography proposes the study of how we navigate and use available media rather than privileging the idea of "medium". The largely forgotten campaigners and proselytisers who are the characters brought to life in this collection do not seem to have been primarily motivated by enthusiasm for the lantern or the cinematograph, but rather by the uses they could make of these instruments – to lay bare the evidence of poverty, deprivation, discrimination, and to mobilise reform, or even revolution. We should surely respect their priorities, while trying to challenge the imminent erasure from history of 150 years of analogue projection systems and rescue their surviving artefacts. There is perhaps a cautionary parallel with the present-day British Museum proudly displaying the fragments of early inscriptions that are our link with antiquity. In addition to initiatives like the Lucerna Magic Lantern Web Resource project (covered elsewhere in this volume), which aims to use new technologies to open pathways to understanding of the uses and materials of older ones, why not a Magic Lantern and a Cinematograph or Theatrograph on prominent display in Bloomsbury, together with a selection of their vivid representations of poverty?[17] At a time of accelerating media or format innovation, we need to be reminded more than ever how our immediate ancestors experienced audiovisual audiencehood and learned about the less fortunate world around them.

Notes

1. Details of some of the slide collections of the British Museum can be found among the archives of the Natural History Museum; see for example "Printed ephemera of the Natural History Museum 1904-1912", item ref. DF/ADM/1011/3 at www.nhm.ac.uk/research-curation/library/archives/catalogue (accessed June 2013, as are all website references here).

2. "The physical removal of about 60,000 books, thousands of slides, photographs and furniture then followed, and on December 12th, 1933, the little steamers 'Hermia' and 'Jessica' with 531 boxes aboard moved slowly down the Elbe [...]. When the two small steamers docked in the Thames the Institute had reached what proved to be its new permanent home." See warburg.sas.ac.uk/home/aboutthewarburginstitute/history/migration.

3. "Aby Warburg 1866–1929", warburg.sas.ac.uk/home/aboutthewarburginstitute/history.

4. "Slide Libraries", en.wikipedia.org/wiki/Slide_library.

5. A University of Colombo website offers a convenient history of 35mm projectors from the 1950s to 2004. See www.cmb.ac.lk/academic/medicine/ext_pages/physiology/images/book.pdf.

6. I raised the question of the lantern as a "medium" in a conference at the British Academy, *Lantern Projections*, in February 2001. See Ian Christie, "Through a Glass Brightly: The Magic Lantern in History", *British Academy Review*, 5 (2001), 21–23. But a more appropriate concept to apply may be that of "format": see Jonathan Sterne, *MP3: The Meaning of a Format* (Durham, NC: Duke University Press, 2013).

7. The Secretary of the National Education Association, reported in *The Bioscope*, 11 February 1909, and quoted in Rachael Low, *History of the British Film 1906–1914* (London: Allen & Unwin, 1948), 41–42 (my emphasis).

8. "Eyegate" and "Eargate" are two of the five gates of the city of Mansoul in John Bunyan's allegorical novel *The Holy War* (1682), which followed his more famous *The Pilgrim's Progress* (1678).

9. John Locke, *Some Thoughts Concerning Education* (1693), paragraph 156.

10. John Ruskin, *Mornings in Florence* (1881; reprinted Teddington: Echo Library, 2007), 21.

11. David Peters Corbett, *The World in Paint: Modern Art and Visuality in England, 1848–1914* (Manchester: Manchester University Press, 2004), 24.

12. John Ruskin, "Benjy in Beastland", in *King of the Golden River and Other Stories* (1841; reprinted Whitefish, Montana: Kessinger Publishing, 2003), 171.

13. See Ian Christie, "Toys, Instruments, Machines: Why the Hardware Matters", in James Lyons and John Plunkett (eds), *Multimedia Histories: From the Magic Lantern to the Internet* (Exeter: Exeter University Press, 2007), 3–17. See also, on "the vagueness built into the concept of media", W.J.T. Mitchell, "Addressing Media" in his *What Do Pictures Want? The Lives and Loves of Images* (Chicago: Chicago University Press, 2005), 204–205.

14. Jean-Louis Baudry's influential 1970 article, "Ideological Effects of the Basic Cinematic Apparatus" posited cinema as an Althusserian "ideological apparatus", melding technical, psychological and political concepts.

15. See for instance the special issue of *Film History* edited by Dan Streible, Martina Roepke and Anke Mebold (*Film History: An International Journal*, 19:4, 2007); and Gregory A. Waller, "Locating Early Non-Theatrical Audiences", in Ian Christie (ed.), *Audiences: Defining and Researching Screen Entertainment Reception* (Amsterdam: Amsterdam University Press, 2012), 81–95.

16. Recent work in this area includes Nick Couldry, *Media, Society, World: Social Theory and Digital Media Practice* (Cambridge: Polity Press, 2012); Shaun Moores, *Media, Place and Mobility* (Basingstoke: Palgrave Macmillan, 2012); Nanna Verhoeff, *Mobile Screens: The Visual Regime of Navigation* (Amsterdam: Amsterdam University Press, 2012); and Roger Odin, *Les espaces de communication: introduction à la sémio-pragmatique* (Grenoble: Presses universitaires de Grenoble, 2011).

17. Perhaps this would finally answer the suggestion made to the British Museum by the British moving picture pioneer Robert W. Paul in 1896, when he proposed that the Museum might consider collecting "animated photographs" to no avail. See Stephen Bottomore, "'The Collection of Rubbish': Animatographs, Archives and Arguments. London 1896–97", *Film History* 7 (1995), 291–297.

The Contributors

Stephen Bottomore graduated from Cambridge University and film school, worked as a film editor and producer at the BBC, and then spent two decades directing broadcast and corporate documentaries in Europe, Africa, Asia and the Americas, completing his television career as executive producer of two series for Channel 4 educational television. He is the author of many articles on early cinema and other media in such journals as *Sight and Sound*, *History Today*, *Historical Journal of Film, Radio and Television* and *KINtop*. He also published *The Titanic and Silent Cinema* (2000) and *I Want to See this Annie Mattygraph* (1995), a history of early cinema based on satirical magazine cartoons. He was awarded a doctorate at Utrecht University in 2007 for his thesis on early cinema and warfare. He has been an associate editor of *Film History* since 1998, editing issues on non-fiction, silent cinema, war films, fiction about the cinema, and the First World War. He lives in Thailand and the UK.

Ian Christie is a film historian, curator and consultant, and is Anniversary Professor of Film and Media History at Birkbeck College, University of London, and a visiting professor at the Palacky University, Olomouc, Czech Republic. He has written and edited books on early film, Powell and Pressburger, Russian cinema, Scorsese and Gilliam, and worked on numerous exhibitions, radio and TV programmes. He was elected a fellow of the British Academy in 1994 and in 2005–06 was Slade Professor of Fine Art at Cambridge University. Current research interests include the history of production design, early (and new) moving-image media and how we engage with them, and the potential of experimental psychology and cognitive neuroscience to tell us more about what (and how) we experience on screen.

Richard Crangle is Treasurer of the Magic Lantern Society, previously its Research Officer and editor of its *New Magic Lantern Journal* (2001–10). He co-edited *The Encyclopaedia of the Magic Lantern* (2001) and *Realms of Light: Uses and Perceptions of the Magic Lantern* (2005), translated Laurent Mannoni's *Great Art of Light and Shadow* (2000), and has contributed to several collections on early cinema. His Ph.D., awarded by the University of Exeter in 1996, considered the relationship between early moving pictures and other media, particularly lantern slides and illustrated magazines. He is currently researching the output of the British lantern slide trade of the late 19th and early 20th centuries and working on the *Lucerna* web resource.

Marina Dahlquist is an Associate Professor in Cinema Studies at the Department of Media Studies at Stockholm University. She has published articles on cinema and civic education, health discourses and colonial structures. She is a recipient of a research grant from the Swedish Research Council (2011–2013) within the project "Cinema and uplift: health discourses and social activism in the U.S. 1910–1930". Her primary research interests are historical reception, educational films, and issues of globalisation.

Karen Eifler studied Media Sciences, French and Chinese at Trier University. She is currently a Research Fellow on the project *Screen1900: the Social Question in Lantern Shows and Early Cinema* at Universität Trier. Her Ph.D. thesis (to be completed in 2014) examines the distribution of lantern slides and the exhibition and reception of lantern shows for social purposes in Great Britain around 1900.

David Francis , O.B.E., was for 15 years Curator of the British National Film Archive, and subsequently, until 2001, Chief of the Motion Picture, Broadcasting, and Recorded Sound Division of the Library of Congress. His publications include the ground-breaking *Chaplin: Genesis of a Clown* (with Raoul Sobel, 1977), and *Film Curatorship: Museums, Curatorship and the Moving Image Experience* (co-authored, 2008). With Joss Marsh, he is plotting a book on the late-Victorian multi-media celebrity George R. Sims. He and Joss Marsh are co-curators of the Kent Museum of the Moving Image (Kent-MOMI), which is due to open its doors in late 2014.

Frank Gray is the Director of Screen Archive South East (SASE) at the University of Brighton. His research is generally related to the screen collection developed by SASE over the last two decades and focused particularly on Victorian and Edwardian screen culture. The latter engages with popular spectacles and projections of the 19th and early 20th centuries, the uses of the magic lantern, the development of narrative film fiction, the emergence of "news" on film and the introduction of the concept of cinema. The curation of museum exhibitions on these subjects has provided a popular focus for his research.

Caroline Henkes is a Ph.D. student within the Screen1900 research focus at the Trier University, Germany. Her Ph.D. project concerns the representation(s) of poverty in early fictional film and its role regarding the establishment of cinema in general and, more specifically, the long feature film in Germany. Her article "Asta Nielsen and Her Destitute Female Characters" appeared in the second volume of the *KINtop Studies in Early Cinema* series, *Importing Asta Nielsen,* in 2013.

Michelle Lamunière is the John R. and Barbara Robinson Family Assistant Curator of Photography at the Harvard Art Museums. In 2009 she completed her Ph.D. in Art History at Boston University. Among her publications is the exhibition catalogue "You Look Beautiful Like That: The Portrait Photographs of Seydou Keïta and Malick Sidibé" and three essays on Harvard University's Social Museum. She also writes frequently about contemporary photography.

Martin Loiperdinger is Professor of Media Studies at the Trier University. He co-edited *KINtop*, the German yearbook of early cinema, and is currently series editor of *KINtop – Studies in Early Cinema*. He co-curated the DVDs *Crazy Cinématographe 1896–1916* and *Screening the Poor 1888–1914*. He is the editor of *Celluloid Goes Digital* (2003), *Travelling Cinema in Europe* (2008), and *Early Cinema Today: The Art of Programming and Live Performance* (2011). With Uli Jung, he co-edited *Geschichte des dokumentarischen Films in Deutschland*, vol. 1 (2005), and *Importing Asta Nielsen: The International Film Star in the Making 1910–1914* (2013).

Joss Marsh is emeritus Associate Professor of Victorian Studies at Indiana University, Bloomington. She is the author of *Word Crimes: Blasphemy, Culture, and Literature in 19th-Century England* (1998), the forthcoming *Starring Charles Dickens*, and numerous essays on Dickens, Chaplin, the 19th-century novel and film, Victorian visual culture, celebrity, film stardom, and the magic lantern. She occasionally submits to stage and radio discipline, and is probably the only female academic in the world to have played Scrooge, in drag, in a professional theatre. She and David Francis are co-curators of the Kent Museum of the Moving Image (Kent-MOMI), which is due to open its doors in late 2014.

Annemarie McAllister, Ph.D., is Senior Research Fellow in History at the University of Central Lancashire, working on cultural history, particularly representation. She has published widely on temperance history and directed the HLF-funded "Temperance and the Working Class" project in 2012–13, creating several exhibitions: www.demondrink.co.uk still shows one of these. Publications include "The Band of Hope in the North West" in *Manchester Region History Review* 21, "Rational recreation and leisure for children: the Band of Hope in the Twentieth Century" in *Recording Leisure Lives: Everyday Leisure in 20th Century Britain*, online articles, and editing and contributing two articles to a special edition of *Visual Resources* in December 2012 on "The Pleasures and Problems of Drink".

Judith Thissen is Associate Professor of Media History at the Department of Media and Culture of Utrecht University. Her research on Jewish immigrant leisure culture in New York City has been published in journals such as *Theatre Survey*, *Cinema Journal* and *KINtop*, and in numerous anthologies including *Going to the Movies: Hollywood and the Social Experience of Cinema* (2007), *Beyond the Screen: Institutions, Networks and Publics of Early Cinema (2012)* and *Audiences: Defining and Researching Screen Entertainment Reception* (2012).

Ine van Dooren has worked as a Moving Image Archivist since 1990, first at the Netherlands Film Museum (now EYE) and for the last 18 years at Screen Archive South East, University of Brighton. A long-standing member of the Magic Lantern Society, she has held posts including its Research Officer and, since 2009, the Society's first Archivist. She co-edited *Realms of Light: Uses and Perceptions of the Magic Lantern* (2005) and has contributed to *New Magic Lantern Journal* and other publications. Her research interests are in amateur and family film and slide collections and life model slide sets.

Ludwig M. Vogl-Bienek, D.Phil., is senior researcher of the Screen1900 research group at the Trier University, and a founding member of the magic lantern ensemble *illuminago* which performs lantern shows internationally. He has published widely on the art of projection and on screen culture in the 19th century, including his dissertation *Lichtspiele im Schatten der Armut* (forthcoming 2014). He co-curated the DVD *Screening the Poor 1888-1914* and initiated the international conference *Screen Culture and the Social Question* at the German Historical Institute London in December 2011.

Bonnie Yochelson, Ph.D., is a freelance art historian and curator who specialises in the history of photography. She teaches in the MFA Program in Photography, Video and Related Media at the School of Visual Arts, New York City. Formerly Curator of Prints and Photographs at the Museum of the City of New York, she has written two books on Jacob Riis and is currently writing a complete catalogue of the Riis Collection of Photographs and organising a major exhibition on Riis in collaboration with the Library of Congress and the Gammel Strand, Copenhagen.

Picture credits

Stephen Bottomore Collection (28).

Richard Crangle Collection (23).

David Francis Collection (34 upper, 40, 55-61, 64, 67-69, 71, 72, 76, 77 upper, 79).

EYE Film Institute Netherlands (100, 107).

From Magic Lantern to Movies (London: PhotoResearch, 2010. DVD-ROM facsimile edition of *OMLJ*) (36, 38, 54, 62).

George Eastman House, *International Museum of Photography and Film* (140, 145).

Harvard Art Museums/Fogg Museum, Transfer from the Carpenter Center for the Visual Arts, Social Museum Collection, 3.2002.22. Katya Kallsen. © President and Fellows of Harvard College (160 upper).

Harvard Art Museums/Fogg Museum, Transfer from the Carpenter Center for the Visual Arts, Social Museum Collection, 3.2002.132. Harvard College Library Imaging Services. © President and Fellows of Harvard College (168).

Harvard University Archives, UAV 800.150.5p. (160 lower, 164, 166).

Mervyn Heard Collection (16).

illuminago Collection (cover, viii, 8, 34 lower, 37, 39, 41-46, 48-50, 101, 182).

Jack Judson Collection, Magic Lantern Castle Museum (104 lower, 106 lower).

Kirklees Museums and Galleries (51-53).

Lichtspiele und Soziale Frage: Screening the Poor 1888-1914 (München: Film & Kunst Edition Filmmuseum, 2011. DVD-ROM) (96, 102, 104 upper, 106 upper, 108).

Livesey Collection, University of Central Lancashire Archives (126, 130, 133).

Lucerna Magic Lantern Web Resource: images by Robert MacDonald (70, 77 lower) and Richard Crangle (73). Originals from private collections.

Museum of the City of New York, Jacob A. Riis Collection; no accession no. (82); 90.13.4.104 (84 lower left); 90.13.4.105 (84 lower right); 90.13.2.59 (85); 90.13.4.127 (89 upper); 90.13.4.84 (89 lower); 90.13.4.158 (90); 90.13.4.151 (91); 90.13.4.132 (92); 90.13.4.208 (93 upper); 90.13.3.42. (94).

Tom Rall Collection (141).

Wikimedia Commons (172).

All other credits are given with the illustrations themselves.